Byzantine Sources for the Crusades, 1095–1204

The Christian, Greek-speaking Byzantine empire was placed rather uneasily between western Christendom and the Islamic world during the Crusade era. Like all historical topics – particularly medieval – sources on the crusades give a variety of perspectives and accounts, but Byzantine writers provide a unique outlook on these crucial events.

Byzantine Sources for the Crusades, 1095–1204 brings together important sources on the Crusades into one volume. The texts translated here include established accounts, such as selections from Anna Komnene's description of the passage of the First Crusade in 1096–8, John Kinnamos' writings on the Second Crusade and Niketas Choniates' studies on the Second and Third Crusades, particularly covering the passage of German emperor Frederick I Barbarossa during the latter. However, less well-known accounts are also translated and provided, such as Zonaras' and the contemporary letters of the archbishop of Ohrid during the First Crusade, various poems and speeches recorded throughout the reigns of John II and Manuel I Komnenos and smaller accounts about crusaders passing through the Byzantine empire.

This book covers up to the Fourth Crusade, in which Niketas Choniates was an eye-witness to the Siege of Constantinople in 1204 and later a refugee in Nicaea, writing a series of speeches about the capture of the Byzantine capital and rallying the Byzantines to recover the city from the newly created Latin empire.

This book will appeal to scholars and students alike studying the era of the Crusades in the East and the perspectives and accounts of Byzantine writers both at the time and after, as well as all those interested in the history of the Byzantine empire in the 11th, 12th and 13th centuries.

Georgios Chatzelis is currently a teaching fellow at Democritus University of Thrace and at Hellenic Open University. In the past, he held research and teaching positions at Royal Holloway University of London, Aristotle University of Thessaloniki, Centre for Advanced Study Sofia and New Europe College: Institute for Advanced Study. His recent publications include *Byzantine Military Manuals as Literary Works and Practical Handbooks: The Case of the Tenth-Century Sylloge Tacticorum* (2019) and, with Jonathan Harris, *A Tenth-Century Byzantine Military Manual: The Sylloge Tacticorum* (2017).

Jonathan Harris is Professor of the History of Byzantium at Royal Holloway, University of London. His recent publications include *Byzantium and the Crusades*, third edition (2022); *Introduction to Byzantium (602–1453)* (2020) and *The Lost World of Byzantium* (2015). His first novel, *Theosis*, appeared in 2023 and he is currently editing *The New Oxford Illustrated History of the Crusades*.

Crusade Texts in Translation
Editorial Board
Peter Edbury
(Cardiff), Norman Housley *(Leicester)*
Peter Jackson
(Keele)

The crusading movement, which originated in the 11th century and lasted beyond the 16th, bequeathed to its future historians a legacy of sources which are unrivalled in their range and variety. These sources document in fascinating detail the motivations and viewpoints, military efforts and spiritual lives, of the participants in the crusades. They also narrate the internal histories of the states and societies which crusaders established or supported in the many regions where they fought. Some of these sources have been translated in the past but the vast majority have been available only in their original language. The goal of this series is to provide a wide-ranging corpus of texts, most of them translated for the first time, which will illuminate the history of the crusades and the crusader-states from every angle, including that of their principal adversaries, the Muslim powers of the Middle East.

Titles in the series include

On Warfare and the Threefold Path of the Jerusalem Pilgrimage
John D. Cotts

The Road to Antioch and Jerusalem
The Crusader Pilgrimage of the Monte Cassino Chronicle
Francesca Petrizzo

The Latin Continuation of William of Tyre
Edited and translated by James H. Kane and Keagan J. Brewer

Byzantine Sources for the Crusades, 1095–1204
Edited and translated by Georgios Chatzelis and Jonathan Harris

For more information about this series, please visit: www.routledge.com/Routledge-Handbooks-in-Religion/book-series

Byzantine Sources for the Crusades, 1095–1204

Edited and translated
by Georgios Chatzelis
and Jonathan Harris

LONDON AND NEW YORK

First published 2025
by Routledge
4 Park Square, Milton Park, Abingdon, Oxon OX14 4RN

and by Routledge
605 Third Avenue, New York, NY 10158

Routledge is an imprint of the Taylor & Francis Group, an informa business

© 2025 selection and editorial matter, Georgios Chatzelis and Jonathan Harris; individual chapters, the contributors

The right of Georgios Chatzelis and Jonathan Harris to be identified as the authors of the editorial material, and of the authors for their individual chapters, has been asserted in accordance with sections 77 and 78 of the Copyright, Designs and Patents Act 1988.

All rights reserved. No part of this book may be reprinted or reproduced or utilised in any form or by any electronic, mechanical, or other means, now known or hereafter invented, including photocopying and recording, or in any information storage or retrieval system, without permission in writing from the publishers.

Trademark notice: Product or corporate names may be trademarks or registered trademarks, and are used only for identification and explanation without intent to infringe.

British Library Cataloguing-in-Publication Data
A catalogue record for this book is available from the British Library

ISBN: 978-0-367-85840-7 (hbk)
ISBN: 978-1-032-89444-7 (pbk)
ISBN: 978-1-003-01534-5 (ebk)

DOI: 10.4324/9781003015345

Typeset in Times New Roman
by Apex CoVantage, LLC

In Loving Memory of our Cherry Lady (1952–2022)
In Memory of Joseph A. Munitiz S.J. (1931–2022), translator

Contents

Maps		*viii*
Preface		*x*
List of Abbreviations		*xi*
Glossary		*xii*
	Introduction	1
	List of Source Extracts	4
I	The First Crusade	7
II	Alexios I, John II and the Latin East	30
III	The Second Crusade	59
IV	Manuel I and the Latin East	90
V	The Third Crusade	151
VI	The Fourth Crusade	173
VII	After the Fourth Crusade	206
	Bibliography	*223*
	Index	*228*

Maps

Map 1 *The Byzantine Empire c.1180.*

Maps ix

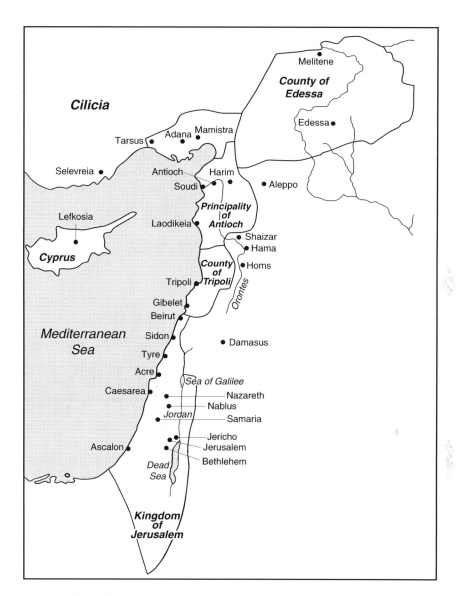

Map 2 *The Latin East.*

Preface

The task of translating the Greek texts in this book fell principally to Georgios Chatzelis, with Jonathan Harris providing suggestions and amendments to his versions. The division of labour was reversed with the small number of Latin texts that we included [3, 11 & 13]. The book introduction, text introductions, footnotes and index were likewise all initially compiled by Harris, with Chatzelis providing the suggestions and amendments. Our volume is by no means comprehensive. For example, the 1174 speech of Eustathios of Thessalonica, which includes an account of the Second Crusade, the speeches of Manganeios Prodromos about Manuel I's expedition to Antioch and the funeral oration of Nicholas Mesarites for his brother John have not been included as they have recently been translated by Andrew Stone, Elizabeth and Michael Jeffreys and Michael Angold, respectively: details are included in the bibliography. Earlier translations of our texts into English and other languages may also be found listed there. We initially planned to omit Anna Komnene as well because her work is freely available in the translation by Sewter and Frankopan but it soon became apparent that the early sections of our book would not make much sense without her work. We have therefore included selected passages from the *Alexiad* in the translation of Elizabeth Dawes (1864–1954), albeit with the spellings of personal names adapted to fit in with the rest of the volume. Throughout the book, square brackets in the text ([]) indicate where we have supplied words to bring out the sense of the passage or omitted sections for reasons of space. . . . We are grateful to Routledge for their permission to reproduce the Dawes translation of Anna Komnene. We would also like to record our appreciation to our editors at Routledge, Michael Greenwood and Louis Nicholson-Pallett, to Andreas Gkoutzioukostas, Martin Hall and Chrysa Zizopoulou for their advice on points of language and to Gilbert Rajkumar and his colleagues at Apex CoVantage for their careful and thorough copy editing of our text.

Georgios Chatzelis and Jonathan Harris
Thessaloniki and London, May 2024

Abbreviations

PBW (2016)   Jeffreys, Michael et al. (2017), *Prosopography of the Byzantine World, 2016* (London: King's College London). Available at: http://pbw2016.kdl.kcl.ac.uk.

Glossary

Domestic   A military official
Dromon   A Byzantine galley mostly used as a warship
Ekphrasis   Description of a place, building or work of art
Encomium (plural: encomia)   Laudatory speech
Eparch   Governor of the city of Constantinople
Forerunner   St John the Baptist
Hagarenes   A Byzantine word for Arabs or for Muslims generally
Lavra   Monastery with dispersed cells and a central church
Logothete   A civil official
Nazirite   Orthodox monk
Pansebastos   Literally 'most august', the sixth highest-ranking Byzantine title
Protostrator   A high official
Sebastos   An honorific title, usually reserved for members of the imperial family
Thema (plural: themata)   Province of the Byzantine empire

Introduction

This volume presents translated extracts from contemporary texts which throw light on the first four Crusades and the subsequent Latin presence in the east. All were written between 1095 and 1330 from within the Byzantine empire (also known as Byzantium). This Christian state could claim direct continuity with the eastern half of the Roman empire, which had survived after the western provinces had been lost to Germanic invaders during the fifth century CE. It had contracted over the years and had had to fight for survival against the expansion of Islam during the seventh and eighth centuries CE. By 1050, it was centred on Asia Minor and the Balkans, along with the islands of Crete and Cyprus and part of southern Italy. The link with the empire of the Caesars remained an important part of its official ideology and, as readers will notice in the extracts, its inhabitants generally described themselves as Romans. Their predominant language, however, was not Latin but Greek.

That is an important point to bear in mind when reading the extracts. Only three of them, connected to external relations [3, 11 & 13], were originally in Latin, a language which very few Byzantines understood. Most were in Greek but it has to be remembered there were varying forms of the language. That used by the mass of the people for everyday spoken communication was developing into the Demotic that prevails in Greece and Cyprus today. The Church used something closer to Koine or Common Greek, the language of the New Testament and the liturgy. Monastic chronicles were often penned in this idiom.[1] The court and administration preferred Classical Greek, especially the version known as Attic, which had developed in Athens in the fifth and fourth centuries BCE. The Greek texts translated in this book are mainly in Attic, with two in simpler language [45 & 47]. They were almost all authored by intellectuals employed in some capacity or other in the state administration and based at the palace of Blachernae in the capital city of Constantinople. Securing such a post was dependent on completing a course of higher education, which involved reading and internalising works of ancient authors such as Homer, Plato and Demosthenes. Students were required to write

---

1 Horrocks (2010), pp. 207–30, 245–53, 273–322; Neville (2018), pp. 13–15.

and even to speak in that Attic language and were expected to use it in the literary works that they produced in their subsequent careers.[2]

Those writings fall into a number of clearly defined genres. History was one of them, and most of the texts translated in this book are from historical works which were modelled on those of ancient historians such as Thucydides and Plutarch. But there were several other forms of writing produced at the Byzantine court that discussed the crusades and the Latin East. Members of the Byzantine political and literary elite often exchanged letters [4, 19 & 32]. There was *ekphrasis*, a description of a place, building or work of art [37 & 41], poetry [9, 20, 28, 31, 33, 38, 46 & 51] and the encomium or laudatory speech. The last was the most public form of Byzantine writing. Encomia could take the form of a eulogy at a funeral [54] but most often they were in praise of a reigning emperor in whose presence they would be delivered on important feasts of the year, such as Epiphany on 6 January [24, 25, 43, 49 & 53]. However, all these works were intended to be read out loud at court, not just encomia. Even letters were often not so much private, intimate communications as exercises in literary skill, designed to be admired for their virtuosity in the ancient language, even if their subject was something as dry and practical as tax exemption.[3]

Byzantine writings present some challenges when they are approached as sources of historical information. They can be difficult to read, even in translation, coming across as stilted and long winded. They were deliberately so because their authors considered it good style to use the most archaic and obscure vocabulary that they could muster. They also demonstrated their erudition by cramming in as many allusions to ancient mythology, history and literature as they possibly could so that the matter in hand can often be hard to discern.[4] This deliberate archaism can also have the effect of making Byzantine writings appear remote from their own times. To preserve the purity of the ancient language, authors preferred not to use contemporary names. So the Turks were called Persians and Western Europeans Celts and even their capital city of Constantinople was sometimes given its old name of Byzantion. Byzantine authors also mirrored the world view of their ancient models, replicating their sharp distinction drawn between 'civilised' peoples and others: those who did not speak Greek and who did not accept the authority of the emperor were labelled 'barbarians'.[5] Finally, it has to be remembered too that these works only represent the views of a tiny segment of the Byzantine population, albeit a very influential one. They circulated only among the very small caste of palace administrators. Some of them, such as the history of John Kinnamos, survive in just one manuscript, suggesting that they were not widely read even within that group. Others, like those of Niketas Choniates, do survive in numerous manuscripts but these date from several centuries later. In any case, their language and style would have rendered them incomprehensible to the vast majority of Byzantines. These

---

2 Neville (2018), pp. 10–13; Harris (2022), pp. 26–31.
3 Mullett (1981), pp. 75–93.
4 Simpson (2013), pp. 251–6.
5 Treadgold (2013), pp. 459–78.

points should be borne in mind before using them as a guide to 'the Byzantine view' of the crusades.

On the other hand, in spite of the obscure language, deliberate antiquarianism and the plethora of classical allusions, the extracts translated in this book can provide an intriguing glimpse into how the policy makers at the Byzantine court perceived the crusades and the Latin East. They reflect not only the literary genre in which their authors were writing but also the way in which they used those conventions to present and construct the crusaders and the Latin states of Outre Mer and to defend and promote the policies pursued by their own rulers. Thus Anna Komnene, Michael Italikos and John Kinnamos championed the actions of Emperors Alexios I, John II and Manuel I, respectively [5, 6, 10, 15, 24, 34, 36 & 39]. Some provide eyewitness testimony: Constantine Manasses and John Phokas gave their impressions of the Latin East when in the area on official business [37 & 41] and Niketas Choniates recounted his own experiences during the Third and Fourth Crusades [42 & 50]. Joel and Ephraim of Ainos voiced the perspective of later generations looking back on these events, about which they were not always well informed [9, 20, 28 & 52]. There is even a set of advice left by an emperor for his son [21]. These viewpoints are, of course, highly partisan but that is only to be expected.

What is even more intriguing, however, is the way that Byzantine authors could express real concerns and even criticism as a kind of subtext behind the formal façade. Two of the letters translated here, for example, leave the reader in no doubt about their authors' uneasiness at the approach of western crusade armies and the intentions of their leaders [4 & 32]: they do not always display the blithe confidence in the emperor that fills the pages of Komnene and Kinnamos. Similarly, while the hyperbolic praise of the encomia reads like vapid sycophancy, skilful orators could subtly subvert the convention by weaving in 'advice' to the emperor which effectively amounted to criticism of a particular action or policy [43].[6] Nikephoros Chrysoberges, for example, subtly expressed his doubts as to the wisdom of Alexios IV's dealings with the leaders of the Fourth Crusade [49]. The same applies to histories. While Komnene and Kinnamos adhered closely to the convention to praise Emperors Alexios I and Manuel I [5, 6, 10, 34, 36 & 39], Niketas Choniates manipulated it to suggest criticism of Byzantine policy in the years leading up to the sack of Constantinople in April 1204 [42 & 48]. None of this was stated openly, merely hinted at: for the art of Byzantine writers was, as one contemporary put it, 'to weave webs of phrases, and transform the written sense into riddles, saying one thing with their tongues, but hiding something in their minds'.[7]

---

6 Angelov (2006), pp. 58–9; Mullett (2013), pp. 247–62; Chrissis (2019), pp. 248–9.
7 Mesarites (2017), p. 88.

List of Source Extracts

I. The First Crusade

1. Theodore Skoutariotes: The Origins of the First Crusade (1095–6)
2. Anna Komnene: Alexios I and the Count of Flanders (1089)
3. Pope Urban II: Letter to Alexios I (1096)
4. Theophylact of Ohrid: A Letter on the First Crusade (1097)
5. Anna Komnene: The Crusaders reach Constantinople (1096–7)
6. Anna Komnene: Alexios I and Bohemond (1097)
7. John Zonaras: The Passage of the First Crusade (1097–9)
8. Michael Glykas: The Passage of the First Crusade (1097–9)
9. Ephraim of Ainos: The Passage of the First Crusade (1097–9)
10. Anna Komnene: The Meeting at Pelekanon (1097)
11. Alexios I: Letter to the Abbot of Monte Cassino (1097)
12. Anna Komnene: Tatikios withdraws to Cyprus (1097–8)
13. Alexios I: Letter to the Abbot of Monte Cassino (1098)
14. Anna Komnene: Bohemond captures Antioch (1098)
15. Anna Komnene: Alexios retreats from Philomelion (1098)
16. Anna Komnene: The Third Wave of the First Crusade (1101)
17. Nicholas of Methone: Crusaders at Athens (1101?)

II. Alexios I, John II and the Latin East

18. Anna Komnene: Alexios I and the Latin East (1101–5)
19. Theophylact of Ohrid: A Letter on Bohemond (1103)
20. Ephraim of Ainos: Bohemond's invasion (1103–8)
21. Alexios I: *The Muses*, advice to his son John (c.1116)
22. John Kinnamos: John II's First Syrian Expedition (1137–8)
23. Niketas Choniates: John II's First Syrian Expedition (1137–8)
24. Michael Italikos: Speech on John II's First Syrian Expedition (1137–8)
25. Nikephoros Basilakes: Speech on John II's First Syrian Expedition (1137–8)

26. John Kinnamos: John II's Second Syrian Expedition (1142–3)
27. Niketas Choniates: John II's Second Syrian Expedition (1142–3)
28. Ephraim of Ainos: John II's Syrian Expeditions (1137–8 and 1142–3)

III. The Second Crusade

29. John Kinnamos: The Passage of the Second Crusade (1147–8)
30. Niketas Choniates: The Passage of the Second Crusade (1147–8)
31. Ephraim of Ainos: The Passage of the Second Crusade (1147–8)
32. John Tzetzes: Letter to the wife of the grand hetairiarch (1147)
33. Manganeios Prodromos: Two poems on the Second Crusade (1147)

IV. Manuel I and the Latin East

34. John Kinnamos: Manuel I, Antioch and Jerusalem (1158–9)
35. Niketas Choniates: Manuel I, Antioch and Jerusalem (1158–9)
36. John Kinnamos: Manuel's search for a bride from the Latin East (1160–1)
37. Constantine Manasses: Poem about his journey to Jerusalem (1161–2)
38. Ephraim of Ainos: Manuel I and the Latin East (1158–61)
39. John Kinnamos: Manuel I and the expedition to Egypt (1169)
40. Niketas Choniates: Manuel I and the expedition to Egypt (1169)
41. John Phokas: Description of the Holy Land (1177–85)

V. The Third Crusade

42. Niketas Choniates: Frederick Barbarossa in the Balkans (1188–90)
43. Niketas Choniates: Epiphany speech to Isaac II (1190)
44. Niketas Choniates: Richard I's conquest of Cyprus (1191)
45. Neophytos: On the calamities of Cyprus (1191)
46. Ephraim of Ainos: The Third Crusade in the Balkans and Cyprus (1188–91)
47. Theodosios of Byzantion: Philip II Augustus visits Patmos (1191)

VI. The Fourth Crusade

48. Niketas Choniates: The Fourth Crusade comes to Constantinople (1203)
49. Nikephoros Chrysoberges: Epiphany speech to Alexios IV (1204)
50. Niketas Choniates: The capture and sack of Constantinople (1204)
51. Ephraim of Ainos: The Fourth Crusade and the fall of Constantinople (1203–4)
52. Joel: On the fall of Constantinople (1204)

VII. After the Fourth Crusade

53. Niketas Choniates: Speech to Theodore Laskaris (1206)
54. Niketas Choniates: Lament for the death of his brother-in-law (1206)
55. Theodore Laskaris: Speech written for him by Niketas Choniates (1208)
56. Constantine Stilbes: Memorandum against the Latins (c.1215)

I   The First Crusade

The origins of the First Crusade are closely connected with events in the Byzantine empire from the mid-eleventh century, when its Christian rulers were struggling to defend their eastern border from incursions by subjects of the Great Seljuk Sultan. In August 1071, Sultan Alp Arslan inflicted a significant defeat on the Byzantines at the Battle of Manzikert and in the years that followed Byzantine authority in Asia Minor evaporated as Turkish and Armenian warlords carved out their own principalities in the region. Distracted by Norman and Pecheneg invasions in the Balkans, the emperors had little option but to leave Asia Minor to itself. By 1095, the situation had changed. With the defeat of the Normans and Pechenegs, Emperor Alexios I Komnenos was ready to embark on the reconquest of Asia Minor. It was probably in connection with that project that he sent an embassy to Pope Urban II at Piacenza in March 1095. A Latin chronicler, Bernold of St Blasien, described how the Byzantine envoys told of the depredations of the Turks in Asia Minor and implored the pope to encourage western knights to come to the rescue. It was in response to this appeal that Pope Urban II preached his famous sermon at Clermont in France during November 1095 that launched the First Crusade.[1]

1. Theodore Skoutariotes: The Origins of the First Crusade (1095–6)

The *Synopsis Chronike* or *Summary Chronicle* is a record of events from Creation up to 1261. Although the surviving manuscript, written in the 1340s, does not preserve the name of the author, it is usually attributed to Theodore Skoutariotes, who was archbishop of Cyzicus during the late thirteenth century.[2] The extract that follows is intriguing as it appears to suggest that Emperor Alexios did more than just ask for help against the Seljuk Turks: he allegedly took advantage of the known reverence of western Christians for Jerusalem and the Holy Sepulchre to encourage them to head east. The evidence of the *Synopsis Chronike* should be treated with some caution as it was written almost two hundred years after the

---

[1] On the relations between Urban II and Alexios I, see Frankopan (2012), pp. 19–24, 87–100; Harris (2022), pp. 57–60.
[2] On Skoutariotes, see Zafeiris (2011), 253–64; Neville (2018), pp. 232–6.

8   *The First Crusade*

First Crusade but it cannot be dismissed altogether. The author makes it clear in the preface that his work was a compilation of that of others so he may have derived this story from a contemporary source now lost to us. Consequently, the precise nature of Alexios' involvement in the genesis of the crusade remains a matter of debate.

Skoutariotes (1894), pp. 184–5:

Considering, therefore, that it is impossible to undertake alone the struggle for the safety of everybody, he knew that he had to enrol the Italians as allies and that this [ought to be done] with planning by deep thought, manipulation and a certain concealment of his thoughts. So, he used as a pretext the fact that these peoples considered the Persian predominance in the area of Jerusalem and of the life-giving tomb of our saviour Jesus Christ unbearable.[3] Regarding this state of affairs as a windfall, he dispatched ambassadors to him who rules the older Rome as an archpriest[4] and to the local kings and lords as they call them. Since he employed notable ambassadors, he managed to convince many of them to leave their country and to proceed wholeheartedly with the undertaking. Many of them accordingly assembled in corps numbering thousands and myriads and after they had crossed the Ionian gulf they marched on foot for a while and appeared at Constantinople. After he had concluded treatises with them and made oath pledges of good faith, he moved to the east. Soon, through divine support, their assistance, and his personal planning, he managed to drive the Persians out of Roman territory, to liberate the cities, and to restore the eastern possessions to their former glory. This emperor was just like that, ambitious and able to perform great deeds.

2. Anna Komnene: Alexios I and the Count of Flanders (1089)

Anna Komnene (1083–c.1150), also known as Anna Comnena, was the eldest child of Emperor Alexios I Komnenos and his wife, Irene Doukaina. By her own account, she started writing history, after the death of her husband, Nikephoros Bryennios, in 1138. Bryennios had begun a history of his times but had only covered the years 1070–9 so Komnene resolved to continue the story up to 1118 in a laudatory biography of her father that has become known as the *Alexiad*.[5] An account of the First Crusade from the Byzantine point of view occupies a significant portion of the work but, unlike Skoutariotes, Komnene makes no mention whatsoever of any negotiations with Pope Urban and suggests that the news of the approach of the crusade in 1096 came as a complete surprise to the emperor.[6] However, she does

---

3   Not literally the Persians. This is an example of the use of a classical word to denote a contemporary foreign people, the Seljuk Turks. 'Italians' is another example and is used here to mean western Europeans in general.
4   i.e. Pope Urban II.
5   On Anna Komnene, see PBW (2016): Anna 62; Horrocks (2010), pp. 238–40; Treadgold (2013), pp. 354–86; Neville (2018), pp. 174–85.
6   Komnene (1928), pp. 248–9; Komnene (2009), pp. 274–5.

reveal that Alexios had earlier made use of the pilgrim traffic to recruit western knights to fight in his armies, describing here how, during his 1087–91 campaign against the Pechenegs, the emperor met with Count Robert I of Flanders, who was on his way home from Jerusalem.[7]

Komnene (1928), pp. 179–80, 182, translated by Elizabeth A. Dawes:

In the meantime the emperor recuperated at Beroë[8] and fitted out the captives he had redeemed and all his hoplites with arms. At that time, too, the Count of Flanders on his way back from Jerusalem visited the emperor there, and took the customary Latin oath and also promised to send to his succour five hundred horsemen directly he reached home. Consequently the emperor showed him great honour and then dismissed him to his own country. . .

The horsemen sent by the Count of Flanders, about five hundred picked men, arrived and brought as a present to the emperor one hundred and fifty selected horses: moreover they sold him all the horses they did not require for their own use. The emperor welcomed them very graciously and returned hearty thanks. Next he received a message from the East saying that Apelchasem, the governor of Nicaea (whom the Persians usually call a 'satrap', and the Turks, who now imitate the Persians, an 'ameer'), was all but starting on an expedition against Nikomedeia, so he sent those horsemen to protect that district.[9]

3. Pope Urban II: Letter to Alexios I (1096)

During the summer of 1096, following his sermon at Clermont the previous November, Urban II sent a letter to emperor Alexios, to update him on preparations for the great military expedition and to inform him that the first contingents would be arriving at Constantinople later in the year. Note how the pope does not address Alexios by his correct title of 'emperor of the Romans'. The popes reserved that style for the western emperors whom they themselves had crowned.

Urban II (1853), col. 485:

Urban the Second, the Roman pope, to Alexios, emperor of Constantinople, etc.

After it had been decreed by public vows at Clermont in Arvernia[10] that war would be waged against the Saracens, such a multitude of men was signed with the cross that as many as three hundred thousand were counted. It is, however, in the zeal of

---

7 A few years later, Alexios despatched a letter to the count, apparently on the same topic of military assistance, although the version of it that has come down to us is clearly not the original text. See Robert the Monk (2005), pp. 219–22.
8 Modern Stara Zagora in Bulgaria.
9 Abu'l Kasim (d.1092) was emir of Nicaea, modern Iznik, from 1086. Nikomedeia is now Izmit.
10 Clermont today is in the French département of Auvergne-Rhône-Alpes. Urban is using the old Latin name for the area.

the brave leaders that we must place most hope for the recovery of Jerusalem. First of all, Peter the Hermit has made himself leader of countless numbers.[11] Godfrey, Eustace and Baldwin, the counts of Boulogne, have added themselves to him and they have prepared even greater forces.[12] From here comes the bishop of Le Puy, the leader of the campaign, and Count Raymond of Saint-Gilles,[13] from there Hugh the Great, brother of King Philip of France, and the counts Robert of Normandy, the other Robert, of Flanders, and Stephen of Chartres.[14] What shall I say of that Bohemond who with great generosity of soul has joined himself to them as a partner with seven thousand chosen Italian youths, having left the care of everything to his brother, with whom he had contended in conflict for a long time.[15] To these great men of war, one preparation is needed, that they should be assisted by your protection and by the provisioning of such a host. Therefore, I beseech you in the strongest possible terms to show favour to the just and glorious war in whatever ways you can. Though I have no doubt that you will have already taken this in hand, I wanted you to know all the same through my letter that this would be most welcome both to me and to the whole of Christendom. Farewell. Rome etc.

4. Theophylact of Ohrid: A Letter on the First Crusade (1097)

Theophylact Hephaistos (c.1050–c.1128) was archbishop of Ohrid in North Macedonia from around 1088. He was well connected with court circles, serving as the tutor of Constantine Doukas, the son of Emperor Michael VII who was for a time betrothed to Anna Komnene.[16] He was a prolific writer of letters, such as this one addressed to the bishop of the Macedonian town of Kitros, ancient Pydna, whose name is not recorded.[17] It can be dated from context to early 1097 and refers to the passage of the First Crusade through the Balkans in 1096–7. It is a rare example of a contemporary source written while the outcome of the expedition was not yet known.

Theophylact of Ohrid (1986), pp. 303–5:

To [the Bishop] of Kitros

---

11 Peter the Hermit led the first wave of the Crusade which arrived six months before the other contingents.
12 Only the eldest of the three brothers, Eustace III, was count of Boulogne. Godfrey of Bouillon was duke of Lower Lotharingia while Baldwin was merely a knight.
13 Adhémar (d.1098), bishop of Le Puy, was to be papal legate on the crusade. Raymond of Saint-Gilles (c.1041–1105) was count of Toulouse.
14 Hugh, count of Vermandois, Robert Curthose, duke of Normandy, Robert II, count of Flanders, and Stephen, count of Blois and Chartres.
15 Mark Bohemond, lord of Taranto and Apulia, left his half-brother Roger Borsa as duke of Apulia and Calabria.
16 On Theophylact, see PBW (2016): Theophylaktos 105.
17 See PBW (2016): Anonymous 221.

Most holy brother and lord, we have maintained silence between each other for a long time. If you know, however, the reason behind your silence, tell us what it is. On my part, it was first the passage of the Franks that shut my lips, or their invasion, or however else one might express it. It drew and diverted our attention so much that we lost our senses. So intoxicated did we become from its bitter bowl and so amazed with unusual fervour. Rather to quote a few words from our texts, having drunk out the wine full of sediment, which is reserved for the sinful, we were thrown into confusion.[18] We lurched around like drunken men, and all our wisdom was consumed. This is the reason why I was rendered heedless and discouraged towards you and refrained in silence from any good and pleasing correspondence with your honour. This was then the first obstacle for my tongue. The second was my inability to find someone reliable to bear the letter. For most people are eager to take letters but torpid to carry them and deliver them to the recipient, as if they had no hands.

Since, however, we have now become accustomed to the harassment of the Franks, we bear our sufferings more easily than before, for time brings ease and is a teacher for us all, and thanks to this we sometimes recover our minds [....]

5. Anna Komnene: The Crusaders reach Constantinople (1096–7)

Anna Komnene gives a very detailed account of the passage of the First Crusade through Byzantine territory and the central theme of her narrative is Alexios' wary reception of an expedition that he had not expected and which he feared might have designs on Byzantine territory. She presents Godfrey of Bouillon and the other crusaders as conventional 'barbarians': fearless and intrepid, but also greedy and boastful.[19]

Komnene (1928), pp. 250–4, 257–8, 261, translated by Elizabeth A. Dawes:

According to universal rumour Godfrey, who had sold his country, was the first to start on the appointed road; this man was very rich and very proud of his bravery, courage and conspicuous lineage; for every Frank is anxious to outdo the others. And such an upheaval of both men and women took place then as had never occurred within human memory, the simpler-minded were urged on by the real desire of worshipping at our Lord's Sepulchre, and visiting the sacred places; but the more astute, especially men like Bohemond and those of like mind, had another secret reason, namely, the hope that while on their travels they might by some means be able to seize the capital itself, looking upon this as a kind of corollary. And Bohemond disturbed the minds of many nobler men by thus cherishing his old grudge against the emperor. Meanwhile Peter, after he had delivered his message, crossed the straits of Lombardy before anybody else with eighty thousand men on foot, and one hundred thousand on horseback, and reached the capital by way of

---

18 Psalms 107:27.
19 On Komnene's account of the First Crusade, see Harris (2022), pp. 65–7.

12 The First Crusade

Hungary.[20] For the Frankish race, as one may conjecture, is always very hot headed and eager, but when once it has espoused a cause, it is uncontrollable. The emperor, knowing what Peter had suffered before from the Turks, advised him to wait for the arrival of the other Counts, but Peter would not listen for he trusted to the multitude of his followers, so crossed and pitched his camp near a small town called Helenopolis.[21] After him followed the Normans numbering ten thousand, who separated themselves from the rest of the army and devastated the country round Nicaea, and behaved most cruelly to all [. . .].[22]

One Hugh, brother of the King of France, and as proud as Novatus of his nobility, riches and power,[23] when on the point of leaving his native land, ostensibly to go to the Holy Sepulchre, sent a ridiculous message to the emperor, with a view to arranging beforehand that he should have a magnificent reception. 'Know, O emperor', he wrote, 'that I am the king of kings and the greatest of those under heaven; and it behoves you to meet and treat me on arrival with all pomp and in a manner worthy of my nobility' [. . .]. Hugh, who, as has been said, travelled through Rome to Lombardy and was crossing from Bari to Illyria, was caught in a very severe storm and lost the greater number of his vessels, crews, soldiers and all, and only the one skiff on which he was, was spat out, so to say, by the waves on to the coast between Dyrrachion, at a place called Palus, and he on it half-broken.[24] After he had been thus miraculously saved, two of the men who were on the look-out for his arrival, found him, and addressing him by name, said, 'The Duke is anxiously looking for your coming, and is most desirous to see you'.[25] Thereupon Hugh at once asked for a horse, and one of the two men dismounted and very willingly gave him his horse. Thus the Duke met him after his deliverance, and welcomed him and asked him about his journey and his country, and heard about the disaster which overtook him on his crossing; so he comforted him with fair promises, and finally set a rich banquet before him. After the feast he detained him and left him, not without supervision, but certainly free. He speedily acquainted the emperor with the facts, and then waited to receive further instructions. On receipt of the news the emperor quickly sent Boutoumites to Epidamnos (which we have often called Dyrrachion) to fetch Hugh and escort him to the capital,[26] but not to travel along the direct road, but to deviate from it, and pass through Philippopolis.[27] For he was afraid of the Frankish hosts and armies which were coming behind him. The emperor received

---

20 Peter the Hermit's army reached Constantinople on 1 August 1096.
21 Probably the modern village of Hersek.
22 Peter's army was severely mauled by the Turks near Nikomedeia in October 1096 and the survivors fled back to Constantinople.
23 i.e. Hugh, Count of Vermandois, who was the brother of King Philip I of France: Anna calls him Ubus. Novatus or Novatian (c.200–258) was a presbyter of the early Roman Church whose pride allegedly led him into doctrinal error.
24 Dyrrachion is modern Dürres in Albania.
25 The duke of Dyrrachion was Alexios I's nephew, John Komnenos: see PBW (2016): Ioannes 128.
26 Manuel Boutoumites, a prominent commander in Alexios' army. See PBW (2016): Manuel 62.
27 Philippopolis is now Plovdiv in Bulgaria.

him with all honour and showed him much friendliness, and by also giving him a large sum of money he persuaded him to become his 'man' at once and to swear thereto by the customary oath of the Latins [. . .].[28]

Now Count Godfrey crossed about this time, too, with more Counts, and an army of ten thousand horsemen and seventy thousand foot, and on reaching the capital he quartered his army near the Propontis, and it reached from the bridge nearest to the monastery of Kosmidion right up to the church of St. Phokas.[29] But when the emperor urged him to cross the straits of the Propontis, he let one day pass after another and postponed doing so on one pretext after another; the truth was that he was awaiting the arrival of Bohemond and the rest of the Counts [. . .]. But the emperor, aware of their rascality from previous experience, sent an order by letter that the auxiliary forces with their officers should move from Athyra to Phileas (a seaside town on the Euxine)[30] and station themselves there by squadrons, and watch whether any messenger came from Godfrey to Bohemond and the other Counts behind, or contrariwise one from them to him, and if so, to prevent their passage. But in the meantime the following incident occurred. The emperor invited some of the Counts with Godfrey in order to advise them to suggest to Godfrey to take the oath; and as time was wasted owing to the longwinded talkativeness of the Latins, a false rumour reached the others that the Counts had been thrown into prison by the emperor.[31] Immediately numerous regiments moved on Byzantion, and to begin with they demolished the palace near the so-called Silver Lake. They also made an attack on the walls of Byzantion, not with siege-engines indeed, as they had none, but trusting to their numbers they actually had the impudence to try to set fire to the gate below the palace which is close to the chapel built long ago by one of the emperors to the memory of Nicholas, the greatest saint in the hierarchy [. . .].[32]

On the following day Hugh went and advised Godfrey to yield to the emperor's wish, unless he wanted to have a second experience of the latter's military skill, and to swear that he would keep good faith with him. But Godfrey reprimanded him severely and said, 'You who came from your own country as a king with great wealth and a great army have brought yourself down from that high position to the rank of a slave; and then just as if you had won some great success you come and advise me to do the same?' The other replied, 'We ought to have remained in our own countries and not have interfered in foreign affairs; but as we have come as far as this where we sorely need the emperor's protection,

---

28 *Gesta Francorum* in Hill (1962), pp. 5–6, says that Hugh was arrested and sent to Constantinople as part of a 'treacherous plan' to make him swear the oath.
29 Godfrey's contingent arrived on 23 December 1096. The Kosmidion monastery was just outside the Land Walls, on the upper reaches of the Golden Horn.
30 i.e. on the Black Sea.
31 Albert of Aachen (2013), i. 48, suggests that it was the news of the imprisonment of Hugh of Vermandois and others that strained relations between Godfrey and Alexios.
32 The fighting took place on 2 April 1097, around the north-western area of Constantinople, known as Blachernae, where there was a church dedicated to the legendary saint, Nicholas of Myra. Anna claims that her husband, Nikephoros Bryennios, inflicted a severe reverse on Godfrey's troops.

matters will not turn out well for us if we do not fall in with his wishes'. But since Godfrey sent Hugh away without his having effected anything and the emperor received news that the Counts coming after were already near, he sent a selected few of the generals with their troops, and enjoined them again to advise, nay even to compel, Godfrey to cross the straits. Directly the Latins caught sight of them, without waiting even a minute or asking what they wanted, they betook themselves to battle and fighting. A severe battle arose between them in which many fell on either side, and [all] the emperor's [men] were wounded,[33] who had attacked him too recklessly. As the imperial troops fought very bravely, the Latins turned their backs. In consequence Godfrey shortly afterwards yielded to the emperor's wish. He went to the emperor and swore the oath which was required of him, namely, that whatever towns, countries or forts he managed to take which had formerly belonged to the Roman Empire, he would deliver up to the governor expressly sent by the emperor for this purpose.[34] After he had taken this oath, and received a large sum of money, he was invited to the emperor's hearth and table, and feasted luxuriously, and afterwards crossed the straits and encamped near Pelekanon.[35] Thereupon the emperor gave orders that abundant supplies of food should be conveyed to them.

6. Anna Komnene: Alexios I and Bohemond (1097)

Bohemond looms much larger in Anna Komnene's account of the First Crusade than the other leaders, as a villain of almost superhuman stature. She alleges that he was planning from the outset to use the crusade as a cover for seizing Byzantine territory and constantly emphasises his cunning and duplicity. She contrasts him with the count of Toulouse, Raymond of St Gilles, whom she presents as Alexios' friend and ally from the outset and whose name she hellenises to 'Isangeles', which has the connotation of 'like an angel'. Recent research suggests that Komnene, writing with decades of hindsight, is probably exaggerating both Alexios' mistrust of Bohemond and his friendship with Raymond at this point. The *Gesta Francorum* describes how Raymond was the most resistant of the crusade leaders to swear the oath demanded by Alexios. Bohemond, on the other hand, threatened to take the emperor's side against the count if he refused to swear. The likelihood is that in the spring of 1097, Alexios regarded Bohemond as his ally and Raymond as the potential enemy.[36]

---

33 There was a lacuna in the text used by Dawes at this point. The text has been supplied from Komnene (2009), p. 288.
34 The Latin sources give a different account of the oaths, leaving out the promise to return conquered cities and stressing Alexios' undertaking to supply the expedition with provisions. See *Gesta Francorum* in Hill (1962), p. 12.
35 Pelekanon is now Eskihisar.
36 Hill (1962), p. 13. See Harris (2022), pp. 70–4.

Komnene (1928), pp. 264–8, translated by Elizabeth A. Dawes:

Now when Bohemond reached Apros with the other Counts,[37] he reflected that he was not sprung from the nobility, nor was he bringing a large force owing to his poverty, but he was anxious to win the emperor's goodwill and at the same time conceal his own designs against him, so leaving the other Counts behind he rode ahead with only ten Franks and hastened to reach the capital.[38] As the emperor knew his machinations and had been long aware of his treacherous and scheming nature, he desired to talk with him before the other Counts arrived, and to hear what he had to say, and to persuade him to cross into Asia before the others in order that he might not join those who were on the point of arriving, and corrupt their minds also. So when Bohemond entered, he smiled at him cheerfully and asked him about his journey and where he had left the Counts. All these things Bohemond explained clearly as he thought best, and then the emperor joked and reminded him of his former daring deeds at Dyrrachion and his former enmity.[39] To this the other replied, 'Though I was certainly your adversary and enemy at that time, yet now I come of my own free will as a friend of your Majesty'. The emperor talked of many things with him, and lightly sounded his feelings, and as he perceived that he would agree to take the oath of fidelity, he dismissed him saying, 'You must be tired from your journey and must go and rest now; tomorrow we can talk of whatever we like'. So Bohemond went away to Kosmidion where a lodging had been prepared for him,[40] and a rich table spread for him, laden with all manner of meats and eatables. The cooks also brought in the uncooked flesh of land-animals and birds, and said, 'You see, we have prepared the food in our usual fashion; but if those do not please you, see, here is raw meat which shall be cooked in whatever way you like'. For they prepared the food and spoke in this way by the emperor's orders. For he was wonderfully clever in judging a man's character, clever, too, in penetrating to the heart and ferreting out a man's thoughts, and as he knew Bohemond's suspicions and maliciousness, he guessed at the truth. Consequently, to prevent Bohemond suspecting him, he ordered those raw meats to be taken to him at the same time in order to allay any suspicion. Nor was he wrong in his surmise. For that dreadful Bohemond not only refrained from tasting the viands at all, or even touching them with the tips of his fingers, but pushed them all away at once, and, though he did not speak of his secret suspicion, he divided them up amongst the attendants, pretending to all appearance to be doing them a kindness, but in reality, if you look at it aright, he was mixing a cup of death for them. And he did not even conceal his craft, for he treated his servants with contempt. The raw meats, however, he ordered his own cooks to prepare in the usual Frankish way. The next day he asked the men who had eaten the supper how they felt. When they replied that they felt

---

37 Apros, now Kermeyan, was in Thrace about 180 kilometres west of Constantinople.
38 He arrived at Constantinople on 5 April 1097.
39 Bohemond had been with his father Robert Guiscard when he had invaded the Byzantine Balkans and defeated Alexios I at the battle of Dyrrachion in October 1081.
40 The Kosmidion was later known to westerners as 'Bohemond's castle' in memory of his stay there: Geoffrey of Villehardouin (2008), p. 43.

exceedingly well and had not suffered even the slightest discomfort from it, he discovered his hidden thought, and said, 'When I recalled my wars with him and that terrible battle I must own I was afraid that he would perhaps arrange my death by mixing poison with my food'. So spake Bohemond. I have never seen a wicked man who did not act wrongly in all his words and deeds; for whenever a man deserts the middle course of action, to whatever extreme he inclines, he stands far away from goodness.

The emperor sent for Bohemond and requested him to take the customary oath of the Latins. And he, mindful of his own position, namely, that he was not descended from illustrious ancestors, nor had a great supply of money, and for this reason not even many troops, but only a very limited number of Frankish retainers, and being moreover by nature ready to swear falsely, yielded readily to the emperor's wish. Then the emperor selected a room in the palace and had the floor strewn with every kind of riches, . . . and so filled the chamber with garments and stamped gold and silver, and other materials of lesser value, that one could not even walk because of their quantity. And he told the man who was to show Bohemond these things, to throw open the doors suddenly. Bohemond was amazed at the sight and exclaimed 'If all these treasures were mine, I should have made myself master of many countries long ere this!' and the attendant replied, 'The emperor makes you a present of all these riches to-day'. Bohemond was overjoyed and after thanking for the present he went away to rest in the house where he lodged. But when these treasures were brought to him, he who had admired them before had changed his mind and said, 'Never did I imagine that the emperor would inflict such dishonour on me. Take them away and give them back to him who sent them'. But the emperor, knowing the Latins' characteristic fickleness, quoted the popular proverb, 'Let bad things return to their own master'. When Bohemond heard of this and saw the porters carefully packing the presents up again, he changed his mind – he, who a minute before was sending them away and was annoyed at them, now gave the porters pleasant looks, just like a polypus that changes its form in an instant. For by nature the man was a rogue and ready for any eventualities; in roguery and courage he was far superior to all the Latins who came through then, as he was inferior to them in forces and money. But in spite of his surpassing all in superabundant activity in mischief, yet fickleness like some natural Latin appendage attended him too. So he who first rejected the presents, afterwards accepted them with great pleasure. For he was sad in mind as he had left his country a landless man, ostensibly to worship at the Holy Sepulchre, but in reality with the intent of gaining a kingdom for himself, or rather, if it were possible, to follow his father's advice and seize the Roman Empire itself, and as he wanted to let out every reef, as the proverb has it, he required a great deal of money. But the emperor, who understood his melancholy and ill-natured disposition, did his best cleverly to remove anything that would assist him in his secret plans. Therefore when Bohemond demanded the office of Great Domestic of the East, he did not gain his request, for he was trying to 'out-Cretan a Cretan'. For the emperor feared that if he gained power he would make the other Counts his captives and bring them round afterwards to doing whatever he wished. Further, he did not want Bohemond to have the slightest suspicion that he was already detected, so he flattered him with fair hopes by saying, 'The time for that has not come yet; but by your energy and reputation and above all by your fidelity it will come ere long'.[41] After this conversation and after bestowing gifts and honours of many kinds on them, the next day he took his seat on the imperial throne and summoned Bohemond and all the Counts. To them he discoursed of the things likely to befall them on their journey, and gave them useful advice; he also instructed them in the Turks' usual methods of warfare, and suggested the manner in which they should dispose the army and arrange their ranks, and advised them not to go far in pursuit of the Turks when they fled. And after he had in this way somewhat softened their savage behaviour by dint of money and advice, and had given them good counsel, he suggested their crossing into Asia. Raymond of St Gilles he liked especially because of his superior wisdom and genuine sincerity and purity of life, also because he recognised that he valued truth above everything; for he 'shone' amidst all the Latins 'as the sun amidst the stars of heaven'. And for this reason he kept him by him for some time. After the Counts had all taken leave of the emperor and reached Damalion by crossing the Propontis,[42] and the emperor was relieved from the disturbance they caused, he often sent for Raymond and explained to him more clearly what he suspected would happen to the Latins on their journey, and he also laid bare to him the suspicions he had of the Franks' intention. He often repeated these things to Raymond and opened, so to say, the doors of his soul to him and, after stating everything clearly, he enjoined him to be ever on the watch against Bohemond's wickedness and if the latter tried to break his oath to check him and by all possible means frustrate his plans. Raymond replied to the emperor, 'Bohemond has acquired perjury and treachery as a species of ancestral heritage, and it would be a miracle if he kept his oath. However, I will endeavour as far as in me lies always to carry out your orders'. And taking his leave of the emperor, he went away to rejoin the whole Frankish army.

7. John Zonaras: The Passage of the First Crusade (1097–9)

Anna Komnene was not the only Byzantine historian to describe the passage of the First Crusade. Her contemporary John Zonaras (c.1074–c.1160) held office at the court of Alexios I although his political career seems to have come to an end with the emperor's death in 1118. He became a monk and produced numerous theological works and commentaries, as well as a history from Creation to 1118.[43] Given that he would have been an eyewitness to the arrival of the First Crusade at

---

41 The Domestic of the East was the commander of the Byzantine forces on the Syrian and Armenian frontiers based in border cities such as Antioch. This alleged conversation could therefore be compared to the claim of the *Gesta Francorum* the Alexios promised Bohemond: 'lands beyond Antioch'. See Hill (1962), p. 12.
42 Damalion or Damalis was a settlement on the Asian side of the Bosporus, probably modern Kızkule.
43 On Zonaras, see PBW (2016): Ioannes 6007; Treadgold (2013), pp. 388–99; Neville (2018), pp. 191–9.

18 *The First Crusade*

Constantinople in 1096–7, his account is disappointingly brief and at times inaccurate. He claims that the crusaders took their first objective Nicaea by storm and then sold it to Alexios. In fact, the city surrendered directly to the Byzantine emperor on 19 June 1097 after a six-week siege.[44] Moreover, while Zonaras mentions the capture of Antioch in 1098 he leaves out the subsequent seizure of the city by Bohemond and Alexios I's demands that it be yielded to him, elements that are central to Komnene's account.

Zonaras (1897), pp. iii, 242–3:

Next, the Franks marched from the west and approached the Queen of Cities[45] so as to be ferried from Constantinople over to the east. Some kind of divine sign foretold their march. For an innumerable multitude of locusts which originated from the west, so dense that it resembled a flying cloud which obscured the sun, flew over the mightiest of cities and its walls and rushing towards the east it rested there.[46] The Franks, then, after they had been ferried over, struck against Nicaea in Bithynia which was occupied by the Turks. After some time and many casualties on both sides, the Franks finally seized the city for a while.[47] Then they sold Nicaea to the emperor in turn for a large amount of money and marched further east. Some conquered Antioch which lies by Orontes after much hardship and slaughter, while others, after a great struggle, conquered the city of Jerusalem.

8. Michael Glykas: The Passage of the First Crusade (1097–9)

Michael Glykas worked as a secretary at the court of Alexios I's grandson, Manuel I Komnenos. His short account of the First Crusade was probably copied from Zonaras, reproducing the locusts and the inaccurate details about the capture of Nicaea.[48]

Glykas (1836), p. 621:

[621] At that time, the nation of the Franks arrived in our empire from the west so as to cross over to the east. A sign from God foretold their march, for an innumerable multitude of locusts from the west had been seen, resembling a mass of clouds which rode over and darkened the sun in the midst of the Greatest of Cities, flew across its boundaries, rushed to the east, and rested there. And so, the Franks were ferried over, took Nicaea from the Turks who occupied it, and sold it to the emperor like some market ware.

---

44 Cf. Komnene (1928), pp. 274–5; Komnene (2009), pp. 300–2; Hill (1962), p. 17; Albert of Aachen (2013), i. 72–3.
45 i.e. Constantinople.
46 The locusts are also reported by Komnene (1928), p. 249; Komnene (2009), pp. 275–6.
47 Compare Komnene (1928), pp. 274–5; Komnene (2009), pp. 302–4.
48 See Treadgold (2013), pp. 403–7; Neville (2018), pp. 205–9.

9. Ephraim of Ainos: The Passage of the First Crusade (1097–9)

Nothing is known about Ephraim except that he was probably writing in the early fourteenth century and was connected with the port of Ainos in Thrace, now the Turkish town of Enez. He was the author of a chronicle in verse that recounts events from 37 to 1261 CE, with much of the information about the period of the crusades being derived from the works of Zonaras and Niketas Choniates. This passage is clearly taken from the former, with Ephraim turning Zonaras' prose into verse. The numbers in square brackets, for example [3575], refer to the lines of the original poem.[49]

Ephraim of Ainos (1990), pp. 132–3:

And an army of Italians emerged from the West
and marched towards Constantinople,
[3575] aiming for the East.
A throng of locusts which flew
from the West towards the East,
through the borders of Thrace and Macedonia,
clearly foretold the advent of these troops.
[3580] The army of the Franks crossed the straits.
It arrived before the city of Nicaea
which was shamefully under the sway of the Turkish hand.
After some time, a dreadful battle
and many losses on both sides,
[3585] the Franks took the city by storm.
They sold it to the emperor
for a large amount of money and proceeded further.
They attacked the city of Antioch
and conquered it with battle and ruses.
[3590] After Antioch, they also captured Zion,
God's city, with fierce struggles and battles.

10. Anna Komnene: The Meeting at Pelekanon (1097)

Following the capture of Nicaea in June 1097, Alexios I crossed the Bosporus and encamped at Pelekanon. This was his last opportunity to exercise any direct control over the crusade before it departed on the next stage of its journey towards Jerusalem and to receive the oath from those leaders who had not yet sworn. Unwilling to go with the expedition himself, he appointed one of his officers, Tatikios, to accompany it with a small force.

---

49 On Ephraim, see Neville (2018), pp. 249–51.

Komnene (1928), pp. 275–6, translated by Elizabeth A. Dawes:

The emperor was still staying at Pelekanon and as he wished that those Counts who had not yet sworn fealty to him, should also take this oath, he commanded Boutoumites by letter to advise all the Counts together not to start on their way to Antioch before they took leave of the emperor, for if they did so, it might be that they would receive still further gifts. Directly he heard the words 'money' and 'gifts', Bohemond first of all gave his assent to Boutoumites' advice and urged all the others to go with him to the emperor, so insatiably greedy of money was he. When they reached Pelekanon, the emperor received them with great ceremony, and treated them with much consideration; later he called them and said, 'You remember the oath you all took to me, and if you are not going to be transgressors of it, advise those who you know have not yet sworn fealty to me, to take the same oath'. And the Counts at once sent for those who had not yet sworn fealty; and they all came together and consummated the oath. But Bohemond's nephew, Tancred, a youth of independent spirit, maintained that he owed fidelity to Bohemond alone, and that he would keep it to his death.[50] His own friends standing by and even the emperor's kinsmen kept importuning him, and then he said, feigning indifference, as it were, and with a glance at the tent in the front of which the emperor was sitting (it was larger than any had ever seen before), 'If you will give me this tent full of money and as much more as you have given to the Counts, then I too will take the oath'. Now because of the respect he bore to the emperor, Palaiologos could not stand Tancred's conceited speech, and turned him away with contempt.[51] Whereat Tancred, who was very hasty, rushed at him and the emperor observing it rose from his throne and stood between them. Bohemond too held him back with the words, 'It is not fitting for you to behave in such an impudent way to the emperor's kinsman'. Then Tancred, ashamed of having acted like a drunken man towards Palaiologos and also influenced to a certain degree by Bohemond's and the others' counsel, took the oath.[52] When they had all taken leave of the emperor, he assigned them Tatikios, who was then Great Primikerios,[53] and the troops under his command, partly to assist them on every occasion and to avert danger and partly to take over the towns from them if God allowed them to take any. So the Franks once again crossed the straits the next day, and all took the road leading to Antioch. The emperor guessed that not all the men would necessarily depart with the Counts and accordingly signified to Boutoumites to hire all the Franks, who remained behind when their army left, for the garrison of Nicaea.

---

50 Tancred was the son of Marquis Odo the Good and Bohemond's sister Emma.
51 George Palaiologos was Alexios' brother-in-law, being married to his wife's sister Anna. See PBW (2016): Georgios 61.
52 This incident is also described in Ralph of Caen (2005), pp. 40–3.
53 See PBW (2016): Tatikios 61.

11. Alexios I: Letter to the Abbot of Monte Cassino (1097)

The monastery of Monte Cassino, which lies about 130 kilometres southeast of Rome, had been founded by St Benedict of Nursia in around 529. The Byzantine emperors had for some time bestowed their patronage on it, Alexios' predecessor Michael VII having granted it an annual pension of 23 pounds of gold in 1076. The abbots may well have been useful to the emperors for the influence that they could wield at the papal curia.[54] That might explain why this first letter, written in Latin rather than Greek, was despatched to Abbot Oderisius I by Alexios in August 1097. By that time, the crusaders had defeated a Turkish army at Dorylaion (modern Eskişehir) on 1 July. It was not until October, however, when the army reached Antioch. In the letter, the emperor appears to be responding to a request from the abbot to assist the expedition, similar to that already made by Pope Urban II [3]. The effusive tone of the letter was typical of Byzantine diplomatic practice, the French monk Odo of Deuil later complaining that envoys from Constantinople were 'too affectionate'.[55]

Alexios I (1901), pp. 140–1:

Our Majesty has been kept informed, close servant of God, by all those noble and courageous counts and dukes who have come from those parts and also indeed by the revered leaders themselves! Most prudent and wise abbot of Monte Cassino! By reason of your great virtues, just as you have always work to do, occupy yourself ceaselessly with all those things that are pleasing to God. Not only your labour but also your penances and admonitions concerning such matters are acceptable to God and enlightening to men. At least, although Our Majesty has particularly considered you and has been fulfilled by your holy words, if only it could be arranged that we might see Your Venerableness with our own eyes every day and speak with you constantly. We wish that with your holy and venerable prayers you should make a foundation in God, so that I will be brought to his remembrance, and that you should write to us more often by means of your honourable letters, telling us of your deeds and of those of your subordinates and of events in those parts. Of these matters and of the pilgrims, this should be said: Just as we hoped, God has been with us and them up to the present time. Our Majesty knows what you are hearing from many people. You will hear it more plainly from these our envoys.

Sent in the month of August, fifth indiction, from the most holy city of Constantinople.

---

54 On relations between Byzantium and Monte Cassino, see Bloch (1946), pp. 195–222.
55 Odo of Deuil, 1948, pp. 26–7.

12. Anna Komnene: Tatikios withdraws to Cyprus (1097–8)

The crusade army reached Antioch on 21 October 1097. The siege dragged on for months, throughout the autumn, winter and spring, during which time the army suffered considerable hardship. Anna's chronology is awry here. Eager to present Bohemond's every move as part of his plot to seize Antioch, she connects the withdrawal of Tatikios with the negotiations with an Armenian to admit the crusaders into the city in June 1098. In fact, Alexios' representative probably left Antioch much earlier, in February.[56]

Komnene (1928), pp. 277–8, translated by Elizabeth A. Dawes:

Now there happened to be an Armenian on the tower above guarding the portion of the wall assigned to Bohemond.[57] As he often bent over from above Bohemond plied him with honeyed words, tempted him with many promises and thus persuaded him to betray the city to him. The Armenian said to him, 'Whenever you like and as soon as you give me a signal from outside, I will at once hand over this tower to you. Only be quite ready yourself and have all the people with you ready too and equipped with ladders. And not only you yourself must be ready but the whole army must be under arms so that directly the Turks see you after you have come up and hear your war-cry, they will be terrified and turn in flight'. And this arrangement Bohemond kept secret. While these matters were in contemplation, a messenger came saying that an immense crowd of Hagarenes sent from Chorosan against them was close at hand, under the conduct of the man called Kerbogha.[58] When he heard this, as he did not wish to cede Antioch to Tatikios according to the oath he had previously sworn to the emperor, but rather longed for it for himself; Bohemond planned a wicked plan which would force Tatikios to remove himself from the city against his will. Accordingly he went to him and said, 'I want to reveal a secret to you, as I am concerned for your safety. A report which has reached the ears of the Counts has much disturbed their minds – it is, that the emperor has persuaded the Sultan to send these men from Chorosan against us. As the Counts firmly believe this they are plotting against your life. And now, I have done my duty by warning you beforehand of the danger that threatens you. And the rest is your concern, to take measures for your own safety, and that of the troops under you'. Then considering the severe famine (for an ox-head was being sold for three gold staters) and also because he despaired of taking Antioch, Tatikios departed, embarked on the Roman fleet which was in the harbour of Soudi, and made for Cyprus.

---

56 See France (1971), pp. 137–47.
57 *Gesta Francorum* in Hill (1962), pp. 44–5, gives this individual the name Firuz.
58 Qiwam al-Dawla abu Said, atabeg of Mosul from 1096. 'Hagarenes' refers to the Arabs who were supposedly the descendants of Hagar, the second wife of the Biblical patriarch Abraham, through their son Ishmael.

13. Alexios I: Letter to the Abbot of Monte Cassino (1098)

News of the long siege of Antioch and the desperate conditions being endured by the crusaders had apparently been conveyed back to Italy, where Abbot Oderisius had heard about it. He had apparently written to Emperor Alexios to request that he march east to assist the Christian army. This letter is Alexios' reply. In spite of his reassuring words, the emperor does not seem to have been in any hurry to bring relief to his co-religionists. The letter is dated from Constantinople in June 1098, indicating that the emperor had still not yet set out.[59]

Alexios I (1901), pp. 152–3:

How much have I read that you have written to Our Majesty, most venerable and wise servant of God, abbot of the monastery of Monte Cassino! Your letter declared honour and praise to Our Majesty and toward me and our subjects there is most certainly great clemency and innumerable blessings from our Almighty and Most Merciful God. Through His mercy and grace, He has honoured and exalted Our Majesty. I, however, not only have no good within in me, but because I sin more than all men, I pray every day that His patience and mercy may take pity on me and sustain my weakness. You, on the other hand, who are full of goodness and virtue, judge me, sinner that I am, a good man, and truly you have a certain achievement: in as much Our Majesty is praised without having done deeds worthy of praise, he holds the accolade to his own condemnation. Your most sagacious letters said: 'I urge you strongly to provide succour to the army of the Franks'. Let your venerable holiness be in no doubt that since Our Majesty has been concerned about them, I will help and advise them in all matters. I have already worked with them in so far as lay within my power, not as a friend or acquaintance but like a father. The expense that I have gone to on their account is more than can be reckoned. Had Our Majesty not done this and aided them in this way, who else after God would have come to their aid? Nor is Our Majesty reluctant to assist once more. By the grace of God, they have succeeded until today in the mission which they began, and they will continue to succeed in the future as long as right intention goes before them. Many knights and foot-soldiers have departed to the Eternal Tabernacle: some of them were killed, others died. They are indeed blessed, since they gave their lives in a good cause! For that reason, we should not regard them as dead at all, but as living and as having passed over to an eternal and incorruptible life. In token of my good faith and of my high regard for your monastery, Our Majesty sends you a vestment, decorated on the back with sparkling gold.[60]

Sent in the month of June, sixth indiction, from the most holy city of Constantinople.

---

59 On these events, see Frankopan (2012), pp. 156–72; Harris (2022), pp. 72–7.
60 The emperor uses the word *epiloricum*. Presumably this was some kind of clerical vestment, chosen as an appropriate gift for an abbot.

14. Anna Komnene: Bohemond captures Antioch (1098)

Anna Komnene now describes how Bohemond was able to bring the crusaders into Antioch and capture it. In her construction of events, he was careful to do so in a fashion that prepared the way for his future rule over the city.

Komnene (1928), pp. 278–9, translated by Elizabeth A. Dawes:

After [Tatikios'] departure Bohemond, who still kept the Armenian's promise secret, and was buoyed up by the great hope of gaining possession of Antioch for himself, said to the Counts, 'You see how long we have already persevered in this siege, and yet have accomplished nothing useful up to the present, and now we are within an ace of perishing by starvation unless we can devise something better for our salvation'. On their enquiring what that could be, he replied, 'God does not always give victory to the leaders by means of the sword, nor are such things always accomplished by fighting. But what toil has not procured, words have often effected, and the greatest trophies have been erected by friendly and propitiatory intercourse. Let us therefore not spend our time here uselessly, but endeavour to accomplish something sensible and courageous for our own safety before Kerbogha arrives. Let each one of us studiously try to win over the barbarian who guards our respective section. And if you like, let there be set as prize for the one who first succeeds in this work, the sovereignty of this city until such time as the man who is to take it over from us arrives from the emperor. Even in this way perhaps we may not be able to accomplish anything worthwhile'. All these things that artful and ambitious Bohemond did, not so much for the sake of the Latins, and the common weal, as for his own advancement, and by this planning and speaking and deceiving he did not fail to gain his object as my history will show further on. All the Counts agreed to his proposition and set to work. And at dawn of day Bohemond at once made for the tower, and the Armenian according to agreement opened the gate to him; he immediately rushed up with his followers more quickly than can be told and was seen by the people within and without standing on the battlements of the tower and ordering the trumpeters to sound the call to battle.

And then indeed a strange sight was to be seen; the Turks, panic-stricken fled without delay through the opposite gate, and the only ones of them who stayed behind were a few brave men who defended the citadel; and the Franks from outside ascended the ladders on the heels of Bohemond, and straightway took possession of the city of Antioch. Tancred with a small body of men pursued the fugitives, many of whom were killed and many wounded.

15. Anna Komnene: Alexios retreats from Philomelion (1098)

Antioch fell on 3 June 1098 but the crusaders' troubles were not at an end. The Turkish garrison held out in the citadel while a large relieving force under the command of Kerbogha, atabeg of Mosul, surrounded the city. Alexios meanwhile had sent a large part of his army south under the command of his brother-in-law John

Doukas to reconquer Smyrna and western Asia Minor. He himself finally set out with the rest of the army in June but only reached Philomelion, modern Akşehir, about halfway to Antioch. There he made a fateful decision.

Komnene (1928), pp. 282–4, translated by Elizabeth A. Dawes:

Before Doukas had returned, whilst he was still fighting with the Turks, the emperor prepared to go to the assistance of the Franks in Antioch, and reached Philomelion with all his forces after killing many barbarians on the way and destroying several towns hitherto held by them. Here he was found by men from Antioch, Gehelmus Grantemanes, Stephen, Count of France and Peter, son of Aliphas;[61] these had been let down by ropes from the walls of Antioch, made their way through Tarsus and reported to him the terrible straits into which the Franks were driven and upon oath they told him of their utter fall. This news made the emperor still more anxious to hasten to their assistance although everybody sought to restrain him from this enterprise. And then a report was spread abroad everywhere that an incredible host of barbarians was on its way to overtake him. For the Sultan of Chorosan, hearing of the emperor's departure to go to the assistance of the Franks, had collected innumerable men from Chorosan and the further provinces, equipped them all thoroughly and putting them under the command of his own son, Ishmael by name, had sent them forth with instructions to overtake the emperor quickly before he reached Antioch.[62] And thus the emperor's expedition, which he undertook for the sake of the Franks, and with the desire of wiping out the Turks who were fighting furiously with them, and above all their leader Kerbogha – this expedition was stopped both by the report which the Franks had brought and by the news of Ishmael's advance against him. For he calculated what would probably happen in the future, namely, that it was an impossibility to save a city which had only just been taken by the Franks and while still in a state of disorder was immediately besieged from outside by the Hagarenes; and the Franks in despair of all help, were planning to leave only empty walls to the enemy and to save their own lives by flight. For the nation of the Franks in general is self-willed and independent and never employs military discipline or science, but when it is a question of war and fighting, anger barks in their hearts and they are not to be restrained; and this applies not only to the soldiers but to the leaders themselves for they dash into the middle of the enemies' ranks with irresistible force, especially if their opponents yield a little. But if the enemy with strategic skill often sets ambuscades for them and pursues them methodically, then all this courage evaporates. In short, the ranks cannot be resisted in their first attack, but afterwards they are exceedingly easy to master both because of the weight of their arms and from their passionate and irrational character. For these reasons, as his forces were insufficient against such numbers, and he could not change the

---

61 These were William of Grandmesnil, Count Stephen of Blois and Peter of Aulps.
62 The 'Sultan of Chorosan' is the Turkish emir Danishmend, who had ruled Sebasteia, modern Sivas, since 1084. See PBW (2016): Danishmend 101.

26   *The First Crusade*

Franks' decision, nor by better advice convert them to their advantage, he considered he had better not proceed any further, lest by hastening to the assistance of Antioch he might cause the destruction of Constantinople. He was afraid, too, in case the countless Turkish tribes overtook him, that the inhabitants of the regions of Philomelion would fall victims to the barbarians' swords, so he arranged to have the approach of the Hagarenes announced throughout the country. The announcement was immediately made and the order given that each man and woman should leave their homes before the Turks arrived, and thus save their persons and as much property as each could carry. They all elected at once to accompany the emperor, not only the men but the women too.[63]

16. Anna Komnene: The Third Wave of the First Crusade (1101)

What Alexios could not have known as he retreated from Philomelion was that on 28 June 1098 the leaders of the crusade decided to launch an attack on Kerbogha's army. Although heavily outnumbered, the crusaders triumphed and compelled the relieving force to withdraw. Antioch was now secure and the main body of the crusade began the march south to Jerusalem. Bohemond remained in Antioch and in December ejected the troops stationed there by Raymond of St Gilles and became the effective ruler of the city. Six months later, on 15 July 1099, the main crusade army took Jerusalem. When news of the triumph reached western Europe, many were inspired to take the Cross and new armies were formed to march to Jerusalem. Anna Komnene is much less informative about this third wave and appears not to know much about it. She describes only one of the armies that passed through Constantinople in the spring and early summer of 1101, saying that it was composed of Normans. In fact, the participants were Lombards and Germans, led by Anselm IV, archbishop of Milan, and the imperial constable, Conrad.[64]

Komnene (1928), pp. 288–90, translated by Elizabeth A. Dawes:

At this time a Norman army arrived whose leaders were two brothers called Flanders. The emperor repeatedly advised them to travel by the same road as the armies that had gone on before, and to reach Jerusalem by the coast and thus join the rest of the Latin army. But he found that they would not listen as they did not wish to join the Franks, but wanted to travel by another route more to the east and march straight to Chorosan in the hope of taking it.[65] The emperor knew that this plan was quite inexpedient and as he did not wish such a large crowd to perish (for they were fifty thousand horse and a hundred thousand foot) he tried 'the next best

---

63   The *Gesta Francorum* gives a similar account of Alexios' withdrawal, including the evacuation of non-combatants. See Hill (1962), pp. 63–5.
64   On these events, see Lilie (1993), pp. 66–70; Harris (2022), pp. 85–6.
65   i.e. to the Danishmendid emirate and Sebasteia. They may have hoped to liberate Bohemond, who had been captured by Emir Danishmend.

thing', as the saying is, when he found they would not listen to him. He sent for Raymond of St Gilles and Tzitas and asked them to accompany the Normans,[66] to advise them to their advantage and to restrain them as far as possible in their mad enterprises. After crossing the straits of Kibotos[67] they hastened on to Armenia and on reaching Ankyra took it by assault;[68] next they went over the Halys and reached a small town. This was inhabited by Romans and consequently the citizens feared nothing; the priests clad in their sacred vestments, and carrying the gospel and crosses went out to meet their fellow-Christians. But the Normans in an inhuman and merciless fashion slaughtered not only the priests but the rest of the Christians also, and then quite heedlessly continued their journey, moving in the direction of Amaseia. But the Turks, long practised in war, seized all the villages and food supplies, and burnt them, and when they caught up with the Normans they attacked them at once. It was on Monday the Turks got the better of them. The Latins fixed their camp on the spot where they were, and deposited their baggage, and the next day both armies met in battle again. The Turks next encamped in a circle round the Latins, and did not allow them to move out either for foraging or even to lead the beasts of burden or horses to water. The Franks now saw destruction staring them in the face, and with utter disregard of their lives, armed themselves strongly the following day (this was Wednesday) and engaged the enemy in battle. The Turks had them in their power, and therefore no longer fought with spears or arrows, but drew their swords and made the battle a hand-to-hand fight and soon routed the Normans, who retreated to their camp, and sought a counsellor. But the excellent emperor to whom they would not listen when he gave them sensible advice, was not at hand, so they appealed to Raymond and Tzitas for advice, and at the same time enquired whether there was any place under the emperor's jurisdiction nearby to which they could repair. They actually left their baggage, tents and all the infantry where they were, and rode off as speedily as they could on their horses to the seacoast of the Armenian theme and Paurae. Then the Turks made a sudden descent upon the camp and carried off everything and afterwards pursued and overtook the infantry and [290] annihilated them completely, except for a few whom they captured and carried back to Chorosan as specimens.[69] Such were the exploits of the Turks against the Normans; and Raymond and Tzitas with the few surviving knights reached the capital.

---

66 Raymond had returned to Constantinople in 1100, angry at Bohemond's seizure of Antioch. Tzitas was another of Alexios' military commanders. See PBW (2016): Tzitas 101.
67 i.e. across the Bosporus to modern Mudanya.
68 Ankyra, modern Ankara, was captured on 23 June 1101: Albert of Aachen (2013), ii. 63–4.
69 The Lombard and German army was severely mauled by the Danishmendid Turks at Mersivan on 7 August 1101: Albert of Aachen (2013), ii. 66–72.

28 *The First Crusade*

17. Nicholas of Methone: Crusaders at Athens (1101?)

Nicholas was bishop of Methone from c.1150 to 1166 and was the author of a number of theological works and speeches in praise of Emperor Manuel I.[70] The extract translated here comes from his hagiography of St Meletios the Younger of Myoupolis, who founded a monastery on the slopes of Mount Kithairon near Athens. Meletios died in around 1105, so it is likely that the arrival at Piraeus of westerners headed for the Holy Land was connected with the First Crusade or the waves of pilgrims who followed in its wake. This text makes an interesting parallel to Komnene in that the governor of Athens is suspicious of the travellers and thinks that they might have hostile intentions. Meletios persuades him that they are genuine pilgrims, on their way to the Holy Land.

Nicholas of Methone (2018), pp. 127–31:

27. It would have been unfitting had not the Romans, I mean those of Old Rome,[71] also benefitted from the gracious deeds of the saint. On the contrary, it was only right for them to experience the latter and to become unimpeachable witnesses and strident heralds of his miracles. On one occasion, as they were travelling by sea to Jerusalem, they encountered contrary winds near the bay of Aegina, and put in at Piraeus, the port of Athens. He who was at that time the governor of Athens regarded these men with suspicion. Since they had requested no permission from us and were supposedly very ill-disposed towards the emperor, he considered them as enemies and did not permit them to resume their journey. The men remained in Athens and learned about the saint. For truly, with need [comes] also inquiry and discovery of what is beneficial. They appealed to him, movingly reported the situation they were in, and asked for his assistance. Almost immediately, they received it, and it went far beyond they had asked for. For since the saint knew that these men happened to be well-disposed towards God and the emperor, he proved to the governor of Athens that they were men of this kind. The governor respected the credibility of the mediator more than anything else. At once, he behaved towards the Romans in a kindlier fashion, absolved them from suspicion, and relaxed their involuntary dwelling there, a product of his mistrust. They were even given an imperial letter which granted them safe conduct to wherever they wished without hindrance. That is how they were delivered at that time. Later, remembering the benefaction of the spiritual father, many arrived every year and visited the monastery, frequently in groups of fifty and sixty people, and sometimes of more. They arrived ever more frequently, obtaining the prayers of the father and sharing the communal table. And so, on one occasion, when the monastery was rather short of supplies, and the legumes being prepared were scarcely enough for the monks, one of the latter approached the father and indignantly reported the scarcity. He said, 'Give me the order, and I will send them away'. The father replied 'On no account,

---

70 On Nicholas, see Angelou (1981), pp. 143–8.
71 An unusual instance of the word 'Roman' being used to describe western, Latin Christians.

my child, on no account! On the contrary, welcome them with open arms. For God takes care of everything and can feed tens of thousands with very little'. After he had spoken, the table was shared by the Romans and the monks, and all ate their fill. Four days later, some people arrived at the outer gateway and knocked at it. The father summoned the monk who had been indignant and said, 'My child, go to the gateway and find out what all that noise is'. He went, opened the gate and found some mules, not few in number, carrying wheat, sent to the monastery by devout men. As soon as he found them, he recalled his displeasure and the greatness of the father's soul. In addition, he realized the father's ability to understand the future and that, beyond all doubt, he had ordered him to go to the gateway as a reproach for his mean – spiritedness. He was amazed by it all and rightly blamed himself. In this way he improved himself through repentance.

II Alexios I, John II and the Latin East

The capture of Jerusalem and the subsequent defeat of the Fatimid army at Ascalon on 12 August 1099 were followed by the establishment of a permanent Latin presence in Syria and Palestine. The county of Edessa had already been set up by Baldwin of Boulogne and his brother Godfrey of Bouillon now took the title of Defender of the Holy Sepulchre as the first ruler of the kingdom of Jerusalem. Bohemond had seized Antioch in December 1098 and now, with his nephew Tancred, he began to conquer the area around the city to create a viable principality with an outlet to the sea. At the same time, Raymond of St Gilles set his sights on the port of Tripoli, which was to become the centre of the county of Tripoli.[1]

18. Anna Komnene: Alexios I and the Latin East (1101–5)

In Komnene's rather brief and confused account of these years, she highlights the different attitude that Alexios took to the emerging county of Tripoli and principality of Antioch. To Raymond of St Gilles and his successor he afforded every assistance in the conquest of Tripoli and the land around. Antioch was a different matter because it had been part of the Byzantine empire as recently as 1084. The passage begins with Raymond and the other survivors of the 1101 debacle at Mersivan still in Constantinople.

Komnene (1928), pp. 290–1, translated by Elizabeth A. Dawes:

The Emperor received them, and gave them plenty of money, and after they were rested asked them whither they wanted to go; and they chose Jerusalem.[2] Accordingly he lavished more presents upon them and sent them by sea, leaving everything to their discretion. But Raymond on leaving the capital desired to return to his own army and therefore went back to Tripoli, which he longed to subdue. Afterwards he fell a victim to a mortal disease and, when breathing his last, sent for his nephew William and bequeathed to him as a species of inheritance all the towns he had conquered and appointed him leader and master of all his troops.

---

1 On these developments, see Lilie (1993), pp. 61–72; Harris (2022), pp. 81–7.
2 Komnene is here referring to the survivors of the Lombard and German army, defeated by the Danishmendid Turks in August 1101.

DOI: 10.4324/9781003015345-4

When the news of his death was brought to the Emperor, he immediately wrote to the Duke of Cyprus, and ordered him to send Niketas Chalintzes with plenty of money to William in order to propitiate him and influence him to swear on oath that he would maintain unbroken fidelity to the Emperor just as his deceased uncle Raymond had preserved his to the end.[3]

Soon the Emperor learnt of the seizure of Laodikeia by Tancred,[4] and therefore sent a letter to Bohemond which ran as follows: 'You know the oaths and promises which not only you but all the Counts took to the Roman Empire. Now you were the first to break them, by retaining possession of Antioch, and then taking more fortresses and even Laodikeia itself. Therefore withdraw from Antioch and all the other cities and do what is just and right, and do not provoke more wars and troubles for yourself'. Now Bohemond after reading the Emperor's letter could not reply by a falsehood, as he usually did, for the facts openly declared the truth, so outwardly he assented to it, but put the blame for all the wrong he had done upon the Emperor and wrote to him thus: 'It is not I, but you, who are the cause of all this. For you promised you would follow us with a large army, but you never thought of making good your promise by deeds. When we reached Antioch we fought for three months under great difficulty both against the enemy and against famine, which was more severe than had ever been experienced before, with the result that most of us ate of the very foods which are forbidden by law. We endured for a long time and while we were in this danger even Tatikios, your Majesty's most loyal servant, whom you had appointed to help us, went away and left us to our danger. Yet we captured Antioch unexpectedly and utterly routed the troops which had come from Chorosan to succour Antioch. In what way would it be just for us to deprive ourselves willingly of what we gained by our own sweat and toil?' When the envoys returned from him, the Emperor recognised from the reading of his letter that he was still the same Bohemond and in no wise changed for the better, and therefore decided that he must protect the boundaries of the Roman Empire, and as far as possible, check his impetuous advance. Accordingly he sent Boutoumites into Cilicia with numerous forces and the pick of the military roll, all very warlike men and devotees of Ares.[5]

19. Theophylact of Ohrid: A Letter on Bohemond (1103)

This letter can be dated from context to the summer of 1103 and is addressed to Gregory Taronites, the duke of Trebizond, in celebration of his recent victory over the Turkish emir of Sebasteia, Danishmend. Undoubtedly designed to be read out at court, it served also as an encomium.[6] It includes a discussion of the prince of

---

3 Raymond died on 28 February 1105. His nephew was William II Jordan, count of Berga and Cerdanya, who became regent of the county of Tripoli: Anna calls him Gelielmus. On Niketas Chalintzes, see PBW (2016): Niketas 15001.
4 Tancred probably took Laodikeia, modern Latakiah in Syria, in early 1103.
5 Ares was the ancient Greek god of war.
6 See PBW (2016): Gregorios 106.

Antioch, Bohemond, who had been captured by Danishmend at Melitene on 15 August 1100.

Theophylact of Ohrid (1986), pp. 427–33:

To the Lord Gregory Taronites

My most illustrious son in the Lord and my master, how and with what shall I return your favour for always distinguishing me as the most faithful of all people and for deeming me worthy of praise for the exaltations with which I think you fit to be extoled? For declaring that this praise is not a piece of the sophist's rhetorical flattery but the impulse of a heart which delights in what is truly fair, and the songs of a mouth which knows how to honour virtue. For tell me now, how much shall my honest and envy-free ears value these recent reports?

With a single victory you have destroyed the arrogance of two peoples. You took down together both the tower of senseless Persian daring and the motte of Frankish arrogance. You emerged as a new Phinehas for us, piercing simultaneously with your mighty lance two peoples unclean in the eyes of the Lord.[7] For Danishmend was accustomed to levy tribute from all the rest of the Greek cities in Pontus, for I omit the Mariandyni, the Galatians and the Cappadocians who are their neighbours, located between the Tanais river and lake Maeotis, as well as in the district of Colchis which lie ahead and has the Phasis as its border, and also in the land of Lesser Armenia which lie above on high peaks, and in all of Armenia.[8] As soon as he had become rich and strong from the tributes, his tribute-collecting hands were cut off by the edge of your sword, and he became accustomed to paying tribute himself instead. After he had been humbled in his incursions, which were similar to those of bandits, he spoke insolently. In addition, he gave up his ambushes as pointless, since he was more obvious to Taronites than a city situated on a mountain. With regard to pitched battles, he realised that he was clumsy and unskilled, and he lost the populous cities which he had captured with difficulty up to that time more quickly than it takes to tell. That is how the die of fortune turned his affairs for the very worst, or rather how the scales of God turned upon him the beam of your virtue which was as heavy as the virtue of those who had been mocked by him before you assumed command was light. Consequently, he was convinced that the celebrated victories of the ancient Romans were no myths, or rather that what has been written about them did not do them justice. It is by your deeds that he realised

---

7 Phinehas was a priest during the Exodus from Egypt who was credited with stemming the descent of the Israelites into idolatry. See Numbers 25:1–9; Psalms 106:28–31.
8 Theophylact draws on mythological and classical names here to overstate the extent of Danishmend's influence. In Greek mythology, Jason and the Argonauts sailed along the River Phasis, which was located somewhere in Colchis, the western side of modern Georgia, in their search for the Golden Fleece. In ancient times, the Mariandyni were a tribe in north-western Asia Minor and Galatia was a state on the Anatolian plateau. Lake Maeotis is the Sea of Azov and the Tanais is the River Don, both in southern Russia. Lesser Armenia refers to Cilicia as opposed to the area occupied by the republic of Armenia today.

the extent of their greatness. I would even argue that he regards you as so much greater than them, because even though you campaign with inferior equipment and supplies, you live up to them. To such an extent your very heavy weight on the scale outbalanced the lack of means. On the one hand, he wishes you had not been born in the first place, but on the other, he admires how you have become virtuous. He curses your birth, but envies your parents. He prays to God that you remain childless so as for your line to end with you, but hopes that he himself will beget children like you. And now, for the first time, he feels unfortunate. He had been so much extoled due to his victories before you came along that, having experienced great losses, he suffered more greatly. His only consolation is that he experienced such a great defeat at the hands of the most illustrious man among the Romans, for the loser is customarily glorified in the splendour of the victor. If Homer were here now, he would have said to you 'the brave fled first, but he who pursued him was so much more brave'.[9]

Neocaesarea, the most beautiful of cities, you too should be full of hope: Gregory your liberator is not far away from you! You are not unused to having Gregories as your benefactors. After you scrape off the cast skin of your present misery, you shall be truly manifest as a new Caesarea.[10] You have the neighbouring towns as your guarantors. Receive the fair husband who shall be united to you in victory and crowned with a crown of precious stone. For Christ erects trophies for Taronites. The most ungodly Turk, on the other hand, inclines his head downwards for you and looks only at what is near his feet, he who yesterday turned the insolent pupil of his eye in all directions and contrived to obliterate all of the earth and the sea. And so, that is why he perceives peace negotiations as his only help and deliverance, and reaches no longer to draw the sword but to pledge good faith. Having dropped his bow, he takes up the caduceus, and wants to have as a reliable friend, he whom he had rightly regarded as an invincible enemy.[11]

As regards the Frank,[12] whose neck was previously hard and unyielding like iron, he has proven to be softer than warm wax, and bows to you on account of your superiority and through you to our most powerful emperor. And now? Is he not going to see the one who welcomed him with such respect being held in honour, and the one who used to bind others in chains being bound on the orders of Taronites as if by more secure fetters? And being so completely mastered by them, that the emperor has granted his release as a favour? The emperor has been striving to this end for some time now and regarded it the worthiest deed to own as a bought slave the man who considered himself to be the liberator of all the East and was so

---

9 Possibly an allusion to the flight of the Trojan Hector from the Greek hero Achilles. See Homer (1924), ii. 462–3 (*Iliad* XXII. 136–40).
10 Neocaesarea, modern Niksar, lies to the west of Trebizond (Trabzon). Its first bishop and patron saint was Gregory Thaumaturgus (c.213–270). Theophylact is punning on its name, which means 'New Caesarea'.
11 A caduceus is a wand entwined with serpents, which in Greek mythology was carried by the god Hermes, the messenger of the gods.
12 i.e. Bohemond.

much deluded by his farfetched fantasies that he was not even satisfied to hold the second place in imperial honour. He will also see the emperor prosper and you the sole person responsible for the success of his plan. For the Turk, having been compelled by your hands, agreed unwillingly to a truce and, along with other terms, to surrender the Frank to our invincible emperor.[13]

In addition to the above, I owe you gratitude in another way too, not only for proving me to be faithful, as I have already said, but also for enjoying as a shared thing the common good. All Christians and those who deliberate and join in prayer for the wellbeing of the Roman empire are also indebted to you. For, as far as our beneficent emperor is concerned, what should I say about how worthily he will reward your prudence and courage, he who always prefers you above all others and puts you forward for duties which particularly require the most attentive care, employing you as some kind of most skilful doctor against serious diseases and as a shipmaster who withstands rough seas? For who of all the emperors has been more talented than him in discerning the character of men?

Unfortunately, such are the requirements of letter-writing. They are a bit and bridle which thoroughly restrain the mouth of the rhetor, and do not allow him to persist in resonating good deeds. I am held back by them from my willingness to say more. Because if I were allowed to speak in an uncontrolled way, I would run races of eloquence for you. It is not even possible to express how much inferior they would be to your chariot of virtues, for you move it by wings. And so, it will probably render us unworthy to utter a word at the gatherings of eloquence, even though we are skilful enough. I will only say the following and then I shall stop.

Lift your eyes to the hills, whence comes your help,[14] and it will come again and again. Do not lower your gaze and do not turn it to yourself. For such great [deeds] are not [the result of] human force, at least not exclusively, but they are totally or mostly [the outcome] of divine grace. Draw your power from God who crushes the enemy.[15] If you are grateful to Him who showers grace upon you, you will assure it for yourself or even attract more. You will achieve these things if you imitate Him in his beneficence which overflows upon the rich and the poor, on those who lead a priestly or secular life, namely in a more divine or human fashion, as much as each requires of it. May you be delivered from wickedness and the Evil One by His benignity, so that you never become defective and base.

20. Ephraim of Ainos: Bohemond's Invasion (1103–8)

After his release by Danishmend, Bohemond returned to Antioch and resumed his campaign to subdue the area around the city. By then the Byzantines had recaptured Laodikeia and Bohemond failed to retake it in the summer of 1104. He accordingly

---

13 Not entirely accurate. Albert of Aachen (2013), ii. 107–9, describes how Alexios I offered to pay the ransom but Danishmend preferred to accept a payment from Antioch and Edessa, allowing Bohemond to escape the emperor's clutches.
14 Psalms 121:1–2.
15 Psalms 60:12.

decided to travel to Italy with a view to mustering reinforcements and stirring up resentment against Alexios I.[16]

Ephraim of Ainos (1990), pp. 133–4:

Raymond, whose father was Robert,[17]
became one of the leaders of the Italians
and he made a sworn oath to the emperor.
[3595] A friendship was confirmed with him
and an everlasting relationship of servitude and benevolence.
On account of this, he received money and gifts
from the emperor, but also unusual honours,
and rushed against Syria and Cilicia.
[3600] After he prevailed over Antioch in battle,
he immediately abrogated the oaths and
the awe-inspiring treaties he had made with the emperor,
and became an irreconcilable enemy of the Romans.
Thus, full of fear,
[3605] he had to leave the East for the West,
and his impure heart spread lies about his own death.
He was then put into a small coffin.
as if he were dead, but more accurately a dead man breathing,
and he was carried off to his country by the hands of his servants
[3610] who falsely repeated over and over that he was dead.[18]
When he cunningly escaped to this homeland,
he accused the emperor unjustly of many things,[19]
and after he had assembled an army of Latins,
he sailed against the city of Epidamnos[20]
[3615] and rushed to conquer it by siege.
But his hopes were false, and he achieved nothing.
And so, devoid of hope, he sent ambassadors
and came to negotiate with the emperor,
and he concluded treaties and agreements.[21]

---

16 On these events, see Komnene (1928), pp. 296–358; Komnene (2009), pp. 325–96; Lilie (1993), pp. 72–5; Harris (2022), pp. 86–90.
17 'Raymond' is an error. It is Bohemond, son of Robert Guiscard, who is being referred to here.
18 According to Komnene (1928), p. 298; Komnene (2009), pp. 329–30, a dead cockerel was placed in the coffin with Bohemond to give an authentic stench of decay.
19 Bohemond visited the courts of Pope Paschal II and the king of France, Philip I.
20 Bohemond laid siege to Dyrrachion (Epidamnos) in October 1107.
21 Bohemond concluded the treaty of Devol with Alexios in September 1108.

21. Alexios I: *The Muses*, advice to his son John (c.1116)

Towards the end of his life, Alexios I wrote or commissioned a poem of 501 surviving lines in three distinct sections: an introduction, the main poem and a second, shorter poem. The manuscript is headed *The Alexian Komnenian Muses* and carries a subheading *The Final Admonition and Instructions of Alexios Komnenos, lover of his mother, autocrat, to John Porphyrogennetos, victor, autocrat, lover of his father, his son.*[22] In the main poem, Alexios refers to the passage of the First Crusade through Byzantine territory in 1096–7 and draws out some of the lessons he had learned on how to handle such dangerous events.

Alexios I (1913), pp. 356–8, 361–2:

Only one thing brings safety, virtue, depend on it.
[255] If, my child, you arm
and shield yourself with it, all around from every direction,
you shall slumber sweetly, even if you sleep for many hours.
If you find yourself amid hostile men,
unarmed, that is unprotected by armour,
[260] you will not suffer harm; you will escape unscathed.
For you shall neither be troubled, nor afraid of tens of thousands.
You will suffer nothing terrible from ambushes
or from numerous deep formations.
The arrow of the enemy, released to inflict a mortal wound,
will become blunt for you.
[265] You will break the dense enemy lines.
You will fall upon the enemy unarmed, like a lion.
You will require no protective helmet.
You will not care for armour, nor bother
to cover yourself with a long shield.
[270] You have virtue as your breastplate and helmet,
and this is your long-protecting shield.
The Celt trembles at this breastplate.
The Norman sees this support
and sails back to his country, shaken and restrained.
[275] The Persian, the Scythian horde,[23]
and the tribes of the Arabs stand in dread before it.
The Abkhaz, the daring Celtiberian
the race of the Indians, the army of the Moors,
and the horde of the opposite side which stands facing
[280] the northern wind and the south sky,
as they say the Ethiopians do.
In the first years of my reign

---

22 See Mullett (2012), pp. 197–8.
23 'Scythians' probably means the Pechenegs here.

I was hard pressed by barbarians from all directions.
They were pushing forward, attempting to confine
[285] the children of Rome and its provinces from every quarter.
Ten thousand Scythian troops and the Italian mentality, arrogant in battle,
inflicted harm on the empire,
on the lands stretching on the western territory.
The coastal territory and the one which lies in the dawn-bringing east,
[290] [was harmed] by the force of Persian arms,
Mytilene and Rhodes were occupied by them,
Lesbos was conquered, Chios afflicted,
and every island in the Cyclades.[24]
The people of Crete rebelled in despotic rule
[295] and the Cypriots ceased to regard the law.[25]
I will not refer to those people who are on our side and take up arms,
those who ever attempt to break the authority
which was given from the heavens,
even though the Trinity is my assistant and master,
[300] strengthening and delivering me in the most splendid manner,
intervening to weaken the determined.
Over the past few years, and in the present times,
I have had no opportunity nor time
to see myself breaking down my thoughts
[305] which have been in flux and changed by the intrusion of foreign matters.
I will learn, oh child, I will contemplate and I will discover
what human nature is after all,
how it was put together, and, after it has been dissolved
how it flows towards the four elements which composed it in the first place.
[310] Since I have just begun to recollect,
I hasten to teach you. Do the right thing and listen to me!
Treat the Queen of Cities as a fount of gold,
so that the Divine attends to her from the heavens
and bestows every distinction on her,
[315] as a pear tree full of good fruits.
Some men she nurtures, while from others
she receives a stream of fine gold
which ever flows with great babbling.
Give, therefore, abundantly and abundantly accept the flow.
[320] Rejoice much, both giving and receiving.
Do this over and over and may you live for many years.
But you should save a large amount in your coffers

---

24 In 1090, Chaka, the emir of Smyrna, had constructed a fleet and used it to raid and occupy Byzantine islands in the Aegean.
25 Crete and Cyprus revolted against Alexios in 1091. See Komnene (1928), pp. 217–9; Komnene (2009), pp. 240–2, 510.

and preserve it for a day of necessity.
so as to halt the greed of foreign peoples
[325] who, just as in past, are marching from every direction.
The numerous multitudes are dangerously opening their mouths,
trying to devour the envy-inspiring city.
Are you not now beginning to recall the affairs I dealt with?
Are you not taking into account and directing your mind
[330] towards the marching of armies from the west to our lands,[26]
lest time, bringing troubles,
tests and puts to shame the
venerable status and majesty of the throne of New Rome?
For this reason, child, you should take care to store up
[335] those things which will fill the open jaws
of the barbarians who also breathe hostility towards us,
in case a force of countless troops somehow rises,
flashing against us while many of the enemies surrounding
the City march in hostility against us [. . .]

[The text after this point belongs to the second, shorter poem. It carries the sub-heading: *The second Alexian, Komnenian Muse. Second final advice of Alexios Komnenos, autocrat.*][27]

You are honourable and with a strong mind.
[45] You look noble, my child, and you are full of authority,
since the throne grants to you great power.
You are worthy of my teachings
and a fulfilment of a father's wishes.
Your palm is thick with strong fingers
[50] matching the muscularity of your ankle joints.
Your mighty arm raises the shield,
and the Norman, the Scyth, the tribes of
the Persians and the daring Celtiberian can confirm all these.
You have an excellent chest and fine shoulders.
[55] The ideal interval between your shoulders
strengthens by flexing and contracting
so as to bear the weight of the well-worked brass breastplate,
easily, painlessly, all day long,
and all night when necessary.
[60] You have prodigious strength, and thanks to your courage,
you have acquired glory, undertaken great enterprises and gained experience in battle.

---

26 A reference to the First Crusade.
27 Mullett (2012), p. 197.

It appears to me that you carry and manoeuvre your shield well,
On your shoulders, like no other Roman,
and that you immediately move the Celt to terror,
[65] whenever you march out armed like a knight.
You are, therefore, inferior to none in intellect,
and you do not fall short of those who are recognized as brave.
For how vigorous, swift and noble you are
in thinking and acting against foreigners.
[70] Your army is clamorous and countless.
Nonetheless, you are in need of divine assistance.
You are in need of divine force,
even if you muster and march into battle
with an army completely exceeding the thong of the stars,
[75] fully furnished with brilliant arms and armour.
Because it is not by prowess and countless troops,
by weapons and the swiftness of horses
that you will be seen overcoming sudden calamities,
that you will be proven to be superior to missiles and blows.
[80] I was not either, for my helmet bears witness to it,
damaged as it was by a Celt at Phthia.[28]

22. John Kinnamos: John II's First Syrian Expedition (1137–8)

By the treaty of Devol of September 1108, Bohemond had promised to hold Antioch as a vassal of the Byzantine emperor. But he never returned to Antioch; he died in Italy in 1111 so that the terms of the treaty were never put into effect.[29] For more than ten years after he succeeded his father in 1118, Emperor John II Komnenos was engaged in securing the Byzantine frontiers in the Balkans and Asia Minor against the Pechenegs and Seljuk Turks of Ikonion (Konya) and did not attempt to intervene in the affairs of the Latin East. Then, in 1130, Bohemond's son and successor as prince of Antioch, Bohemond II, was killed in battle, leaving only a two-year-old daughter, Constance, to succeed him. Hoping to exploit the situation to bring Antioch back under Byzantine suzerainty, John II made an agreement with the regency council in Antioch that Constance should marry his youngest son, Manuel. In April 1136, however, the regency broke their undertaking and instead gave her hand to a younger son of the duke of Aquitaine, Raymond of Poitiers, who thus became prince of Antioch. In the summer of 1137, John marched southeast with a powerful army. He entered Armenian-ruled Cilicia and deposed its prince

---

28 A mythical city in Thessaly. Perhaps a reference to the battle of Larissa in October 1083, where Alexios defeated the Normans under Bohemond.
29 See Lilie (1993), pp. 75–82. The full text of the treaty is preserved in Komnene (1928), pp. 348–58; Komnene (2009), pp. 385–96.

Leo who was sent as a prisoner to Constantinople. He then moved on towards Antioch.[30]

John Kinnamos, who takes up the story, was the personal secretary of John II's son and successor Manuel I Komnenos and he wrote a history that covers the period from 1118 to 1176.[31] As with most Byzantine historians, Kinnamos displayed a marked political bias in favour of the reigning emperor. He is more neutral in his account of the reign of John II and much less well informed. Consequently his version of John's Syrian expedition lacks the eulogistic element that marks his account of Manuel I's in 1158–9 **[34]**.

Kinnamos (1836), pp. 18–21:

[18] In this manner, therefore, Anazarbos was conquered by the Romans.[32] Now Raymond and Baldwin, who was the ruler of Marash at that time, as long as danger did not stand at their door yet, assembled a sufficient army and marched quickly to Palestine so as to deliver the king there from danger. For the Saracens who dwelled near Palestine had prevailed over him in battle and besieged the fortress of Montferrand where he had taken refuge.[33] Since the emperor was already at Anazarbos, he advanced against a fort named Vahka. Fearing for Antioch, Raymond and Baldwin returned to it at all haste. In response, the Roman army put off the siege of Vahka and pitched camp in the area of the river which flows beside their city.

At first, the Antiochenes were undaunted, trusting in the strength of their walls and their steadfastness in general. Then, they suddenly sallied out against our conscripts and slew many. For by that time the siege had been prolonged for a considerable length of time and some of our conscripts, as usually happens in large armies, had headed towards the gardens at the outskirts of the city and gathered fruit. When it became clear what was happening, and the Roman soldiers had swiftly come to their aid, the Antiochenes fled and threw themselves at the gates, suffering many casualties during their flight. As the Romans had already embarked on an assault on the walls, they experienced all kinds of great terrors.

[19] Consequently, Raymond often came before the emperor and earnestly begged to surrender the city to him, on the condition that the emperor would become and be proclaimed the lord of the city, while Raymond would be appointed as its governor through the authority of the emperor. Failing in the things he had entreated, he retired unsuccessful. A few days later, however, when

---

30 Leo I had ruled Cilician Armenia from c.1129: PBW (2016): Leon 17002. On these events, see Lilie (1993), pp. 109–14; Harris (2022), pp. 91–5.
31 PBW (2016): Ioannes 17001; Treadgold (2013), pp. 407–16; Neville (2018), pp. 186–90; Hobbs, (2020), pp. 65–92.
32 John II captured Anazarbos, now Ain Zarba, in August 1137: William of Tyre (1943), ii. 84.
33 In March 1137, Count Pons of Tripoli had been killed fighting the ruler of Damascus. At the request of King Fulk of Jerusalem, Raymond of Poitiers and his brother Baldwin of Marash had gone south to offer their assistance to the new count Raymond II. William of Tyre (1943), ii. 82–3, 85–6.

the Roman council voted on the matter, he was favourably received on account of his proposals, and the rest of the Latin forces offered their allegiance to the emperor, both the so-called Orders and the inhabitants of the region. That was what took place so far.[34]

Not wishing to waste such a favourable situation, Emperor John invaded upper Syria with the aforementioned forces. He took the fortress of Piza by right of conquest.[35] Having acquired a rich haul of booty, he dispatched it to Antioch along with the captured men, putting in charge Thomas, a man born from an insignificant family but selected from childhood, I believe, as deputy clerk by the emperor. The emperor then advanced against Berroia,[36] an ancient and very noteworthy city. Soon, however, the enemy suddenly fell upon Thomas, who lost the booty and the crowd of captives he was escorting, barely escaping the danger himself.[37] When the emperor arrived at Berroia, he bypassed it since he perceived that its surroundings were totally waterless. He conquered the fortress of Hama and Kafarthab by assault and arrived at Shaizar, a prosperous and populous city[38] [20]. Although he captured the city after a siege, he was repelled when he reached the citadel. As he was planning to make a second attempt on it, envoys arrived declaring that they would offer both immediate payments and thereafter a sort of tribute to the Romans every single year. Such was the decree of their embassy. At that time the emperor dismissed them as he was hoping to overcome them too in battle. Afterwards, however, after he attacked them many times, he realised he was attempting the impossible. He received the ambassadors and agreed to the terms.

Thus, a large amount of money was sent to John and a cross was added too, a remarkable piece of considerable size, a gift worthy of emperors. It was made from red marble. After it had been hewn into the shape of a cross, it had lost only a little of its natural colour in the process of chiselling. It is said that the Apostle Constantine[39] had commissioned it when he was emperor, but in some way it fell at the hands of the Saracens.[40] Having accepted the aforementioned gifts and received pledges for future tributes, John marched once more to Cilicia. After he had subdued the strong fortresses of Vahka and Kapniskerti, he himself remained at the region, but he detached a division of the army and dispatched it to assault the rest [of the castles]. I think that narrating these deeds in detail exceeds my principles though, because I resolved to record these matters in a summarised form. For I was not an eyewitness to these [events] and as a result I have not secured a credible testimony. [21] Whatever the case, since fortune gazed at the emperor favourably, much was achieved in two years. Consequently, emperor John won great repute for

---

34 This agreement was probably made in September 1137: William of Tyre (1943), ii. 93.
35 The fortress of Piza (Buza) was captured on 9 April 1138.
36 i.e. Aleppo.
37 On Thomas see PBW (2016): Thomas 17001.
38 John laid siege to Shaizar in late April 1138. William of Tyre (1943), ii. 94–6, gives a very different account of the siege.
39 i.e. Constantine the Great (306–37), the first Christian Roman emperor.
40 In the next extract [23], Niketas Choniates explains how this object came to be in Shaizar.

his struggles in Asia, except for the matter of Neocaesarea which did not turn out according to his plan.[41]

23. Niketas Choniates: John II's First Syrian Expedition (1137–8)

Niketas Choniates (c.1155–1217) held high office under the Angelos emperors Isaac II and Alexios III. It was during that time that he began composing his history, starting with the death of Alexios I in 1118 and taking the story down to 1202. Following capture and the sack of Constantinople in 1204, he decided to revise and rewrite it, extending the coverage to 1207 and making the work more critical of Isaac II and Alexios III.[42] Thus, like Kinnamos, Choniates was writing some time after the events described on this extract and was reliant on second-hand sources of information. He differs from Kinnamos on one or two important details. For example, he plays down the hostilities at Antioch, described by Kinnamos at some length. On the other hand, he recounts an abortive attack on Aleppo and John's triumphant entry into Antioch, both of which Kinnamos omits altogether.

Choniates (1975), pp. 27–31:

[27] John went to Coele Syria and entered the fair city of Antioch which is traversed by the Orontes and surrounded with the sound of the west wind. He was received with open arms by Prince Raymond and all the citizens. After he had spent some time in the city and proved that the prince and the count of Tripoli were his vassals, he determined to attack the Syro-Phoenician cities near Antioch which were occupied and oppressed by the Hagarenes.

Thus, he approached the Euphrates and reached a fortress called Piza by the locals. Since the enemy there displayed great bravery in the engagement, the Romans were repulsed and the vanguard was pursued for some distance, unable to withstand the insane fury and unexpected onrush of the barbarians. After a while, the emperor approached them and many men from the phalanx around him engaged the enemy. The latter, unable to resist the Roman impetus against them, shut themselves behind the walls with the intention of making no more forays. The fortress was surrounded by an inner and an outer wall; a deep trench partly girded it while in some places it was protected by natural rock. However, when many of the towers had been damaged [28] by the thick shower of stones and had collapsed to the ground, the Hagarenes lost their vaunting spirit. As soon as their walls had been breached, the bold and immensely arrogant enemy, begged for their lives and offered in exchange all their possessions, stretching out their hands in supplication to the emperor.[43]

---

41 In December 1139, John laid siege to Neocaesarea but failed to capture it.
42 PBW (2016): Niketas 25001; Treadgold (2013), pp. 422–56; Simpson (2013), pp. 11–23; Neville (2018), pp. 219–25.
43 The fortress fell on 9 April 1138.

After this, the emperor dispatched a portion of the army against the cities and fortresses beyond the Euphrates. He gathered a large quantity of booty and bestowed Piza on the Count of Edessa.[44] John bypassed Vempetz, judging it to be an easy target because it lay on a level field, and, at the request of the Prince of Antioch who was campaigning as the emperor's ally, he marched against Aleppo and Ferep. When he reached Aleppo (which was called Berroia in ancient times), he saw a populous city which was garrisoned by a great number of men at arms. As soon as they saw the Romans, they sallied out from the walls and made a headlong charge against the troops around the emperor. They were worsted, however, and they found refuge within their fortifications. This did not happen only once, but they made sorties again and again and every time they were defeated. At times, they cunningly planned to harm the emperor himself by shooting missiles from afar as he was riding around the city and reconnoitring the walls, but this plan failed as well.

Unable to do anything immediately or at once, due to the city's stout walls and its well-equipped and well-mounted garrison, as well as due to the lack and shortage of supplies, firewood and water, the emperor departed from Aleppo.[45] After he had taken Ferep by assault, he bestowed it on a count from the city Antioch, and marched to another city, called Kafarthab in the native tongue. Kafarthab ruled over a very large district. [29] It boasted the mastery of many fortresses round about and bragged about the stoutness of its walls. Nevertheless, the emperor quickly subdued it and marched on. Taking the road to Shaizar, he encamped near Nistrion, another city in Mesopotamia which was situated a short distance from Shaizar and was outstandingly built in every respect. Since it was on the way, the city was captured and was left to be despoiled by the soldiers, and especially by the conscripted Pechenegs, who had seized it. The emperor departed from Nistrion and reached Shaizar.

The inhabitants of Shaizar and the nearby satrapies joined forces and assembled a very large number of men at arms. Thus, united in one army, they formed a league, and having strengthened themselves, they crossed the winding local river. Brandishing reed spears and mounted on swift-footed horses, they engaged the emperor's phalanxes. After several clashes, the emperor emerged victorious. Some of the enemy were thrown into the river, while others were impaled by spears, because their fragile reed-poles proved totally insufficient and were of very little help, providing them, to put it bluntly, brittle, reed-like assistance. So, they retreated behind their walls and made no further sorties. Although they resisted the Romans by popping up from their earth shelters and by enjoying the extensive protection of their walls, they allowed their countryside to be pillaged and looted, and their fortresses to be subdued without resistance.

With these things accomplished, the emperor arranged the companies carefully, dividing them by race and faction, so that race might assist race. [30] He

44 Joscelin II.
45 20 April 1138.

arrayed the Macedonians in one corps, the Celts in another, and the Pechenegs in yet another. The latter originated from Persia and had defected to the Romans in earlier campaigns. On account of these homogenous and manifold divisions of the army, each bearing different kinds of arms and armour, the enemy was seized by great fear. They slackened their firm resistance and, withdrawing from the outer wall, they took their posts on the inner wall.

For many days, hand-to-hand engagements took place, skirmishes and struggles, as well as duels between the bravest, flights, retreats and pursuits on both sides. The Romans, however, always emerged victorious. Even though the enemy was cut down by the sword in great numbers and put to eternal sleep by arrows, while the stones of the siege engines shattered their walls and parapets and made them collapse to the ground, they still remained unshaken and numbering tens of thousands. After all, they were fighting for their lives and those of their wives and children, as well as for their great wealth and divers material possessions.

Shaizar would have been captured, submitted to the emperor and emptied of all its wealth, and the Romans would have won more brilliant renown than ever before on account of its submission. Horrible reports, however, diverted the emperor from the enterprise against his will. The reports croaked that Edessa was to be surrounded by the Turks and in danger of suffering the worst of fates, unless the emperor came to its aid as fast as possible. The emperor lifted the siege and took the road to Antioch. In return, he received magnificent gifts from the besieged, made of all kinds of precious goods: excellent arched-neck horses, silk sutures woven with gold, a table well worth looking at, and most importantly, he accepted as a gift a cross, a very beautiful object, astonishing to look at, carved from red marble on which the craftsman had engraved an inscription of natural colours. It was almost as beautiful as the divine, and an absolute delight for the eyes. The Saracens of Shaizar asserted that, among the gifts offered to the emperor, [31] they had acquired the cross of glittering marble and the luxurious and magnificent table as spoils of war in former times, when they had captured Romanos Diogenes, who then had charge of the Roman empire, looted his tent and, after capturing the camp, distributed what they had found.[46]

During his departure from Shaizar, the rear-guard of the emperor was attacked by the Turkish troops of Zengi and some other eminent chieftains.[47] They made cowardly skirmishes on horses that were almost as swift as the wind, contemptuous of the Romans in their mad barbarian arrogance. In the event, their hopes proved vain: not only did they accomplish nothing courageous whatsoever, but in exchange for their boasting and bragging they were punished by divine retribution and lost two of their chieftains, the son of Atabeg and the brother of Amir Samouch, who were captured alive.

When the emperor entered the blessed city of Antioch, every single citizen flocked to him so as to hold for him a splendid reception by bearing holy images

46 A reference to the defeat of Byzantine Emperor Romanos IV by the Seljuk Sultan Alp Arslan at Manzikert in August 1071.
47 Zengi was governor of Mosul and Aleppo from 1127.

and adorning the streets.[48] He [left] the city with fervent acclamations and appropriate farewells and approached the borders of Cilicia. Then he departed from that place and took the road which leads to Byzantion.

24. Michael Italikos: Speech on John II's First Syrian Expedition (1137–8)

Michael Italikos (fl.1126–56) was a deacon of the cathedral of Hagia Sophia in Constantinople and later metropolitan of Philippopolis. Niketas Choniates later describes his role in receiving the armies of the Second Crusade in Philippopolis in 1147 **[30]**.[49] His speech contains all the features of a Byzantine encomium in its ancient language, hyperbolic praise and endless allusions to classical literature and mythology. It must have been delivered at the Byzantine court shortly after John's return from Syria in the summer of 1138.

Italikos (1972), pp. 245–70:

Imperial oration to emperor John Komnenos, the purple-born, on his battles in Syria:

[245] Most divine emperor! Plato described Socrates sitting under a plane tree by the Ilissus and engaging in his usual philosophical discussion.[50] He was discussing with Phaedrus the Myrrinusian fearing that the cicadas, chirruping above his head and composing their midday tunes, might go the Muses and denounce him to Calliope, the most senior of the Muses, unless he also discussed the art of poetry and rhetoric. For these two are rites of this particular Muse. Thereafter, the philosopher would firmly dedicate himself to this kind of discourse as well. I shall not be afraid that cicadas and other chirruping will tell on me to Calliope because I have neglected eloquence (for this truly corresponds to being overwhelmed with dread, where there was nothing to dread,[51] as tales are the bugbears of children). Since I am already old,[52] oh divine emperor, I will fear the truth itself, that I might be removed from the company of scholars and philosophers if I do not recount your battles and struggles. [246] For in this manner, I would have truly neglected eloquence if I just let your battles remain in their great splendour. Because your struggles grant brilliance to eloquence, rather than the other way round. For how can any bright image of glory, reflected by the struggles into rhetoric, sparkle in oratory in the same way as the deed is reflected in the mirrors themselves? How could I not be reproached by all the Muses and by eloquence itself, oh emperor, for depriving oratory in such a way of your great splendour which derives from your

---

48 John arrived back at Antioch on 22 May 1138 and made his ceremonial entry shortly afterwards.
49 PBW (2016): Michael 20130; Magdalino (1993), pp. 332–60.
50 The Ilissus river in Athens is the setting for Plato's dialogue *Phaedrus*, written in 360 BCE.
51 An echo of Psalms 53:5.
52 Not to be taken literally as the word had a double meaning in Byzantium: both an old man and one with wisdom and authority, especially a monk.

deeds? If you have filled both continents with wonders but we remained silent, at least let envy be cast down, let slander be expelled, as well as he who secretly fabricates and spreads these things, a true effeminate worshiper of Cotys who behaves in this manner and secretly inflicts injuries.[53]

[. . .]

[252] And so, you amazed the Cilicians, you put the Celts to flight, you conquered Tarsus, you occupied Adana, you captured Mamistra by force.[54] We applauded these deeds; we did not keep them concealed, nor your battles in Cydnus[55] and [253] the destruction of the barbarians at the Saros River. With loud and open mouth, we celebrated and recited the calamities you inflicted on the Celts in these areas. Thence you passed over from one Cilician city to another. From the barbarian Celts to the Armenian barbarians. From Tarsus to Anazarbos. From plains suitable for riding to mountainous outcrops impassable even on foot.

[. . .]

[256] Oh the great wonder, now Israel is saved because of you! Pharaoh is ruined, the rider and the horse fall not in the sea but in the mountains, in wilderness and in ravines.[56] We were amazed at the sack of the cities all around Coele-Syria and at the marvels you accomplished by the banks of the Tigris and Euphrates rivers and against the Arabs. Which eloquent Lysias will give voice to them? Who will match the voice of Demosthenes, the sweetness of Herodotus, the charm of the words of Isocrates, surpass the lyre of Amphion, [257] the lyre of Pindar, the solemnity of Thucydides?[57] The deeds of the Macedonians have been silenced, those who fell at Marathon and drew up in Plataea were worthless, the [deeds] of the Achaeans have faded away.[58] Only your deeds are celebrated and proclaimed by everybody. What can I say on my part? Every tongue and every mouth refer to you, oh emperor, but I, more intensely than the others!

[. . .]

[259] But let us now come to the issue which regards the people of Antioch. Celebrating with those who are fond of honour, let us narrate your wonders against them. When I say people of Antioch, I mean the Syrian Celts. For they should be called in this manner due to the natural passage of time, as for example, we call some of the Celts Iberians. At first, the Antiochenes used to behave like giants, walking on the tips of their toenails, and raising their eyebrows higher than a cubit. Their arrogance was completely in the clouds. When you removed your kindness from them, you showed them your thunderbolts and cast your lightning flashes roaring with fire. After being harmed by the sufferings of war as if by a hurricane,

---

53 Cotys, or Cotytto, was a Thracian goddess of immorality and debauchery.
54 John took Adana and Mamistra in July 1137. William of Tyre (1943), ii. 84.
55 Cydnus is the ancient name for the Berdan River which runs through Tarsus.
56 A reference to the parting of the Red Sea in Exodus 14:28.
57 Lysias, Isocrates and Demosthenes were Athenian orators of the fifth and fourth centuries BCE. Pindar was a Theban poet while Herodotus and Thucydides were historians. Amphion was a mythological figure. Son of Zeus, he built a wall around Thebes by luring the stones into place with the sweetness of his lyre.
58 Marathon (491 BCE) and Plataea (479 BCE) were victories of the ancient Greeks over the Persians.

one man ran faster than the other to hiding places and lairs. Even though they had declared that they took great pleasure in weapons and spears, they raised the sign of the cross instead of spears and swords, and adopted a piteous bodily posture. They who otherwise scourged the sky with their heads and threatened to ruin the land with their spears, now only spoke words of humility and weakness. Nevertheless, there is neither Rhine here, oh Celts, nor earthquakes and the dashing of waves at which you are angry, and having armed yourselves fully, you will not dip your spears in land and sea, covering everything with frantic energy and throwing things into confusion! Our neighbour, Ishmael, who sometimes wins, and at others loses, is not here either,[59] [260] only the unconquered emperor and general who is completely undefeated! You proved, oh [emperor], that the Celtic ashen spear can in no way match your spear. You moved all Asia to wonder. You are the master of bodies through arms and the ruler of souls through clemency. You are eager to surpass your predecessors in their love for toil and to leave for your successors no reason for struggle!

For, as if you were anxious lest some future general acquire a gift of honour in the struggle against the city, while you might depart unrewarded, you followed the deeds of Achilles against Hector.[60] In equal manner, you were the first to partake in fighting so that nobody else may succeed in acquiring glory with his struggles, and you included Antioch in the epic circle of your achievements as well. How then, you who are mighty in arms and had earlier written their death sentence with your spear, would you rather fill your soul with mercy towards those who bend their necks and receive life as a gift from your right hand? Then what? You contained their might with a few syllables, saying thus far shall you come, and no farther, and here shall your proud waves be stopped,[61] and your imperial letter had the same effect on them as God's command towards the sea. From that point onwards, the rulers of the Phoenicians have subjugated themselves to you and extended their right hand from afar as a sign of friendship. The ruler of Edessa has joined your army and wishes to brandish his spear on your behalf. The ruler of Jerusalem, having thrown his bronze-edged spear from his hand, [261] bows to your spear tip, and removing the crown from his head, he grants it to you alone and deems only you worthy of the imperial title. For when the sun is not visible, it is natural for the other stars to shine, but when it emerges from the horizon and shows its all-illuminating sphere, every star loses its lustre. If some star in the sky is bolder than others and desires to outshine the great fire, it deserves to be laughed at, since its light is dimmer than daylight.

How shall I not admire your fearlessness, oh emperor, your firmness towards toil? For you are a man by nature, but fair and unbeatable in fighting. Because even though you subdued foreign cities, populous rich and prospering, despoiling some and leaving them only with their name and soil, others you granted as a gift as they were along with their riches and money to those of the Celts who were

---

59 Probably a reference to the sultan of Ikonion, Masud I Rukn al-Din.
60 The Greek hero Achilles killed the Trojan Hector in single combat, thrusting his spear into his neck. Homer (1924), ii. 476–7 (*Iliad* XXII. 326–7).
61 Job 38:11.

enslaved by the enemy, as if to compensate their plundered cities with others given as counterbalance from other districts. The same man both takes away and gives. The first is an act of justice and the other one of munificence. Because receiving by force those things which had been snatched away in the past is the act of the sword of retribution which is always glittering against those who desire to mutilate and to plunder the Roman empire. To be honoured with gifts, on the other hand, is the imperial right hand's act of largess. For since you became the master of all their domains, you wish your beneficiaries to be satisfied with the imperial hand, and not to join forces with one another, due to lack of counter measures and by ruses to take control of as many of their cities which are already greedy.[62]

Noblest emperor, who shall count the conquered cities? Who shall begin counting and not straightaway lose count of the final sum, much like those who attempt to count the waves of the Icarian Sea? Wise Homer, can you speak of such a king, ravager of cities, among your heroes? Your Achilles sacked twelve cities with curved ships and eleven on foot, a fraction compared to our amazing deeds, [262] and their swiftness is more admirable than their numbers, because most of them were achieved in less than a week. Who shall recount the great amount of plunder, the herds of camels, the many tens of thousands of horses, the captured men, and all the other things which completely amaze the human mind? I will innovate for you, oh emperor, so as to render this praise a little more novel than the usual rhetorical speeches! Borrowing from the discipline of strategy, I will herald your most brilliant victories, not those in which you held the advantage over the enemy, but rather those in which your spear was not more powerful. Because in the first case one might say that fortune helped to the greatest extent, whereas in the second prudence achieved everything. For what need is there to pursue he who is in flight, or to put it more specifically the barbarian from Aleppo or Berroia who is fleeing in Cyrrhestica?[63] For they say that he who pursues those in flight is out of his mind. Therefore, having turned your reins from that place, from Aleppo (I mention the name frequently because the sun had not witnessed the Roman standard in that city for many days), [263] you dispatched the army to Shaizar, the city which we call Larissa in the Greek language. For Shaizar is the strongest fortress in the district of Kasiotis.[64] You were angry at this particular city, because it turned out to be unsuitable for a siege, with everything having been removed from its vicinity: water, wheat and all sources from which a soldier and a horse may be provisioned, all this which . . .[65] a siege. So, you plundered many Arab cities but one, you subdued a total of a hundred, among them stood the remarkable Kasiotic fortress. Once more there were thunderbolts and the hurling of stones. The governor of the city averted disaster by asking for mercy, and he was not disappointed; rather he was washed all around with entire rivers of benevolence. He whom they knew as thunderbolt

---

62 Proverbs 11:21.
63 i.e. into the area around the town of Cyrrhus, to the north of Aleppo (Berroia). John II reach Aleppo on 18 April 1138.
64 John laid siege to Shaizar in late April 1138.
65 There is a lacuna in the text here.

wielder, as one descending in thunder and lightning and as a burning force while they were resisting, they recognised as saviour, friend and protector while they were making supplication. They learned that the titles of Greek gods were fitting for you, since these changed according to time and the situation. As soon as you brought the barbarian [264] to terms, you followed the example of Alexander and set him free at once. After your victory, you granted the city to those who had been conquered. Having achieved your price of victory, you did not sell the city back to the barbarians, but you granted it as a gift, much like Alexander did with Porus. For having removed his kinship from him, he appointed him king once again.[66] This is your honour fitting of Alexander. Do not censure me, oh emperor, for this comparison, for you do not envy of the sovereignty of others, but like a pillar, loftier than anything else and acting as a guardian, you fasten on yourself the reins of all sovereignties!

[. . .]

[265] We sang along with the voices of the Antiochenes, most excellent emperor, when you held a triumph [266] after your many victories in the midst of Coele Syria![67] In a way, we danced and rejoiced with them, weaving procession speeches and preparing artful narratives, not cursorily though, as I now write and read for the sake of [avoiding] prolixity in my speech, but listing all your achievements in a long speech, perhaps as long as the extent of the city. Everything was filled with men, speeches and veils interwoven with gold and fashioned out of all kinds of precious materials. Some were suspended, other bestrewed and still others fastened. The city was another imperial capital, second to the Queen of Cities. The emperor, like another Zeus, was carried by a magnificent horse. Accompanied, praised and escorted by an assembly of ten thousand men, you emitted pure sparkling towards everybody, while compound cheers rung all around and filled the air from every direction. The thing to be heard was the trophy-winner, victorious, undefeated emperor! Then I think even the children shouted triumphantly, if not the hosanna; then they rattled out for you half the hymn in honour of the saviour.[68] All the distinguished Celts, men who ever care for battles and wars, now ceased from the deeds of Ares, and walking on foot, they all participated in the triumph in great numbers. Some were escorting and joined those who were following, while others were lying on the ground, having thrown themselves at the horse's hooves. How you raised the spirits of the Romans, how you shook down the hearts of the barbarians, how you kindled the long-extinguished glory of the Romans! Labourer of great struggles, Pompey once celebrated victories over the Armenians, but it was Lucullus who had prevailed and Pompey held a triumph for the struggles of

---

66 Poros, king of the Parauvas, was defeated by Alexander the Great, king of Macedon, at the Battle of the Hydaspes in May 326 BCE. Alexander was so impressed by Poros' fighting skill that he reinstated him as governor of the region.
67 Italikos is now describing John II's ceremonial entry into Antioch in late May 1138, briefly described by Choniates but omitted by Kinnamos.
68 A reference to Christ's entry into Jerusalem. See Matthew 21:9.

others,[69] whereas you yourself are the conqueror, the winner of trophies, and the one escorted by many rulers on account of your great victories! City of Antiochus, you saw things you had not beheld for many years.[70] You were formerly ravaged and you saw the venerable emperor entering in triumphal procession! The Queen of Cities does not envy your magnificence. Since she is the emperor's mother, she claims glory for her own; she rejoices in victories and exercises royal authority in reality and in name. For those which she overcomes with the emperor's spear she includes in her sovereignty.

[. . .]

[270] I am a philosopher in thinking, a rhetor in speaking, loyal in my way of life, a friend of the emperor in my disposition. Even though I was not entirely part of your inner circle before, I have not been reticent in praising you. What would I do if I were aided by the emperor's right hand? A double stream of words would flow from me, one pouring forth naturally and the other emanating from established custom. And this because we [rhetors] shall hardly be sufficient for your infinite struggles, on account of which we never now see our emperor relaxing from toil. You are only seen [as such] in your painted portraits. I think, however, that if one looks more closely at the imperial depictions, he will find you dropping a trace of perspiration even in your images. May your sovereignty last so long as the light of the moon!

25. Nikephoros Basilakes: Speech on John II's First Syrian Expedition (1137–8)

Nikephoros Basilakes (c.1115–c.1185), also known as Basilakios, served as an imperial notary during the reign of John II. Later, he became a teacher of rhetoric but was exiled to Philippopolis in around 1157 for his unorthodox theological views. It would have been during the earlier part of his career that he wrote and delivered this encomium.[71]

Basilakes (1984), pp. 49–74:

Speech to the glorious emperor, Lord John Komnenos

[49] Most godlike from the emperors of old times, you have returned to us gladdened ones with joy, pleasant, wished for, welcomed! We are now seeing bright rays on dull days, and we are blooming in wintertime thanks to you and your trophies.
[. . .]

---

69 Roman general Lucius Licinius Lucullus achieved many victories in the Third Mithridatic War of 73–63 BCE. In 66 BCE, however, he was relieved of his command and replaced by Gnaeus Pompeius Magnus, also known as Pompey, and it was the latter who celebrated a triumph for the Roman victory on 29 September 61 BCE. See Plutarch (1914–26), ii. (*Life of Lucullus* XXXVI).
70 Antioch was founded in BCE by the Hellenistic King Seleucus I Nicator, who named it after his father, Antiochus.
71 On Basilakes, see PBW (2016): Nikephoros 17003; Magdalino (1993), pp. 279–84.

[50] Rhetoric always is a noble affair; it rejoices in assemblies, loves the stage and desires the podium. If it ever sees beautiful deeds and the impossible timing of events, then it cannot bear to remain quiet, but lets loose its tongue, demonstrates the beauty of its voice, and in the manner of the most accomplished painters, it quickly adapts images which are not ugly to the more beautiful [version], while the images which are not so great, it reshapes to the exact time of the performance of some noble deed, and polishes them fittingly. On account of this, the beauty of the souls gains marvellous dimensions, and, so to say, becomes the other arts' favourite kind of charm.

Now, however, even the boastful rhetorical art itself is humiliated, subdued and thrown to the ground by you and your deeds against the Celts, Persians and Cilicians. Not only did you tie their hands behind their backs with your weapons, but you also bound our tongues with your deeds. Oh emperor, this is another trophy of yours in addition to your others, and another new kind of victory over us!

[...]

[62] What inexpressible deeds must I enumerate? For you are truly formidable, and who shall resist you?[72] Indeed, nobody resisted, and you also captured another more fortified city, and erected one trophy after another. All the Isaurians bowed down before you, all the Cilicians surrendered.[73] And to employ a divine saying most fittingly for the excellent deeds of the devout emperor, 'the swords of the enemy were no more, and you seized their cities'[74] which were large and well-fortified, boastful and rebellious. Just like in the scriptures, you pursued your enemies and you overpowered them, and you did not give up until they were destroyed.[75]

The Celt was strong like an oak, and you pulled him out by his roots. The Cilician was tall like a cedar tree, and you lifted him up, where we could not see him, and you threw him to the ground.[76] Escape by flight was denied, the mighty one was found guilty, and he, who was previously fearless and boastful, came forward as a suppliant, lowly, mourning and wailing. He looked at the ground and trembled, he became a prisoner of fate, a spoil of natural disposition. For truly, the children with their mother and all their loved ones have become subject to you and your right hand.

[...]

[63] The ruler of Antioch saw these things and was amazed. He dispatched his messenger to you and sued for peace. He saw a general whom the all-subduing fire did not overcome, whom the gleaming steel did not scare, and, at once, he appeased his harsh disposition, drew back his right hand, bent his neck, and became an ally.

---

72 Psalms 76:7.
73 Isauria is a mountainous district of southwestern Asia Minor. Basilakes is using the word here as a synonym for Cilicia.
74 An echo of Psalms 9:6.
75 Psalms 18:37.
76 Judges 2:3; Amos 2:9. The Cilician is the Armenian prince Leo.

But you were unlikely, oh emperor, having so easily repelled fiery arrows, to neglect to extinguish 'the inflamed arrows of evil' which someone else had unleashed against you like coals and had burned up all kinship.[77] For he burned you up with your yearning for your beloved brother, but he [64] burned your brother to a cider with his fraternal emotions for you, the emperor and brother-loving brother.[78]

Nevertheless, you ascended into grandeur. For you penetrated further into the land of the barbarians and imprisoned many of them. My Abraham, by the aid of the Father, you turned the ways of your relative like the south wind does to a stream, and you rejoiced greatly, offered thanksgiving, and as from magnanimity, joyful matters are not without tears.[79]

Which kind of motive was there in the heavens? Which of the angels ever praised my Job so as for the archangel of brotherly hate to tempt you and to inflame your emotions?[80] He did not overcome you though, and achieved nothing, as when the wolf opened his mouth.[81] I can picture David chanting your brotherly love with his voice and the harp of spirit.[82] From this victory, first of all you pay a tenth of the spoils to the high priest, and in true accordance with Melchizedek, he announces peace for Zion, the city of God.[83] You receive heavenly bread which strengthens the mortal soul. After you insert all of it into your soul, you praise the latter on account of its brotherly love and great benevolence, and you become immune to the hands of the barbarians.

You whirled about the Isaurians, Pamphylia and the Cilicians, but the swift wings of fame fly around the Assyrian nomads and brought beforehand the trial of fear as far as the Arabs. They were terrified by the vision of the warrior even before the battle and foresaw the capture [of cities] even before the siege.

[. . .]

[71] But, as it seems, the great city of Antioch was from the beginning a fervent one in devotion and pulsating with great love for Christ, and I think that even then, more than any other city, she immediately revered Christ, the true God and King, who mobilised from heaven against the false gods and the apostate demons. Antioch, first among the cities, accepted Christianity as some kind of imperial distinction and precious seal.[84] And even now, she ventures on the same deeds, she has

---

77 Ephesians 6:16.
78 This is a cryptic allusion to events in Asia Minor that had taken place around the time that John was in Syria: his brother Isaac had defected to the sultan of Ikonion. See PBW (2016): Isaakios 102.
79 The Biblical patriarch Abraham resolved his conflict with his nephew Lot peacefully and conceded him a portion of the Promised Land. See Genesis 13:5–13. Similarly, John II was reconciled to his brother Isaac, who accompanied him back to Constantinople at the conclusion of the campaign.
80 The fallen angel Satan is given permission by God to bring misfortunes on Job so as to test his faith. See Job 1:8–12.
81 An ancient fable: a wolf promised a reward to a crane if it would remove a bone from his throat with its beak. Once the bone was gone, the wolf gave the bird nothing, saying that it was reward enough not to have had its neck bitten off. See Babrius and Phaedrus (1965), pp. 200–2 (8).
82 David's playing of the harp made an evil spirit come out of King Saul. See 1 Samuel 16:23.
83 Abraham gave a tenth of his spoils to the priest-king Melchizedek. See Genesis 14:18–20.
84 Possibly a reference to Acts 11:26, which says that the followers of Jesus were first called Christians at Antioch.

the same zeal, she attracts, embraces and pulls towards her [72] the Christ-loving emperor, who is fiery bright like the sun and dissolves all of the barbarian darkness with the flashes cast by the imperial arms.

She loves your beauty and embraces you more warmly. She welcomes you as a lover of Christ, an athlete of the Lord,[85] a zealot against the barbarians, a bearer of the sword of the sun. She wipes your brow and takes you in her arms gladly.

All the numerous citizens of Antioch poured forth.[86] People of all ages and both sexes participated in the bright procession for you and celebrated your great triumph. Who could reproach the elderly as immobile and sluggish on that day? How many of the age of virgins and brides danced for you in the welcome ceremony and composed hymns of praise as songs? The people sang, 'You are my David [who has slain] by the tens of thousands',[87] the civil officials and the families cheered it, while the army sang it as a paean of victory. The cry was so mixed and of different languages. One could hear the Italian language here and the Assyrian there, and from another place, our own tongue, whose speech is more correct and more brilliant. The military chanting was so great, the sound so loud and diatonic, and the acclamations, ceaseless and in order, as if it were the occasion of a succession.

The ground too took a new form. It was covered with the most precious textiles, and myrtles were laid upon it. One might say that Antioch's ground was turned into a meadow. The fragrance of the perfumes contested with the sweet smell of the flowers and produced a mixture of a delightful air. On one side the generals, on the other the captains, and you, the magnificent star, shone in the middle. Those on the podium sang praises to you and thank-offerings to God for favouring you.

Now, however, the Great City clings to your neck more warmly.[88] She is contentious about the emperor. She is jealous of the other city because she sees her embracing you, her passionate lover and dearest spouse. On account of these, she is tormented by even more fiery love for you; she cannot bear to be second to Antioch in loving honour. And so, at some point she confesses to you the following: 'You mistreat, oh emperor, you mistreat so blessed a city by not allowing her to become distinguished. You mistreat those to whom you do not grant your triumph. I cannot accept not to crown the athlete of Christ, who contends lawfully for His legacy and according to His precepts. I cannot bear wrongdoing from the hands which saved me from being harmed by the barbarians. Let me strew the ground for you. For do not I possess more myrtle groves than her and so great a number and variety of most luxurious fabrics? Am I not more well-disposed and [73] more grateful to my benefactor?[89] Even my gold-embroidered robe, I wear for you. So enjoy a fraction of your possessions for a while. I do not wish to see your fair legs, thanks to which the barbarians do not walk on me, on the ground. I shall welcome you mounted on your horse, just as you were back then, overrunning with your

---

85 A reference to I Corinthians 9:24–5.
86 Basilakes is now describing John II's ceremonial entry into Antioch in late May 1138.
87 A reference to 1 Samuel 18:7.
88 The city here is now Constantinople.
89 i.e. more than Antioch.

horse the plains of Persia. I shall soothe your horse, mop your brow, behold you crowned, triumphant. You have accomplished many feats, so accept your prizes. You won many struggles, so accept your proclamation. Why do you endure afflictions but postpone the delights? Why do you pluck out thorns but not enjoy the rose? Why do you command and conquer but not lead the triumph?'

The Church and the priests agree with the Great City: 'I brought you into this world, a child in purple. Since you were a young eagle, I taught you to be sharp-sighted in the face of the rays of truth. . . . If you have learned to be humble, I will not be ungrateful. Do this favour for me. Let the mother force the child a little. I wish to hear Solomon singing about us too, 'come out and look [at him] wearing the crown with which his mother crowned him on a day of victory and festivity [. . .]'.[90]

These are the words of the Great City to the emperor, of the Church of Christ to the anointed and Christ-loving lord. Now, oh emperor, she urges me, who I am insignificant and much lower in rank among our brothers, to offer you as gifts what I can, she did away with the old ancestral weapons and [74] assigned speeches to me. For all of my ancestors were soldiers, and the child used to acquire the art [of war] from the father as an inheritance, and to train to dance in the martial rhythm.

I, however, have changed this military clothing, and instead of a servant of Ares, I have become a servant of Hermes and I follow the cultured one closely. But why do I deal with trifles of the myths? I am rather a servant of the mysterious word which emanates from God.[91] But actually, this does not mean that my gifts are completely devoid of value. I will not reject the ancestral and paternal goodwill. Rather, I will cheer you when you campaign, admire you when you triumph and I will compete with the rest of my family for distinction in an alternative way.

And if the day of battle comes, they first shall take up the sword for you and put on bronze armour, and I shall defend you against time, the other malignant enemy of the good, whom you shall also crush after the barbarians. In this manner, you will become a superhuman general, more sublime than time and truly unforgotten.

I will take advantage of what has been handed down, mould for you those that are vivid, and forge for you many statues out of reason and intellect. Thus, I shall not shame my ancestors, I shall not neglect ancient custom, but I shall do my military service by remaining here, and I shall fight by living in peace. Just be my commander and forge one victory after the other, as if they were bronze weapons. The rank and file of the military formation shall raise up their commander and cry out loud in praise for him who led them well in battle, they who amply fulfilled their military duty. And before them, the friends of the emperor for the beloved emperor, the sub-general for the general, Chrysantas for Cyrus, Craterus for Alexander.[92] We, good with words and skilled in unmartial deeds, shall vividly proclaim and

---

90 Song of Solomon 3:11.
91 In Greek mythology Hermes, the messenger of the gods, was also the protector of language.
92 Chrysantas was a Persian noble and trusted advisor to Cyrus the Great, king of Persia. Craterus was a loyal general of Alexander the Great.

herald. And you may defeat our words with your deeds, like the barbarians with your arms, but not our goodwill.

26. John Kinnamos: John II's Second Syrian Expedition (1142–3)

In September 1142, John II led his army towards Antioch once more. He was to remain in the area until his death on 8 April 1143, apparently from an injury sustained while hunting.[93] Kinnamos' account of this second expedition is very brief and is mostly taken up with a long speech that John allegedly made on his deathbed (omitted here). Kinnamos may have not had access to much information or it may have been that his main interest in these events was to legitimise the accession of John's youngest son Manuel to the throne. There was an older brother, Isaac, who was in Constantinople but since Manuel was with his father in Syria when he died, he was able to take control of the army and engineer his own succession.

Kinnamos (1836), pp. 22–4:

When was informed that Raymond, the prince of Antioch, had rebelled, [23] he immediately marched to Cilicia again. His purpose was to grant Cilicia, Antioch, Attaleia and Cyprus to Manuel as a heritable estate [. . .]. [24] It seems, however, that none of these affairs depend on human planning. For John had not yet arrived at Cilicia when he was deprived of his two first-born children, while one of the two remaining departed to escort the bodies back to Byzantion since he was sick in his body.[94] The emperor spent the last of his days in Cilicia and so Manuel ascended to the imperial throne.

27. Niketas Choniates: John II's Second Syrian Expedition (1142–3)

This time Choniates' version is fuller than that of Kinnamos and includes some interesting details, such as John II's supposed plan to march as far as Jerusalem. Even so, it is still rather brief and historians are dependent on William of Tyre's narrative to establish the sequence of events.

Choniates (1975), pp. 39–40:

[39] After John had arrived in Isauria and had settled matters there accordingly, he took the road back towards Syria, accompanied by his lastborn son, Manuel. The official pretext of this expedition was to bring about a better status quo in Armenia and to establish a firm control of the cities and fortresses which he had subdued during his earlier expedition up from the coast. The deeper motive of this campaign, however, was kept hidden, secret and concealed from the army. He had

---

93 On these events, see Lilie (1993), pp. 134–8; Harris (2022), pp. 95–8.
94 John's eldest son Alexios had died at Attaleia (modern Antalya) on 2 August 1142 and the next in line, Andronikos, shortly afterwards. The oldest surviving son, Isaac, had been given the task of accompanying the bodies back to Constantinople.

always desired to unite Antioch to Constantinople, and then to visit the places trodden by God, to adorn the life-giving tomb of the Lord with generous gifts, and to clear the area all around from the barbarians. He, therefore, employed every possible device in order that the Latins might yield to him the dominion of venerable Antioch willingly, or, if the Latins did not comply, that the Cilicians and Syrians might be favourable to him (for he was very familiar with the stupidity of the Latins and their unyielding spirit).

In the course of this expedition, he wrote to the Antiochenes and did not hesitate for a moment to announce his arrival in the hope that he would receive an embassy before he even crossed the Syrian borders. That would suggest that there were very good prospects for him in the near future. When he was approaching Antioch, however, he found out that the Italians had different intentions because word was already out about the emperor's unspoken and concealed plans.[95] So John found out that, contrary to his expectations, his passage to Antioch would be difficult. Even though he knew that his right of entry was guaranteed by treaties, he pondered in his mind whether it would be seemly for him to do so. For if he had indeed entered, spent some days in the city, received their obedience and been honoured by them, and then departed again in a ceremonial fashion without having achieved anything new in the affairs of Antioch or having altered the established custom, he would have been deceived and annoyed by them. He decided that it would be improper to force his way into the city, because he genuinely wanted to avoid conflict between Christians, but he did allow his soldiers to plunder the city's suburbs, after he had bivouacked there, and to take away anything which could [40] easily be carried off by hand. As a result of this command, which was given on the pretext of a lack of supplies, not even the fruit bearing trees were left unharmed, but were consumed by the cooking-fires. Once he had deemed that this subtle revenge on them was sufficient, he changed his course towards the Cilician borders.[96]

28. Ephraim of Ainos: John II's Syrian Expeditions (1137–8 and 1142–3)

Ephraim, who was probably writing in the early fourteenth century, seems to be following Choniates' account in his verse chronicle.

Ephraim of Ainos (1990), pp. 144–8:

Leading a numerous army,
he campaigned against Leo, the ruler of Armenia,
who pillaged the cities which were subject to the Romans.
[3920] And so, he arrived at Armeno-Cilicia and
he captured Tarsus, the shining city with ingenuity,
as well as Adana and Vahka.

---

95 John reached the area around Antioch on 25 September 1142. William of Tyre (1943), ii. 122.
96 It was in Cilicia that John died in April the following year.

Then he captured well-fortified Anazarbos by force,
a renowned city, tall as a column.
[3925] Next, he marched against all the towns,
forts, fortress and villages surrounding these cities.
Then he appeared in the region of Syria
and entered the city of Antioch.
Raymond, the prince, along with all the citizens,
[3930] received him well with a friendly welcome,
and honoured him with all appearances.
After he had dwelt in the city for some days
and made the prince himself his vassal,
as well as the one who ruled over Tripoli,[97]
[3935] the gracefully-named emperor marched out again
and headed towards the cities which lay near the Euphrates,
which were unjustly ruled by the Agarenes.
From the above cities, he conquered Piza, Aleppo, Nistrion, Kafarthab and Ferep
with arms and siege operations.
[3940] From the rest of the cities he received
numerous and exotic gifts, precious stones and pearls,
much gold and plunder,
including red marble which from above had the shape of the cross,
an object most marvellous, astonishing and unique,
[3945] and, in addition to this, a most brilliant table,
which was fashioned with craft impossible to imitate,
luxurious, colourful, and made out of gold
all of which were captured by the Persians long ago,
when they took emperor Diogenes prisoner.
[3950] John II took the road to the Queen of Cities.
[. . .]
[4005] After he had arrived at the Queen of Cities,
he spent a small amount of time there,
then he campaigned anew with a very large army.
He crossed Phrygia and Lycia
and arrived at the famous city of Attaleia.
[4010] He put the country around the city in good order, as was fitting,
and annexed the lake which is called Pasgouse.[98]
Next, he reached the district of Isauria,
then Syria and the city of Antioch.[99]
He employed diligent zealous actions and words
[4015] so as to liberate the city of Antioch

---

97 i.e. Count Raymond II.
98 Now Lake Beyşehir.
99 Ephraim is now talking about John's 1142–3 campaign.

from the very grievous and despotic Latin rule
and to unite it with Constantinople.
Then he planned to arrive at the city of Zion,
to furnish the tomb of the Lord
[4020] with generous and unique presents and offerings
and to purge all the barbarians from all directions.
And so, when he arrived at the city of Antioch,
he plundered and laid waste to its surroundings.
When the shrewd emperor realized that the things
[4025] he had hoped would not materialize readily,
he departed for the districts of the Cilicians with all his army.

III The Second Crusade

The Second Crusade was launched by Pope Eugenius III in response to the capture of the city of Edessa in 1144 by Zengi, atabeg of Mosul and Aleppo. In response to the pope's call, two large armies were formed, one headed by Louis VII, king of France, the other by Conrad III, emperor-elect of Germany. Both rulers decided to follow the route of the First Crusade and to lead their armies to the Holy Land via Constantinople.[1] By now, John II's son Manuel I was emperor and he had to make the decision on how the approaching armies were to be received.

29. John Kinnamos: The Passage of the Second Crusade (1147–8)

Kinnamos may well have been an eyewitness to the passage of the Second Crusade through Byzantine territory. His narrative begins with Manuel's campaign against the Turks of Ikonion in the summer of 1146 and the conclusion of a peace treaty with them, after which news of the preparations for the crusade reached Constantinople.

Kinnamos (1836), pp. 66–88:

[66] A little later, the emperor advanced once more against the Persians. After he arrived at Ryndakos river, he made preparations to besiege Ikonion and to lay waste to its environs completely. But before the army had moved from that place, ambassadors arrived in the name of the sultan to request peace. At the head of this embassy was a man called Suleyman[2], potent among the Persians and a veteran of many wars. As I have [already] described, he had tested the emperor's might a long time ago when he had engaged the Roman army at the so-called hill of Kalograia and had been severely defeated. The decree of the embassy was as follows: they would restore the city of Prakana to the emperor along with everything else they had previously seized from the Romans. Thus, they agreed that hereafter there

---
1 On the events, see Phillips (2007), pp. 168–206; Harris (2022), pp. 106–9.
2 Solymas in the Greek text.

would be peace between the Persians and the Romans. [67] Complying with the above, the emperor concluded the campaign and arrived at Byzantion.

After that began the western affairs. For Celts, Germans, the peoples of the Gauls, and all the other who dwell around old Rome had been mobilised, the British, the Bretons, and, in a word, the whole western force. The pretext was that they were going to cross from Europe to Asia so as to fight the Persians whom they would encounter in their way, to capture the temple and to visit the holy places in Palestine. The real [reason], however, was to occupy by assault the land of the Romans and to ruin everything in their way. Their army was beyond counting. When the emperor learned that they were very close to the Hungarian frontiers, he dispatched ambassadors, a man called Demetrios Makrembolites and another, Alexander, Italian by race who had been the count of an Italian city, Gravina.[3] Since he had been dispossessed along with many others from his office by the tyrant of Sicily,[4] he defected to the emperor. The emperor commanded them to investigate their intentions and, if they had not arrived to harm the Romans, to confirm it by oaths.

When the ambassadors came before the barbarians' leaders, they said the following: 'It is neither pious, nor decorous in any way for people who possess noble birth and above all superiority of forces to wage an undeclared war upon those who have committed no harm. For if they prevail, should things come to this, they will win without bravery, and if they are bested, they will not have risked their lives for the sake of virtue. [68] Neither is praiseworthy. It will not be possible for you to walk on Roman soil at all, unless you first tender assurances to the emperor that you will inflict no injuries. Consequently, why do you not conduct war openly, if you are going to swear falsely? Certainly, it will be difficult for you to fight the Romans openly, but even more difficult if you pursue the war against them after having perjured yourselves. Because you will have to fight both the Roman might and God. But if there is truly any friendship in you and no guile lies in wait, it is lawful to confirm the matter by oaths so as to transverse the territory with the favour of the great emperor, enjoying proper hospitality and every kind of benevolence'.

These were the words of the ambassadors. The Crusaders met by the tent of Conrad, the king of the Germans, to consult before him, as he was given the first place among the peoples of the western world. They claimed that they had in no way arrived to harm the Romans but so that Palestine and the Persians who plundered the east might experience their assault. They also argued that, if it was necessary to confirm that by oaths, they would readily do so. As that agreed with the intentions of the Romans, all the kings' kinsmen and all among the crusaders who were distinguished, I mean the counts and the dukes, turned their words into actions. These offices differ in that there are various ranks lower than that of emperor, which is a universal and supreme rank. For the duke is superior to the count, the king outranks the count, and the emperor outranks the king. Naturally, he

---

3 On these individuals, see PBW (2016): Demetrios 17002 and Alexandros 17001.
4 i.e. by Roger II, the Norman king of Sicily.

who is currently more inferior yields to the more superior one, supports him in war and obeys his commands. Thus, it is customary for the Latins to call the emperor *imperator*, alluding to his supreme rank, and 'kings' those hold the second rank. That is how ranks are divided.

Once the ambassadors had accomplished those matters for which they had been dispatched to the barbarians, they returned to Byzantion, whereas the kings continued their way further. The armies, however, did not merge together. The German king marched ahead followed by the French. I do not know why they proceeded in this way: either both boasted that individually they were sufficient in strength and number for the enemy, or they were taking measures not to exhaust their supplies. Nevertheless, they were marching, impossible to be counted and more than the grains of sand on a beach. Not even Xerxes made a display of so large number of men when he bridged Hellespont with boats.[5] For when they were about to reach the Danube, the emperor made there preparations for their crossing and ordered a large number of low-ranking secretaries to stand on both banks of the river and to register the load of each ship. When, however, they reckoned them up to 900,000, it was impossible to continue counting.[6]

So large were their numbers. When they arrived close to the city of Naissos,[7] which happens to be the capital of Dacia, [70] Michael, surnamed Branas, who had been entrusted with the command of the region in the name of the emperor, was already providing for their needs there, having been ordered to do so by Manuel.[8] In the meantime, they reached Serdica.[9] Two of the distinguished men there came to them in order to receive them and to supply them with necessities. One of these men was the Sebastos Michael from the family of the Palaiologoi, a man of considerable wisdom and experienced in many affairs, who, had formerly offended emperor John II, I do not know in what way, and had been exiled.[10] He was recalled by emperor Manuel and became his champion and, above all, that of Roman affairs. Such a man was Michael. The other served as *chartoularios* to both emperors. He enjoyed the highest favour of emperor John to the degree that when it happened that his eldest son Alexios departed from the world of men, the emperor's kinsmen, after the latter's death, relied on him to summon Manuel to power and to hand him the imperial office.[11] That is why, therefore, these two were dispatched at Serdica.

---

5 Xerxes, king of Persia, built of bridge of boats across the Hellespont or Dardanelles in 480 BCE to allow his army to march across on its way to invade Greece. See Herodotus (1920–5), iii. 348–51 (VII. 36).
6 Cf. Odo of Deuil (1948), p. 51.
7 Now Niš in Serbia.
8 On Michael Branas, see PBW (2016): Michael 17002.
9 Now Sofia in Bulgaria.
10 On Michael Palaiologos, see PBW (2016): Michael 62.
11 Basil Tzintziloukes, who held the office of chartoularios or archivist: see PBW (2016): Basileios 242. Alexios, the eldest son of John II, had died at Attaleia on 2 August 1142 and Basil had helped to bring Manuel to the throne after John II's death in April 1143, even though he was not the oldest surviving son.

62 *The Second Crusade*

As long as the barbarians found themselves on difficult terrain (for between the Danube river and Serdica many mountains emerge, lofty and highly impassable), they marched quietly and did nothing contrary to the Romans' wishes. By the time they reached the plains, however, those which lay after the many challenges of the Dacian region, they began to manifest their hostility. They unjustly laid their hands on those who sold them goods in return for money. [71] If anybody opposed their plunder, they put him to the sword. King Conrad had a completely obstinate attitude towards what was happening. Either he paid no attention whatsoever to those who appealed to him, or when he did, he attributed everything to the irrationality of the multitude.

When the emperor was informed about these matters, he immediately dispatched an army against them, under Prosouch, a man experienced in warfare.[12] When he met them close to Adrianople,[13] he shadowed them for some time, keeping his distance and holding in check the undisciplined impulses of the multitude. Since he noticed, however, that they were becoming more impudent, he openly came to blows with them on account of the following. When one of the more prominent men of the Germans fell ill, one of the monasteries in Adrianople took him in along with his money and all his baggage. When some Romans from the infantry muster roll discovered this, they set the residence on fire, and having thus killed the man, they took the money. When Conrad's nephew, Frederick, a very pretentious man of extreme arrogance and ungovernable impulses, heard of what had happened, he hastily returned to Adrianople, even though he was two days ahead of Conrad, and burned down the monastery where the German had previously perished. Thus, he gave the Romans and his own people the occasion for battle. Indeed, after Prosouch had engaged with Frederick on account of this, [72] he routed him and caused a great slaughter of barbarians. It was this Frederick who ruled the Germans after Conrad for a reason which will be narrated later.[14] Consequently, having learned first-hand the might of the Romans, the Germans abandoned their previous arrogance.

That is how these things were accomplished then. Andronikos, whom people call Opos, had been dispatched by the emperor for the very same reason.[15] He reminded them of their oaths and reproached them for their unfaithfulness, referring to the things they had earlier agreed on with regard to inflicting no harm to the Romans. Andronikos also advised them to march towards the strait at Abydos so as to cross from there as soon as possible, unless they wished to fall into manifest peril. But even though Andronikos said so much, he returned unsuccessful to Byzantion for he was unable to persuade them. After they had assembled in council, they considered the matters at hand. Since their decision was to keep their course to Byzantion, they took the road from that place and advanced. Those who were

---

12 Also known as Bursuq, he was a Turk in the service of Manuel I; see *PBW* 2016, Prosouch 17001.
13 Modern Edirne in Turkey.
14 Frederick Barbarossa was at that time duke of Swabia but was later to succeed Conrad as king in 1152 and to be crowned emperor by the pope.
15 On Andronikos Opos, see PBW (2016): Andronikos 17003.

arrogant before, were still no less boastful after their defeat. For they slaughtered cattle freely and killed many of the Romans who resisted them. Hostilities thus were no longer taking place secretly.

When the emperor heard of these developments, he knew that he should also make himself ready for war. He immediately garrisoned Constantinople with troops, some stationed in front of the walls and others taking posts inside the gates. In addition, he dispatched Basil, whom people also call Tzikandeles, [73] a man who had gained great glory from his battles and wars in the East against the local barbarians,[16] along with Prosouch, whom I have already mentioned, a Persian by birth who had nonetheless enjoyed the same Roman upbringing and education, to lie both in ambush at a place called the Thicket. The emperor commanded them to attack the Germans as far as possible whenever they attempted to resume their unjust killings. When they arrived close to the place, they carefully observed the German host and discerned how their armies were sometimes in order and sometimes in disorder. They noticed, for example, that their bodies were mighty and completely covered in armour, in the strict sense of the word, but their horses were anything but swift. In addition, after they had noticed that they were conducting their march in great disorder, they concluded that their army could be overcome by Romans who conducted their assault with [tactical] knowledge. Having sent word to the emperor, they explained the matter and inquired as to how to proceed. The emperor still respected the barbarian's pretence, I mean their alleged march to Palestine, and thus shrank from an attack, waiting for them to attempt something against him more openly. Such was then the emperor's decision.

The barbarians continued their march. When they arrived at the plains of the Choirobacchoi, they encamped there for this area is flat and, above all, offers an abundance of grass for the pasturage of horses[17] [74]. On these plains, it is said, an indescribable disaster befell them. From this very thing, one might reasonably infer that God was angry with them because they had broken their oaths and practiced great inhumanity against fellow Christians and people who had done them no harm. For when a violent storm suddenly hit, the rivers which flow through this area, the first is called Melas by the locals and the second Athyra, swelled up far beyond their customary level and flooded the plain. They swept away a large part of the German force, their horses, their weapons, carrying their tents from the land and spitting them out into the sea.[18] When the emperor learned of this, he felt pity for the peoples' souls and sent distinguished men to Conrad to console him for the calamity. In addition, he summoned Conrad to join him in order to discuss and plan important matters.

Since Conrad still had no desire to abandon his arrogance, he demanded that the emperor should come and meet him while he was marching towards Byzantion, estimating his pronouncements to be more valuable regarding this and other matters. On account of these words, the emperor concluded that Conrad's arrogance

---

16 PBW (2016): Basileios 17001.
17 The area around Bahşayış in Turkish Thrace.
18 8 September 1147.

knew no limits and kept an eye out for what was to come. Conrad marched with all his army as far as Byzantion. He camped in the area opposite the imperial walls which people call Philopation. I do not know whether they allude to the pleasant passing of time (for this place offers some relaxation and relief from cares to those who escape from the troubles of the city) [75] or to the plentiful plants which spring up and the abundant grass (for the area is wide-spreading and all its surface green). From this place, Conrad observed the city's wall. When he noticed that the towers were of sufficient height and saw the great depth of the moat which surrounded it, he was greatly astonished. When he observed a thong of women and some unarmed citizens standing calmly on the bulwark (for all those who were accustomed to tasting the enterprises of the enemy, some were stationed to guard the inner walls, while others had been arrayed in front of the city walls, waiting for the Germans to commence hostilities), he came to understand what this signified. He immediately reflected on the truth, that the city awaited him undaunted due to its great might and he withdrew from that place. After he had quickly crossed the bridge, which one might say joins the adjacent river sea, he camped in the suburb which is opposite the north side of Byzantion, called Pikridion.[19] The strait in that area is as follows: the Black Sea creates some kind of outflow by entering from the right as it flows and broadens towards the west, forming an oblong port for the people of Constantinople. A certain river, which emanates from some place at the north of the country, flows down through the local plains. Close to Byzantion, it unites with the tip of the harbour, and mingles with it, where the bridge happens to stand. That is how the area is.

When Conrad reached Pikridion, he sent word to the emperor and included a great deal of chicanery. [76] The letter was as follows: 'Emperor! He who is prudent, should not merely consider what has actually taken place, but examine carefully the reason why it occurred. For he who fixates on a particular purpose often fails to approve what is beneficial and to object to what is obviously harmful. Moreover, contrary to popular belief, one sometimes experiences favour from the enemy and, in turn, injury from friends. Consequently, do not put the blame on us for the past wrongs done to your country by the mob of our army, nor be angry for them. For we are not responsible for these acts. The mob's impulse which proved to be irrational in this case, was capable of acting on its own will. Because I think that when a wandering and foreign army travels and marches across many places, either to reconnoitre the region or to gather supplies, it is likely that some harm will be caused from both activities'. Such were the words of the Germans.

Since the emperor reckoned the letter to be posturing, he replied in this manner: 'It does not escape Our Majesty that the mob's inclination is ever unmanageable and unruly. In fact, we planned to make it possible for you, who are wandering foreigners, to pass through our [land] unharmed, without accusing us of inflicting any kind of injustice on you and, above all, without your experiencing it, so that we

---

19 i.e. he crossed the bridge across the upper reach of the Golden Horn, near the Kosmidion monastery, and moved to the area of modern Hasköy.

might not acquire an ill reputation among mankind for breaching hospitality. Since, however, you think that such behaviour is irreproachable and inasmuch as you are so very wise [77] and assume that you examine the substance of affairs so well, we owe you gratitude. For we will no longer be concerned as to how we may check our people's mass impulse, but we will ascribe it to the irrationality of the mob, as you have fortunately instructed us. Thus, it shall no longer be advisable for you to be scattered on the march, or likewise to wander into unknown territory. Since we have come to this decision, and we both let the mob free to exercise its impulses, it is likely that the strangers will suffer more at the hands of the locals'. After dictating these words, he sent them to Conrad.

The emperor decided on the following course of action, since he knew that although the Roman army was far less numerous than that of the barbarians, it was so much more competent in terms of military science and endurance in battle. He commanded Prosouch, Tzykandeles and many other Roman generals to lead a sufficient force and to make a stand against the Germans. He ordered them to draw up as follows. To deploy first in four units the least warlike and, so to speak, the rank and file. To draw up in front of them, those who were heavily and fully armoured. Next to deploy those who rode swift horses, and last, just beyond the front line, the Scyths, the Persians and the Roman archers. The Romans did as they were ordered. When the Germans observed this, they advanced at full speed with great passion and clamour. Thus, a fierce battle was joined and a great slaughter of the Germans took place. For, even though the Germans attacked, the Romans resisted with tactical skill and slew them.

Conrad, who had not learned anything [78] of what had taken place, stood proud and had high hopes. The emperor, therefore, wished to reproach him for his earlier arrogance and dispatched the following message: 'There is something that we should know well: just as an unbridled horse will do no better service to its rider, even if perhaps it were not to carry him over a cliff, the army which does not obey its generals can put its leaders in great danger. So the generals should not allow their troops each to be carried away by their impulses. Since, however, you were careless on this point, I do not know what you were thinking of back then. You persuaded Our Majesty, who offered you his hospitality, to adopt the same opinion as yours: now think of the injuries that the mob's free rein has inflicted on you! For I have been informed that a small Roman army encountered a German one of considerable size, and mauled it. As a rule, then, natives are likely to prevail over foreigners and aliens. We too, however, cannot punish the mob's insubordination. For, how could we? We permitted them for the first time to be swayed completely by their intentions. Consequently, if you agree, we must both apply the reins fit for sovereigns and restrain the troops' impulses. If you disagree, however, we can keep the present state of affairs. Let us know about your actions in a clear manner'.

That is how the emperor concluded the letter. Since Conrad had not yet learned about the defeat of the Germans [79], he decided not to alter his stance in the slightest. He required the emperor to dispatch the imperial dromons and the regular triremes so that they could be employed for the Germans' crossing and he threatened to surround the city immediately with many thousands of men, if the ships did not reach him quickly enough. The affronted emperor no longer wished to reply to the arrogant man with irony. He, therefore, sent a very harsh reply and confronted him with the following words: 'Those who can comprehend the details are accustomed to judge matters not by quantity, but rather by quality and by the corresponding qualities and defects. Consequently, the champions of Ares should not be distinguished by their number, but by their virtue, experience and skill in warfare. Therefore, even though a very large army follows you (still it does not exceed ours by very much, given the fact that most of our army has been allocated to different provinces of the Roman realm), it mostly consists of common and unwarlike folk. Herds of sheep are scattered easily when a lion rushes upon them, even if each herd happens to have myriad sheep. Are you really unaware that you have already been in our hands just like a sparrow? Should we desire it, you would perish before you even knew it. Bear in mind that those who possess this realm had ancestors who overran the whole earth with their weapons and conquered your own people and every other people under the sun. In addition, you must also take into account the following: you will never embark on the imperial ship, nor will anything you demand be granted by us [80], but your horse's legs will once more carry you on this land. Surely, under no circumstances can we be blamed for being hard on those who desire to harm us. For to inflict harm unjustly is not the same as to defend oneself. The first derives from an evil disposition, the second from self-preservation. Our ancestors would have thought it fit for everything that will be gained from the neighbouring Persians to be acquired by Romans without effort. Therefore, what we did not encourage our people to demand, we are now about to do, because of your propositions'.

When Conrad heard this and simultaneously learned about the misfortune which had recently befallen the Germans, he embarked on a miserable boat which had been dragged somewhere near the sea shore, crossed the strait of Damalis and quickly arrived on the other side, because some kind of barbarous helplessness pressed the man hard. For it is the way of barbarians to boast and to brag beyond measure when they thrive, but they are dejected and humbled more than is proper and without measure when they experience misfortune. Thinking of devastating Conrad's pride even more, the emperor did as follows. He dispatched some Romans to the rear-guard of the German army, rumoured to be innumerable, and with money he persuaded them to withdraw their allegiance towards Conrad. When Conrad was informed of this, he was no longer his former boastful self. He sent word to the emperor and begged for some Romans to be dispatched so as to guide him along the roads and to escort him safely. [81] Therefore, the man who at that time occupied the office of akolouthos was sent to him. The akolouthos and his men were also entrusted with the task of negotiating an alliance. Since, it is inevitable for the Romans and the Germans to contest for mastery over this alliance due to their many disagreements, let Conrad agree with the emperor on an alliance and receive very generous rewards, provided that he was willing to join the emperor in battle against the Persians. Two roads lay ahead and Conrad should take whichever of the two he desired. That is what Stephen told Conrad. After consulting with his men, Conrad turned down the alliance and took the road which leads to Philomelion.

As far as Melangeia and the city of Dorylaion, nothing unpleasant befell the Germans. When they arrived at this place, a Persian called Mamplanes charged their vanguard with a small force so as to test their might and learn their customary way of drawing up.[20] When the Persians appeared before the Germans for the first time, the latter did not advance in formation, but attacked them, seized by anger and agitation. Since the Germans were not far from their camp, the Persians turned tail and feigned retreat. When their cavalry was worn out and, by this time, far from their camp, however, the Persians conducted dreadful charges and slew both men and horses. Since the same thing was repeated over and over again, it threw the Germans into a terror beyond measure. And so, one could see those who had recently been arrogant and boastful and who used to attack like irresistible beasts, [now] cowardly, ignoble and unable either to do or to plan anything. [82] Even Conrad rode against the Persians (for he was daring in battle) and lost the particularly swift horses which emperor had given to him. He came close to being captured by these barbarians.[21]

This was the state of the Germans then. The French king, however, (for it was announced that he had already crossed the Danube and marched further on) determined that he would no longer be more presumptuous than necessary as Conrad had been. For he was glad to see the emperor's envoys who had come to him, I mean Michael Palaiologos the sebastos and Michael who had the surname Branas, and thus confessed his favour for the emperor, making plain that he would no longer do evil to the Romans. Whether he had been chastened by all the things that had already befallen Conrad, or whether the character of this man was such by birth, I am completely unable to say. He, thus, continually enjoyed the emperor's hospitality. When he was already near Byzantion, he sent ambassadors to the emperor, promising him even greater friendship and agreeing to assist him in important matters. Should the emperor desire to meet him in the palace and to share plans with him, the French king did not want to neglect this matter either. The emperor gladly heard these words and urged him to come in good faith. Consequently, upon his arrival, those who were close to the emperor, both by birth and by fortune, as well as those who at the time held high offices greeted him so as to escort him majestically to the palace and to honour him properly.[22]

[83] When he entered the palace, the emperor was on a seat raised from the ground. Some smaller seat was offered to him which those who speak Latin call a *sella*. Having sat on it, he said and heard what was appropriate and then he was dismissed to the suburb outside the walls which, as I have already stated, most people call Philopation, so as to rest. A little later, he went to the palace south of the city along with the emperor, so as to pay a visit to all things which are worthy of admiration and to see the holy items which were in the churches. I mean these which touched the body of Christ the saviour and are protective symbols for the

---

20 On this Turkish military commander, see PBW (2016): Mamplanes 17001.
21 This reverse occurred around 30 October 1147. See William of Tyre (1943), ii. 171–2; Odo of Deuil (1948), pp. 91–5.
22 Louis VII arrived in Constantinople on 4 October 1147. See Odo of Deuil (1948), p. 73n.

Christians.[23] After he had concluded his visit, he pledged on oath that he would be an earnest friend and ally of the emperor for life and he too passed over to Asia.[24]

These were the things which had been negotiated then [. . .] [25] [84] As has been stated, the Germans had been many times repulsed by the Persians and had lost many of their men. Since they had given up their intention of passing through Philomelion by this time, they hurried back to reach Nicaea where they joined the French who were marching on the road and the other kings who were also leading large armies.[26] One of the latter was the ruler of the Czech people, who appears to have been appointed king by Conrad; another was the ruler of the Poles who are Scythians by race and dwell near the western Huns.[27]

When the troops merged, the French said before the eyes of all something which sounded like this 'Bougez, allemand!'[28], a cliché phrase which the French had for years been accustomed to apply to the Germans. I will now, therefore, explain whence this phrase derives. These two peoples do not conduct battle in the same way. For the French are particularly skilful in riding their horses in good order and in charging with lances, while their horses overtake the German ones in terms of speed. The Germans, however, are more capable than the French when it comes to conducting battle on foot and greatly excel in the use of the sword. Thus, whenever the Germans march against the French, [85] they determine to conduct battle as infantry because they distrust their cavalry. Consequently, the French engage the disorderly German cavalry and prevail over it. Then they overrun the more steadfast Germans with their horses. Even though they are considerably less numerous than the latter, they turn them to flight, since the Germans are infantry, and customarily mock them with the aforementioned phrase because even though it is possible to fight on horseback, they prefer to fight on foot. As I have said, this mockery was now repeatedly inflicted on the Germans by the French, vexing them greatly.

For this reason, therefore and since it was dangerous for them to fall behind the French during the march, they marched together as far as Philadelphia but thereafter Conrad could no longer bear it. He decided to return rather than be slighted by the French. And so, he wrote to the emperor and revealed his intention to him. The emperor, desiring both to separate the kings from one another and to show sympathy to the man, sent the following message: 'Men who seek prudence even a little, usually perceive things for what they are, not according to the vagaries of fortune, regardless of the sudden reversal of circumstances. Thus, we decided not to treat you better than your dignity when you were thriving, now at your moderate

---

23 Louis was taken to the chapel of the Holy Virgin of Pharos in the Great Palace at the other end of the city from Constantinople. The relics of the Passion, such as the True Cross and the Crown of Thorns, were kept there.
24 The French army crossed to Asia Minor on 26 October 1147. See Odo of Deuil (1948), p. 73n.
25 John Kinnamos diverts from his narrative at this point to recount the appointment of Nicolas Mouzalon as patriarch of Constantinople.
26 Conrad's III army retreated to Nicaea and joined up with the French force there during November.
27 These were Conrad's bother-in-law, Vladislav, duke of Bohemia, and Boleslav IV, high duke of Poland.
28 i.e. 'Move over, German'! The Greek reads 'Pouge, Alamane'.

misfortune, we do not hesitate to pay you again the same honours as before. We think them appropriate to grant to a relative and to a ruler of so many nations, and to give advice in the present circumstances on account of the aforementioned and of the fact that we are of the same religion.[29] You, however, I do not know how, [86] unaware that you considered that which was advantageous to you of low value, chose the worse course of action. Nevertheless, since it is impossible to undo what has been done, you are now pardoned by us. We must pay attention, as much as possible, to the matters which are before us, to what has not yet passed by. For such is the nature of affairs: they are in perpetual flux, never standing still. If someone manages to draw something [from the flow], he has it all, but if it floats by, it is impossible to retrieve it. Thus, so long as there is a way of cure for your affairs, seek eagerly to seize what is beneficial'.

The letter concluded in such words. By that time, Conrad had already perceived his aberration in the past. He had followed the French not so much voluntarily, but because he was unable to do anything else. Therefore, when the emperor's words reached him, he immediately regarded the event an unexpected piece of luck. He gladly accepted the advice and marched back quickly.[30] When he reached the Hellespont, he crossed to Thrace across the strait in the region. He met with the emperor who was resting there and then he came to Byzantion with him. For the next days, amusements came one after the other for him in the city, imperial residences, spectacles of every kind, horse races and splendid receptions, through which his bodily suffering was alleviated.

After he had been supplied with a sufficient amount of money, he immediately sailed with triremes to Palestine. Nikephoros Dasiotes was the commander of his voyage and was the person who provided for all his other needs.[31] [87] In Palestine he went to meet the other kings and he performed the proper rites at Christ's life-giving tomb. The other kings set out for their homelands as best as each one could. Conrad received orders to sail from Palestine to Thessalonica with the aforementioned ships. In Thessalonica, he saw the emperor for the second time and once more shared plans and discussions with him. The emperor reminded him of the things on which they had previously agreed. These were the following: Italy would be restored to Empress Irene as a wedding gift, for she was Conrad's relative and betrothed to the Emperor.[32] Conrad and Frederick secured their intentions with oaths for the second time and departed from Roman soil.[33] And so, the affairs of Conrad end here.

The French king, however, set sail from Palestine in boats which anchor at the local shores in great numbers and offer voyage to those who wish it in exchange of

---

29 Manuel could claim kinship to Conrad as he was married to his sister-in-law, Bertha of Sulzbach, also known as Irene.
30 Conrad III parted company with the French army during December 1147. See Odo of Deuil (1948), p. 109.
31 PBW (2016): Nikephoros 17002.
32 Bertha of Sulzbach had adopted the name Irene when she married Manuel I.
33 In September 1148.

money. Something like the following befell him. Sicilian ships which had earlier sailed to raid Roman territory were travelling on the sea nearby. A Roman fleet, led by Chouroup, encountered them and engaged them in battle. By some kind of chance, the king was sailing in the midst of the two fleets as they were fighting. Since the Romans had the upper hand in battle right from the start, he was close to being captured on account of the following. When he met the Sicilian ships, as it has been stated, he disembarked from his ship and leaped onto a Sicilian trireme. Had he not perceived the risk quickly and managed to fix standards of one of the Romans' allies in the trireme beforehand, [88] he would have probably been seized by the Romans. As a matter of fact, he lost most of his men who became spoils of war and he himself barely remained unscathed.[34] Nevertheless, he appealed later to the emperor who released the prisoners and restored everything which had been plundered. Here ends the foray of the Western peoples into the territory of the Romans.

A short time after Conrad had returned to his fatherland he passed away, never fulfilling anything on which he had agreed with the emperor.[35] After Conrad, Frederick assumed the rulership. The following story of mine will relate for what reason the German state fell at the hands of Frederick after Conrad. The German king Henry had held his authority most unlawfully, since his father was still alive.[36] He imprisoned him, and he prevailed in war over the high priest in Rome. On account of his actions, the Germans took vengeance on him. When he passed away, they determined not to offer sovereignty to his children (his children were Conrad and the father of Frederick). Instead they called to office Lothair, a man who was very old, and granted to him supreme power over the Germans.[37] The two children, however, could not bear having been excluded from paternal office and they determined to raise revolts. When Lothair realised this, he was very old and generally completely advanced in age but from his birth he had always possessed a noble character and there was nothing he was unable to say or do with sincerity. He promised to pass the office to them whenever his time came. Since he passed away shortly after, the appointment fell on the elder brother, namely Frederick's father. When the latter lost his sight in one of his eyes, he chose his brother to replace him. Conrad had pledged an oath beforehand to pass the office to Frederick the son on his own death. Thus, when Conrad was dying, as I have said, he placed the crown on Frederick. Consequently, that is, more or less, how things took place.[38]

---

34 This naval skirmish took place in July 1149. Louis VII had been unwise in sailing with the Normans of Sicily, who were at that time at war with the Byzantines. On the Byzantine admiral, see PBW (2016): Chouroup 17001.
35 Conrad died on 15 February 1152.
36 A reference to Emperor Henry V, who had overthrown and imprisoned his father Henry IV in December 1105.
37 Lothair III was elected on Henry V's death in 1125.
38 Kinnamos is not well informed here. Conrad III and his brother were not the sons of Emperor Henry V but of Frederick I of Hohenstaufen, duke of Swabia.

30. Niketas Choniates: The Passage of the Second Crusade (1147–8)

Choniates' account has much in common with that of Kinnamos. One difference is that Choniates was writing much later and is clearly less well informed, becoming confused between the contingents led by Louis VII and Conrad III. Another is that while Kinnamos presents the crusaders as boastful barbarians and questions the sincerity of their professed aim of travelling to the Holy Land, Choniates is more ambiguous. The opening passage of his account presents the westerners as barbarians in the classical mould but as the narrative proceeds he becomes more sympathetic. He asserts that their mission was genuine and puts into the mouth of Louis VII a stirring speech that demonstrates that he was familiar with some aspects of crusade ideology. While Kinnamos praises Manuel's wise actions, Choniates is critical, claiming that the emperor incited the Turks to attack the crusaders in Asia Minor. A similar charge is levelled by a French priest who travelled with Louis' contingent, Odo of Deuil.

Choniates (1975), pp. 60–72:

[60] But while the emperor governed the empire in this manner, a terrible and deadly cloud of enemies gathered from the western regions and, after it had uttered a shrill cry, fell upon the Roman borders. I mean the expedition of the Germans and of the corps of kindred peoples which joined them. Women were included among them mounting horses as men do, not relaxing their feet on the side of the saddle but shamelessly riding astride. One could see them bearing lances and arms as men do and clad in men's uniform. They looked utterly warlike and more militant than the Amazons. One of them stood above all the others like another Penthesileia; she was named Gold-footed after the gold which decorated and surrounded the edges and fringes of her garment.[39]

[61] The Lord's empty tomb and the straightening of the crooked and treacherous roads for those of the Germans who wished to rush directly to Jerusalem supplied the pretext for the launch of this expedition. They promised that, for this campaign, they would put nothing unnecessary in their baggage trains, save only what was exclusively needed for the levelling of the roads. By this they did not mean shovels, picks and mattocks, but shields, breastplates, swords and all the other equipment which can prove useful in battle. They, therefore, proclaimed and swore that this was their motive and, as it was eventually proven, their claims were not false.

They dispatched ambassadors and requested from the emperor leave to enter the land of the Romans as friends and that he might prepare for them wayside markets from which they would be able to buy enough to feed the people and to provide for the horses. Understandably, the emperor's mind was thrown into confusion

---

[39] In Greek mythology, Penthesileia was leader of the Amazons, a nation of female warriors. She assisted the Trojans in the war against the Greeks and was killed by Achilles.

on account of the unexpected turn of events. He took care not to neglect what was expedient, though: he genially discussed with the ambassadors the matters pertaining to food supplies, feigned his complete approval of the expedition, and pretended that he admired them for their pious goal. Consequently, he immediately ordered that full preparations be made with regard to their passage and asserted that he would prepare an abundance of wares and thus have them ready, as if they were marching through their own land and not a foreign one, provided that they solemnly swore that they would not embark on hostilities within Roman territory, and that their passage was truly in accordance with God's will.

He devoted himself to these matters fittingly and sent imperial edicts everywhere to prepare food markets on the roads along which the western armies would pass. And the promise was fulfilled! Eying them suspiciously, however, and thinking that they might embrace the ways of the lion and the fox, or that they might be, inversely of the fable, lions hiding under donkey's skin, or even little wolves marching in sheep hides, he assembled the Roman forces[40] [62]. He weighed matters of common concern with public authorities: he expounded on the size of the armies that would pass through, drew attention to the large number of their cavalry, explained how many heavily-armed men there were, commented on the myriads in each infantry unit, described their metallic equipment and bloodthirsty ways, the fiery sight of all their eyes and how they exulted not in the sprinkling of water, as others do, but in blood. He did not report only the above to the senate, the magistrates and the army, but also the actions that the tyrant of Sicily had carried out against the coastal provinces: like a sea monster, the tyrant had beaten the sea with oars, entered the harbours of Roman towns, and plundered on his way, mostly with no resistance.[41] Then, the emperor repaired the towers of the city and rendered the whole perimeter of the enclosure well-fortified. He also supplied the army with lamellar coats, armed it with bronze lances, aroused their spirits with swift horses and encouraged them with distributions of money, which one of the ancients most fittingly called 'the sinews of state-affairs'.[42]

Thus, having rendered the troops, with the assistance of God and the Guardian of our City, the Virgin-Mother, as hard as possible to fight against, some he reserved for the defence of our fair city and deployed along the walls, while he commanded others to follow the German army closely so as to hinder, peacefully rather than in a warlike manner, those of the Germans who deviated into theft and plundering.

40 The observation that he who does not possess the ways of the lion (courage, strength and open confrontation) should use the ways of the fox (cunning and planning) is attributed to the rhetorician Zenobius (fl.117–138): Von Leutsch and Schneidewin (1889), p. 30 (I. 93). The stories of how a donkey dressed in a lion's skin so as to scare the other animals and how a wolf dressed in sheep's fleece so as to infiltrate a flock are attributed to the fabulist Aesop (c.620–564 BCE). See Babrius and Phaedrus (1965), pp. 182–3 (139), 512–3 (451).
41 Roger II of Sicily had sent a fleet to attack Byzantine Greece in the summer of 1147 and had plundered the cities of Corinth and Thebes.
42 Choniates may be referring to the words of the Greek cynic philosopher, Bion of Borysthenes: Diogenes Laertius (1925), ii. 426–7 (IV. 48).

During the march through the more distant provinces, nothing worth mentioning took place between the two armies. When the Germans entered Philippopolis, the troops had absolutely no expectations of a quarrel during their quartering in the city. For the local bishop, Michael Italikos, was of great stature on account of his reasoning and, one would say, his love for wisdom was such that he was most alluring in his manner of speaking and a true magnet.[43] He brought the king [Conrad] completely under his power [63], softening him with the charms of his words and bewitching him with the honey of his speaking. He spoke the opposite of what he thought, advantageously disguising his views for the benefit of the Romans and vigorously adopting new forms, like Proteas of Pharos.[44] To hold the haughty in suspense by his ears, like the suspension of an empty wine-pitcher from its handles, he made him his messmate, and before dinner, he shared wine with him. In addition, with the approval of the king, he fiercely reproached those who brought in grain from various sources without paying in cash.

After the king departed from there and proceeded at the head of the army, an act of retribution took place for the first time between the Romans and the rearguard of the Germans, because allegedly some were treated badly. Soon, the tumultuous opposition of the many made the situation worse and the clamour exacerbated it. Next followed bold words and pugnacity which is what arms hands for battle. Enyo attended, and after being assisted by Phylopis, the strife clearly reached its peak.[45] Since Enyo loves and always desires to grow upwards, despite being a creature of the earth and walking on it, she was close to rising her head up to the heavens, had the aforementioned bishop not outrun the king. Above all expectations, the bishop soothed the king with his charm and persuaded him to calm down. For, in the meantime, the king had become hostile and sent forth an odour of war, like a royal beast, which even though it is already fed, is stimulated by the tail and rushes forward by leaps.

After that, the troops assembled at the well-fortified city of Hadrian.[46] The king had passed through the aforementioned city, but since the body of one of his relatives had fallen into a sickness which needed tending, he bivouacked in Adrianople. Some ignoble Romans, whose hands were trained, not in fighting,[47] but rather in avarice, attacked the residence at night, set it on fire, and burned it along with the tenants, including the [sick] man. When Conrad (for this was the name of the king) learned of this, he assigned to his nephew, Frederick, the task of revenge. [64] Being especially arrogant and, at that time, overcome by his emotions, he returned to the sacred convent in which the German had spent the night and laid it waste by fire. After holding an investigation regarding the lost money, he condemned

---

43 This is the same Italikos who wrote the speech celebrating John II's expedition to Antioch [24].
44 Proteas of Pharos in Egypt was a prophetic sea-god, servant of Poseidon, who, among others, had the ability to transform into all kinds of living creatures.
45 Enyo was a goddess of war associated with Ares. Phylopis literally means 'battle cry' or 'the din of battle', but here Choniates seems to be denoting the goddess of strife, also known as Eris.
46 i.e. Adrianople.
47 This seems to be an echo of Psalms 18:34.

to death those who were arrested. This, among other things, became the cause of strife, but, once again, peace smiled like a woman who nurtures men. While many Roman officials quenched the quarrel, everything was settled especially by Prosouch. For he left the horse on which he was mounted at the rivers, the three which flow below the nearby stone bridge, and came to Frederick so as to change his attitude. Although the latter was angry, Prosouch assuaged his feelings.

Thus, the halts along the road and the day's march were peaceful and quiet again, and the road ahead placid. A few days later, then, the low-lying district of the Choirobacchoi accommodated them. They pitched camp, and, in fact, without building a palisade. This was the case every time they camped, for they trusted the Roman oaths and treaties. A river with a narrow channel and easy to cross, called Melas, flows by the plains of the district. In the summer, however, it suffers from a lack of water and shrinks to a gully that one can stand on. For it does not flow through gravel land, but one which is extremely fertile and dark, cleaved by ploughmen and oxen to form a deep furrow. At the time of winter or downpours, the river expands from small to gigantic, and from a worthless cistern-water it swells into a deep-eddying river. No longer content to be a river and desiring to be reckoned among the seas, it roughens its babbling, and, from passable water, it spreads greatly in width and becomes navigable by ships. In fact, when it is exposed to winds, it raises into waves and, thus, spits out foam. The violent [river] dashes against the neighbouring land, carries away the fruits of the farmer's labours, hinders travellers from journeying, and, as always, improvises a cursed thing.

[65] At that time, therefore, Melas swelled too much because of rain and appeared to be filled with water. By night, it suddenly overflowed. As if the floodgates of the heavens had been unleashed upon it,[48] the Melas carried away from the German camp not only weapons, the horses' cheek-pieces, garments and everything that their pack-animals carried, but also horses, mules and knights. The spectacle was pitiable and an occasion for sincere tears, since [men] fell and died without a battle or a pursuer. Neither their huge stature, almost a stade high, nor their right [hands, which were] insatiate of war, assisted them to repel this evil, but they were cast down like dry hay and chaff and carried away like a light tuft of wool. To put it as the Psalms do, this river carried off the voices of those who shout and sing in a barbarous manner, to the peaks and the hill-tops, through which they were dragged.[49] Through them was swept away a violent and savage music, nothing like the honey-sweetened music of the shepherds, so that those who saw what happened interpreted it, at that time, as the wrath of God, directly visited upon the German camp. Indeed, they were overwhelmed by the river so suddenly that they did not have the means to save themselves. Some, therefore, slept that night to suffer death, others destruction and loss of their belongings. The king was greatly afflicted by what had happened; he gave up some of his boasting and wondered whether the creations of God were subject to the Romans, whether they willingly

---

48 An echo of Genesis 7:11, regarding Noah's flood.
49 Reminiscent of Psalms 93:3.

yielded solely to them, and, whether the seasons paid over to the Romans everything that servants rightly give to their masters. He moved away from this place and carried on.[50]

As soon as he approached the queen of cities, he was compelled to ferry his army over to the other side, even though he was over-proud in the beginning and foolishly refused the crossing, arguing that it was his own decision whether to do so or not. He encamped in the area of Peraia, which is called Pikridion. From that place, every rower and ferry-boat, along with every fishing-boat and horse-transport ship was provided for the ferrying of the Germans. [66] The emperor appointed enumerators of the size of the [German] army, assigning them to record for him how many men were transported across on every trip. The numbers, however, were beyond counting, and so, those who took on this public task resigned and returned unsuccessful because of the multitude.

Thus, for the Romans it was a matter of satisfaction that Conrad had passed over to the eastern part of the empire, like the passing of some sort of ill-omened celestial object of terror. After a while, all those of the Franks who had joined his cause accompanied him. Once more, the emperor took for his provinces the same measures which he had implemented before: he did not neglect to provide for them food supplies, and markets sprang forth along the roads. Nevertheless, Roman troops occupied the defiles and the most strategic places, as was Manuel's plan, and slew many who were out of their camps. In addition, the citizens shut the cities' gates and did not share their markets with the Germans. Hanging ropes upon the wall, they would first haul up the advance payment for their products and then they sent down only as much as they pleased, regardless of whether the commodity was bread or some other kind of food.[51] Since they acted unlawfully, they allowed themselves to insult the All-Overseeing Eye, because they did not weight products properly, neither did they pity the Germans as travellers, nor offer them anything from their household storage as fellow-Christians. Quite the opposite in fact: they scrounged the necessities of life from the mouths of the Germans. The very worst of the inhabitants and all those who were determined to behave inhumanly did not send down even the smallest amount but pulling and dragging up the gold and silver coins, they put them in their pockets and disappeared, never to be seen again on the ramparts between the towers. They were even those who, by mixing lime with flour, made bread poisonous.

I do not know for certain whether the rumour that the above deed was commanded by the emperor holds true. Whatever the case, it was an unlawful and profane deed. One of the emperor's plans was undoubtedly and clearly unlawful though: he minted debased silver into coins and offered them to those from the Italian army who wanted to sell something.[52] To put it briefly, there was no stratagem which this same emperor did not plot or did not exhort others to accomplish, so

---

50 8 September 1147.
51 Cf. Odo of Deuil (1948), p. 41.
52 'Italian' here is being used as a general term for western European Christians. Cf. Odo of Deuil (1948), p. 41.

that these deeds might serve as enduring monuments for future generations sowing seeds of fear that would deter any campaign against the Romans. Once Manuel encouraged them with letters and aroused them to war, the Turks decided to act in a similar manner against the Germans too.[53] Thus, with Mamplanes commanding their army, the Turks killed many and prevailed near Bathys.[54] Afterwards they would attack the army as it marched through Phrygia, although their plan was to fall flat. While ruin was far away, they simply and willingly invited it down on their heads. They fell into the same pit which they had dug with their hands.[55] Let me tell you, therefore, that it was unlawful for the attackers to vex and to compel the beast of wrath, which was hitherto asleep, to awaken it from sleep and to encourage it to man-slaughter. Since the Turks deployed in a solid battle-array and occupied the banks of the river (namely the Meander), they entirely prevented the Latin troops from passing through. At any other season and from any other place, the Meander was difficult to cross, but at that time it was completely impassable for it whirled round, forming whirlpools and changed its shape into eddies.

On this occasion, it was also by their deeds that the western forces demonstrated that it was [only] by refraining from attacking them that the Romans troops were neither plundered, nor their cities ravaged and their inhabitants cut to pieces, slaughtered like cattle. For, when the king reached the bank of the river, [68] there was no bridge joining the two banks, and no river boats at hand with which to cross over. The Turks, both infantry and cavalry, were clearly visible on the opposite side, shooting from afar. The missiles reached those who had arrived at the river and had formed up into the first rank. Shortly after, the king withdrew from the river bank and encamped as far back as to be out of the arrows' range. He ordered everyone to prepare for dinner, to muster the horses, and to attend to their weapons so as to fight with the Turks shortly after dawn.[56]

The king, then, awoke in the dark, before the sun had yoked his chariot,[57] prepared himself for battle while the rest of his army put on their arms and armour. Also bearing their arms and armour, the barbarians drew up for battle. They deployed their archers along the bank and prepared the cavalry as they thought fit, so as to be able to shoot from afar, should the Italians ever advance towards the river. As the king passed along his ranks and exhorted his men, he said the following:

'Fellow-soldiers! Undoubtedly, all of you should know very well that our campaign [was undertaken] for Christ and that we chose it to pursue the glory not of men but of God, for how could it be otherwise? For the sake of this we renounced

53 The events that Choniates subsequently describes befell the French contingent under Louis VII, not the Germans who had already turned back.
54 This attack on the French army took place near Ephesus on 24 December 1147. Cf. Odo of Deuil (1948), pp. 108–9.
55 Psalms 7:15.
56 The events that follow took place around 30 December 1147. Cf. Odo of Deuil (1948), pp. 109–11.
57 A reference to the sun-god Helios, who wore the sun as a crown and drove his golden chariot across the sky every day.

the comforts of home, willingly separating ourselves from our friends and relatives, marching through foreign lands. We have experienced distress, we have exposed ourselves to dangers, we have wasted away from hunger, we have frozen from cold, we have become weary from heat, we have had the earth as our bed, the sky as our roof. We, the nobles, the lords, the masters of glory, wealth and many peoples, we for ever carry our military equipment as involuntary bonds and we grow weary as we bear it, enduring like Peter, the greatest of Christ's followers, who had suffered in the past from double bonds, guarded by sixteen soldiers.[58] And nobody will disagree, unless he is evidently defective in understanding, gazing in front of him without seeing and hearing without listening,[59] [69] that the barbarians, who are separated from us only by this very river, are the enemies of Christ's cross, with whom, long ago, we desired to engage in battle and in whose blood we promised, as David put it, to cleanse ourselves.[60]

And if you truly simply care about your visit to your eternal resting place (because God is not unjust so as not to recognize the purpose of this expedition and not to give a share of Eden's untouched meadows and shady resting places to us, who, having left back our homes, chose rather to die for his sake than to live), and if some kind of memory should come to your thoughts, recall to your mind, at the right time, how those uncircumcised in heart maltreat our kinsmen, the blows they have struck, the unjustified shedding of blood, and you will be delivered from mercy. Stand bravely now and fight stoutly! Let no overwhelming godly fear prevent you from dutifully defending yourselves! Let the foreigners know for certain that as much Christ, our guide and our teacher, excels the prophet, the deceiver of people and initiator of false mysteries, so much we surpass them in everything!

Therefore, since we are a holy camp and a God-chosen army, may we not ignobly prove faint-hearted towards a devout death, everlasting in remembrance. If Christ died for our sake, how much more righteous we are to die for him?[61] From such a virtuous march, let a virtuous end follow! May we fight with confidence in Christ and with good knowledge that we will put the enemy to flight! Victory shall not be difficult, because nobody will be able to resist our assault and they will all yield before our initial charge. If we shall fall, God forbid, dying for the sake of Christ is a fair shroud. Let a Turkish archer shoot at me for the sake of Christ. Let no sinful and inglorious death snatch us away! One should close his eyes just before death with fairer hopes and ought to use the arrow as a conveyance towards the heavenly place of rest.

[70] This very moment we shall punish those whose kinsmen and coreligionists had, with dirty feet, entered, as if it were some common site, the sacred place where Christ, contemporary of God and sharer of His throne, shared the same dwelling

---

58 Acts 12:4–7.
59 Isaiah 6:9.
60 Psalms 58:10.
61 Romans 5:1–8.

place with the dead. Mighty and picked men, all with broad swords, we champion the life-giving and God-receiving tomb like another couch of Solomon.[62] The freemen, then, shall banish the offspring of the slave Hagar and remove them, like stones blocking the path of Christ. The Romans, I do not know how, provide themselves as food to those peoples, like sacrificial animals, and so the wolf's cubs are vulgarly brought up on Roman blood. The Romans, after they take courage and the mindset of a prudent man, should drive them away from their provinces and cities like beasts from the flock.

Since this river is, as you can see, impassable, unless one opens a new way, I myself will propose the following and I will be the first to implement it: protecting ourselves in a massed formation and with lances at hand, we shall ride following the flow of this river-stream and we shall charge headlong into it. I know for certain that the water will stand still, it will draw back along its length and stop flowing in its normal course, as if it had wheeled around towards the opposite direction, exactly as, long ago, river Jordan was crossed on foot by the people of Israel.[63] May this plan and deed be of everlasting remembrance to our offspring, untouched by time, unfading to the flow of oblivion, and a resounding mockery of the Turks, whose corpses will fall around this river, rising up much like a column and declaring, just like a trophy, our immortal glory'.

After he had given the above orders and raised the battle flags, the king loosed the rein of his horse, repeatedly spurring and urging it to pass through the river with force. The others, having chanted a martial song and having raised the usual war cry, assembled at one spot. They closed their ranks, forming a close array like a tower, and, crowded together, they rode out. [71]

Since the current of the river was partly repelled towards the land by the horses' hooves, and partly broken, it checked its forward motion, as if indeed it unnaturally stopped its upward flow or dragged itself backwards. They went through the water as though it were land and suddenly fell upon the Turks. Since the barbarians were truly unable to take safety either in flight (for they were pursued and captured and not even their swift-footed horses, which ran on top of the ears of corn, helped them),[64] or in an attack against the Germans in a hand-to-hand battle, they were torn to pieces in various ways: like ears of corn, one fell on top of the other, or even like grapes, they were trodden out and their life-giving blood squeezed out by the lancers. For some were pierced by lances, others cut, cleft in two by longish swords, especially the light-armed and unarmoured men of the army, others still, wounded by daggers, fell one next to the other with bronze pouring out their guts. Consequently, the Turks who fell there completely covered the fields with their corpses and the ravines were overflowing with their blood. From the Italians on the other hand, only a few were brought down and killed, even though they were shot at by many archers.

62 See Song of Solomon 3:7.
63 See Joshua 3:7–16.
64 An allusion to Homer (1924), ii. 382–3 (*Iliad* XX. 227).

The heaps of bones bear witness to the great number of men who fell here. The piles are so many and so tall, rising up like lofty hills, that all those who are on the [road] which leads to this place look at them with wonder, including the author of this book. Therefore, those, who had perceived that remarkable thing with their eyes and transmitted it to the others via the hearing of the ear, would most accurately know how vast the fences were: those fences which, after Marius the Roman crushed the barbarians, enclosed the vineyards of the Massalians with the bones of the Cimbri. Had it not been for the bombast which drifted to legend and outdid the historical character of the events relating to the Cimbri, without a doubt, the present sight [would have] surpassed the ancient one.[65] Thereafter, the march of the Germans was peaceful, revealing none of the barbarians as an evident adversary.[66]

[72] Having participated in such struggles, the offspring of the Italians arrived in Coele Syria.[67] First, they crossed the Roman borders and reached upper Phrygia, Pisidia and Lycaonia which had been subject to the Romans in the past but were now abandoned to the barbarians who conquered and exploited them due to the fact that the public matters of the Romans are conducted with complete softness and an inclination to stay at home.

The Romans do not regard it as outmost priority to toil and campaign for the regions they once ruled. While the Italians were marching to Jerusalem, Emperor Manuel examined how he might punish the Sicilians, how to set free the citadel of Kerkyra, which is now called Corfu, from their garrison, as well as how to exact justice from them for their inhumane deeds against the Romans.[68]

31. Ephraim of Ainos: The Passage of the Second Crusade (1147–8)

Ephraim's account of the Second Crusade is very short and mentions only Conrad and his army. Interestingly he presents the German ruler in a positive way, suggesting he might, like Choniates, have confused him with the French king, Louis VII.

Ephraim of Ainos (1990), pp. 151–2:

[4120] Manuel established his control of the Eastern regions,
and an army of Germans, just like a cloud,
totally terrible, roaring and destructive,
suddenly came in upon the land of the Romans,
boasting that their goal was to reach Zion.
[4125] Conrad, their king, was the general of the troops,

---

65 It was the Teutons and the Ambrones who were defeated by the Roman general Gaius Marius in Gaul in 102 BCE. So many were killed that for years afterwards the people of Marseille (Massalia) were able to use their bones for fencing posts. See Plutarch (1914–26), ix. 520–1 (*Life of Marius*, XXI).
66 i.e. the French.
67 Louis VII and his army arrived in Antioch on 19 March 1148.
68 The fleet sent by Roger II of Sicily had landed on the island of Corfu in the summer of 1147 and occupied the citadel of its main town.

80 *The Second Crusade*

a reverent king and a great lover of Christ.
He made an honest agreement with the emperor
to cross Roman territory as a friend,
he, along with his troops without harm.
[4130] He reached Constantinople
with his army and the people subject to them,
breaking none of the agreements.
From there, they quickly sailed across the straits
and took the road which lay in front of them.

32. John Tzetzes: Letter to the wife of the grand hetairiarch (1147)

John Tzetzes (c.1110–c.1183) was a teacher and poet who was connected to court circles during the reign of Manuel I. That does not seem to have led to fame and fortune, though, since he frequently complains of poverty in his 107 extant letters. This one was sent to the wife of an unknown official at some point during 1147.[69]

Tzetzes (1972), pp. 87–8:

To the wife of the grand hetairiarch, when the Germans marched against Constantinople.

[87] The dream you saw, most respected lady, is auspicious for us and for the Queen of Cities. For to see her walls made out of bricks is not a sign of weakness, as one would have expected, but proof of an abundance of good crops throughout the land. When cities are full of supplies, they become firmer than the walls of Semiramis,[70] even if they are unwalled, just like Sparta. In addition, to dream of suits of armour filling the Forum of the Ox and of a tawny man, yellow like a lemon, lamenting bitterly next to the bull,[71] [denotes that] you envisaged the legendary saying the ox shall roar and the bull shall mourn, which will now be fulfilled, with God's aid. Do not be troubled by all this though. For we do not jump into conclusions like the unruly and vulgar mind. Instead, you should know that for us the bull is the male ox and the ox the female one. Indeed, all Latins and Romans have learned to call the bull Italian. [88] Consequently, if this bull, the Italian and Latin men, prove disobedient to the emperor's will, the ox, heavily armed with all kinds of weapons, shall roar. [The ox] denotes our Queen of Cities [which was founded] by the race of the Italian bull. Namely, [the Queen of Cities] will shout the war cry and the aforementioned bull will mourn and turn pale, seized by great terror. This is how you should interpret and explain 'the ox shall roar and the bull shall mourn' to the common

---

69 On Tzetzes, see PBW (2016): Ioannes 459.
70 Semiramis or Shammuramat, regent of Assyria in 811–808 BCE, built huge embankment walls to control the River Euphrates. See Herodotus (1920–5), pp. 228–9 (I. 184).
71 A huge bronze bull's head had once stood in the Forum of the Ox but it was melted down for coins by Emperor Herakleios (610–41).

folk, most respected lady, adding the explanation that this is Tzetzes' interpretation, profitable and profound and by no means superficial. In addition, the terrified citizens should perceive the [words] 'woe to you [city] of seven hills, for you shall not live to be a thousand years old' in the following manner: even though you shall not live to be a thousand years old, there will be no grief for you like the other cities which have been razed to the ground. That is to say, [there will be] joy and more brilliance and growth instead, as is the case with the phrase 'for he struck him not the weakest of the Achaeans'.[72] This was and still is the case with our famous city. For in the past, it had been built smaller and less beautiful by Constantine the Great, and Theodosius adorned it and greatly increased its beauty.[73] Then, every emperor after him brightened it anew with churches and buildings, and until today it grows and becomes distinguished. May it never cease to be adorned and to grow in size, guarded by the hand of God. I have written to you as your servant. Please send me, by your favour, a little bit of incense and resin.

33. Manganeios Prodromos: Two Poems on the Second Crusade (1147)

The real name of the author of these two poems is unknown. He is conventionally known as Manganeios Prodromos to distinguish him from Theodore Prodromos (c.1100–c.1170), who was active around the same time.[74] Whoever the author was, he was clearly an eyewitness to the passage of the Second Crusade and was writing for an audience who had witnessed it too. It would appear from internal evidence that he composed the first poem shortly after the German and French armies crossed the strait to Asia but before Conrad III returned to Constantinople in December 1147. The second appears to have been composed later as it refers to events in 1159. Both are written in verse but were clearly designed as encomia, to be read out in the presence of Emperor Manuel, praising him for averting the danger posed by the crusade armies.

Prodromos (1881), pp. 220–5, 228–9, 757:

I.
After [Conrad III] had proclaimed the above, and cloaked his false
pretence of justice in darkness,
the new Doeg, the new Sennacherib
marched with an army of tens of thousands

---

72 Homer (1924), ii. 106–7 (*Iliad* XV. 11). For a discussion of these prophecies, see Magdalino (2005), pp. 41–53.
73 Constantinople had been founded on the site of the city of Byzantion in 324 by Emperor Constantine the Great. Emperor Theodosius I had extended and beautified the city between 379 and 395.
74 On Manganeios Prodromos, see PBW (2016): Manganeios 101; Magdalino (1993), pp. 440–4; Jeffreys and Jeffreys (2001), pp. 101–16 (on the correct number and some additional passages); Jeffreys and Jeffreys (2015), pp. 51–149; Jeffreys (2019), pp. 128–40.

[20] against our New Jerusalem.[75]
[. . .]
[56] He now arrives before Philippopolis,[76]
paying no heed to God, he puts all his trust
in the uncountable numbers of his army.
So arrogant is he as to say the
[60] same things as the first haughty mind before him,
namely that he will take the City as his lair
and that he will reduce everything subjected to it to dust,
turning it all at once into desert places,
should any opponent dare to face
[65] his power eye to eye.
If one hoped to oppose him,
he would not be able to resist even his first charge,
for that is how much the great desires of proud plans
inflame the arrogant.
[70] Having such confidence in the abundance of his numerous troops,
so that even before [fighting] any battle or engagement
he already assumed that victory and dominance
in both were already in his grasp,
[75] and, as it turned out, without serious consideration.
He who is strong and mighty in battle, however,
He who crushes the haughtiness of the arrogant,
shattered his boastings beyond hope.
For God rushes to resist only those who
[80] think that their nature is endowed
with more than natural human strength
without considering who they are and where they come from,
how they were formed and by whom,
and whether their seed is ephemeral and susceptible to decay.
[85] He who coloured the field with roses
put matters in order in such a beautiful way.
For anyone who has come to blows with the soldiers there
understands that he is among those susceptible to the ruin of death,
so he probably realized
[90] when he engaged with the men of Philippopolis
that the substance of all mortals is of the same nature
and how fragile is their mould
and fluid the foundations of their existence.
[. . .]

---

75 Conrad is here being compared to two Biblical figures. Doeg, the chief herdsman of King Saul of Israel, massacred the priests of Nob in I Samuel 22:6–13, 17–19. Sennacharib, king of Assyria, attempted to capture Jerusalem in c.701 BCE, according to II Kings 18:13ff.
76 In late August or early September 1147.

Your existence, however, Manuel, is an imitation of Christ's
it bears the name of Christ for but a syllable,[77]
[100] because when you are named after God,
it is necessary to distinguish between the creator and the creation.
When Conrad realized that,
as he went on, he was encountering more and more unexpected things
and that he was marching out into battle against
[105] the God-protected ruler of the Romans,
he was seized by anger and dominated by fear.
[. . .]
[110] Adrianople, the city which is situated next to three serpents,
I mean the three rivers which all meet together,[78]
by means of the bodies which lay slain before it,
made him finally realise,
that he was going to face the might of men,
[115] their bronze bows and irons arms,
but actually that the hand of God which shatters insolence,
His son and His word come to the aid of these men
and strengthen their arms with might.
Thus, he did not fulfil the hopes
[120] with which he flooded his army.
Even though he was mistaken in his expectations,
he once more became restless when he reached the City.
He was unable to believe in what had happened to him,
but he trusted in his comrades.
[125] as they had joined the army on oath.
Because indeed fondness of strife is an evil that
confers darkness on fortune!
It can turn happy outcomes into unfortunate ones
up to the point that the confident one is brought down, groaning, to a trap of dank decaying darkness.
[130] So he followed the [road] leading this way,
he set up his headquarters in the plain,
fixed his court facing the valley,
where Choirobacchoi meet the mud-smeared
Oistros [which derives its name] from the ancient [word for] Bacchic frenzy.[79]
[135] He encamped and considered suddenly attacking
those around him with some wicked act,
to bring about, oh founder of cities, a quick
and total decimation of the troops in the area,
and then, with the soldiers all around already destroyed,

---

77 Christ is also known as 'Emmanuel', which adds an extra syllable to the name of the emperor.
78 The three rivers that meet at Adrianople are the Maritza, Tonsus and Ardas (Meriç, Tunca and Arda).
79 i.e. the River Melas.

[140] to enter the City triumphantly,
with the vainglory of arrogance.
This, then, was the wicked intent
of the crooked and corrupting barbarian mind.
But He once again commanded and directed
[145] the undefeated army of the Israelites
which crossed the currents of the Red Sea.
This time His miracles were better.
For back then the sea was cut open,
and the army of the Pharaoh's vizier
[150] at once embraced the waters as its grave.[80]
Now, however, the twist and unexpected occurrence
[was that] He re-modelled earth to water in masterly fashion.
He threw valleys and dales into the sea
and immediately an open sea of streams covered
[155] the plain and the waters were raised
covering the heads of the miserable wretches
in the manner of a crown which sits upon a helmet.
[. . .]
Look the sort of new miracles he made.
The river was roaring from afar,
[165] the army was panic-stricken by the noise
and supposed it was the sound of a strong
assembly of thongs of cavalry soldiers.
Immediately, they sought protection in body armour,
greaves and all the usual weapons.
[170] Having clad themselves in iron, as usual,
everybody stood with drawn swords,
veritable giants clad in iron,
prepared for the dance of Ares,
holding their spears ready for the engagement.
[175] A small stream ran forth fiercely,
the Pharaoh, a first-rank knight, at once
fell back to the second rank, but not the third.
The flood of the stream, having been raised up to the heads,
whirled about many of the wicked.
[180] They gave up the ghost in Choirobacchoi,
filled with mud, just as the latter
is piled at the mouth of pigs by the rope's swings,
wallowing in shallow waters,

---

80 A reference to the drowning of Pharoah's army in the Red Sea as it chased the escaping Israelites. See Exodus 14:28–9.

The Second Crusade 85

where he urinates, cleans his face and drinks.[81]
[...]
In this manner, He overturned the plans of the ungodly,
He who by his will makes everything so easy.
By releasing the torrents of the river,
[200] He slackened their treacherous expectations
and denied His support for them.
For some said that they would have laid in ambush
and slain those who had their backs turned.
But when their proposal had been accepted,
[205] what might be called a black stream suddenly rushed forward.
The murky colour concealed the death
of those who were eager to inflict evil
on those who had engaged in no crooked action whatsoever.[82]
Many weapons of those who fled unarmed and barely escaped
[210] were carried away by the stream,
the rush of the newly tempestuous river.
A river which had never before overflowed in earlier times,
which had never resembled the waters of the sea,
flooded only on this occasion once and for all
[215] and drowned
the western and sea-loving knights like latter-day Egyptians.[83]
[...]
[231] Even more now, the motion of the river
gives pleasure to all corners of God's city.
[...]
For that is how God destroys the dissolute,
as I have been able to observe many times,
and I notice that this mostly applies to the insolent.
[265] Namely the rash and mighty perish
in an utterly devastating flood of rain.
[...]
[Conrad], the arrogant man who always looks upwards,
was already feeling agitated
dripping water and barley.
[290] After he had been dried up by the sun,

---

81 The poet is describing the events of 8 September 1147, when the German camp at Choirobacchoi was flooded by the River Melas. Kinnamos and Choniates [29 & 30] also recount the incident. He uses word play here as the first half of the place name means 'pig' (χοῖρος).
82 The poet is playing with different variations of the word 'black' to correlate the muddy and dark hue of the river with the colour of evil.
83 Another probable word play. The author uses two different words which mean 'western' one next to the other (ἑσπέριος and δυτικός). The second word, however, can also denote one who can dive, so possibly the word is used ironically in this context, since the knights were drowned.

he marched inland reluctantly.
He was contemplating the all-seeing judgment,
he was trembling with fear at the river's omens,
lest he should suffer retribution for his evil plans.
[295] He passed by the God-founded city.
He crossed the bridge
where Borbyzes and Byzes meet,
and encamped suitably at Pikridion.
For, when he fixed his gaze at the city from where he was,
[300] he was overwhelmed by bitterness.[84]
After he spent some time there,
he ate bitter herbs with unleavened bread
in perfect accordance with the Jews.[85]
The host of the bitter herbs banquet, the emperor,
forced him who prepared a mixture of
[305] venom for those who had done nothing harmful to him
to eat the bitter food which inflicted no harm on him.
[. . .]
The ruler gave the signal to the guard dogs.
[330] You marched against him and put the wolf to flight.
The king was shattered, he let go of his pride,
he saw the corpses at Derkou[86]
and left the city of Byzas, never to return.[87]
Further away, at Damalis, he who was previously unbreakable,
[335] was completely tamed,[88] as a wolf in a chain collar,
by the Scythian dogs who fell into his way.
Such were the trophies of the Queen of Cities
and the military deeds of the emperor.
They have surpassed both intellect and linguistic expression.

Prodromos (1881), pp. 758–9:

II.
By the City to the emperor, when the kings of Germany and Frankia arrived.
[1] Today, oh emperor, the City discards the wrinkles of old age
and adorns herself like a bride.

---

84 A word play between the word 'bitterness' (πικρία) and the name of the suburb where Conrad encamped (Πικριδίου).
85 Exodus 12:8.
86 Derkou lay about 11 kilometres west of Constantinople, in what is now the suburb of Yeşilköy. There is another word play here: the uncommon verb δέρκω ('to see') matches the name of the village (Δέρκου).
87 Byzas was a legendary founder of the city of Byzantion, on whose site Constantinople was later built.
88 Another word play between the area of Damalis (Δάμαλις), on the Asian side of the Bosporus, and the words 'unbreakable' (ἀδάμας) and 'tamed' (δαμασθείς).

The Second Crusade 87

[. . .]
[8] The beasts learned that my teeth had fallen out
and came to hunt me down and devour me.
[10] But like Christ Emmanuel, Manuel of our times
turned me, the old woman, into a young one with all her teeth.
The beast trembles with fear at the new growth of my teeth,
and flees from its prey even as it howls for food and leaps forth.
[. . .]
[32] Today my emperor dressed me like a bride,
my walls are my bridal chamber, and the towers my women quarters.
[. . .]
[36] The surrounding enemies see me, the old woman, as a young one,
as a fully adorned bride and queen.
My walls burst forth like valleys.
The Germans and the Franks saw them and dropped their jaws.
[40] The white wall blooms like lilies, the red like roses,[89]
the golden-yellow like saffron, the green like grass,
the blue like hyacinth,
like the mauve-blue colour of the so-called blue violet,
and everybody was amazed at the unexpected sight.
[. . .]
[51] You saw how the plains turned black frow the crowds,
and how the hills, the ravines, the glens and the valleys
were covered by heaps of uncountable ants,
more numerous than the stars, more than the sands of the sea.
[. . .]
[88] Oh kings, you saw the light-bringing emperor of New Rome!
You saw the invincible power and the glory of the emperor,
[90] you saw the splendour and the sea of money,
and the countless hoard of gold and silver.
You saw the estates of the pious, the patrimony of the Virgin
of the Queen of Cities, the inheritance of our faithful people.
[. . .]
[142] From some place you came forth, oh emperor and dropped
    your anchor there,
from where the barbarian minds set sail.
I speculated, my lord, I predicted the future.
[145] Because from those who involuntarily crossed
from the area of the now-well known St Mamas,[90]
everybody asked for him and is still looking for him.

---

89 Possibly a reference to inscriptions on the Land Walls, recording the part played by the Circus Factions (Greens, Blues, Whites and Reds) in their erection and maintenance.
90 There was a small harbour at St Mamas on the Bosporus just to the north of the Golden Horn. Presumably this was where the Crusaders embarked to cross over to Asia.

They investigate and call for St Mamas,
and St Mamas is nowhere to be found and they perish by hunger.[91]
[150] Monks of the loudly proclaimed St Mamas,
show regard from now on for the Germans and the Czechs!
For they yearned for the saint more than you,
once again, they call his name as they cross from there,
they chant the seventh ode of supplication,
[155] and raising their arms towards St Mamas they cry:
'We wholeheartedly fall before you in supplication, oh Mamas!
We have reverence for you, do not hide, we now seek your guidance,
we are looking for your face, and if we cannot find you,
please do not put us to shame, dear Mamas!'
[160] The walls of distress surrounded us,
griefs fell upon us and torrents of death,
but he released sharpened arrows,
and scattered our enemies in Pisidia.
[. . .]
Like a new Alexander, reliable and great,
[190] you amazed the Latins, the Celts and the Czechs.
[. . .]
[210] You rendered me strong and vigorous against the enemies,
you scratched off my old skin, concealed my wrinkles,
once more you restored, you embellished, you painted with crimson,
like the redness from the slaughter of the Germans,
and with their blood you adorned me, as with rouge.
[. . .]
[240] Thrice the sovereign, thrice more prosperous than your father and grandfather,
and the third from your family to be Roman emperor,
you gave light and shone like a torch, illuminating everything.
You surpassed your urges and your barriers,
you completed what they had left incomplete,
[245] and became the culmination of ancestral glory.
From the former emperors, the foundations of your sovereignty,
one fought the Latins, back then, and emerged victorious,
later, the other campaigned against Antioch,
but even though they had produced the crowns of victory,
[250] they left them unfinished, both your grandfather and your father.[92]
You, however, received the unfinished round crowns
which they had produced and completed them.

---

91 St Mamas was martyred for his faith at the age of 15 in c.275. The poet may be punning on his name, which sounds like an infantile word for 'food' in Greek. See Jeffreys and Jeffreys (2001), p. 114.
92 A reference to the failure of Alexios I and John II to impose Byzantine overlordship permanently on the principality of Antioch.

You put the great kings to flight here,
and the serpent, the ruler of Antioch,
[255] you made him roll over like a little puppy
at the crimson-booted feet of Your Majesty.[93]
[...]
For your complete victory completely outshone
the unfinished victories of your predecessors against the Latins,
[265] and next to their achievements and distinctions,
you added a much more brilliant crown and glory.

---

93 A reference to Manuel I's later humiliation of Reynald of Châtillon, prince of Antioch, in a ceremony at Mamistra in the spring of 1159 [34 & 35].

IV Manuel I and the Latin East

Manuel I Komnenos inherited his father and grandfather's ambition to establish Byzantine overlordship over Antioch and the Latin East. By dint of astute diplomacy and the occasional use of force Manuel succeeded in bringing Antioch to heel and he was to become the ally and protector of the Crusader States. His reign marks the high point of Byzantine influence in the region.

34. John Kinnamos: Manuel I, Antioch and Jerusalem (1158–9)

An opportunity to intervene in Antioch arose in June 1149 when Raymond of Poitiers was killed fighting against the ruler of Aleppo and Damascus, Nur al-Din. Raymond's son, Bohemond III, was too young to succeed as prince, so in 1152, Manuel stepped in and despatched a Norman called John Roger to Antioch to seek the hand of Raymond's widow, Constance, and so become regent for Bohemond III. Matters did not go as he planned as Constance ended up marrying someone else, a French nobleman named Reynald of Châtillon.[1] Kinnamos' description of Manuel's subsequent dealings with Antioch are predictably laudatory but they are much more detailed than his account of John II.

Kinnamos (1836), pp. 178–90:

[178] Now the emperor advanced against Thoros. For while he was occupied with Western affairs, as already stated, the barbarian had been waiting for the right time and had subdued almost all the cities of Cilicia.[2] Because this man was truly skilful in anticipating opportune occasions and competent in devising plans, and for other reasons which I am going to narrate, the emperor marched to Asia himself.

After Raymond, the prince of Antioch, had departed from this life, Constance, his wife, at first handled her affairs and that of the Antiochenes in accordance with the emperor's wishes.[3] Later, however, as I have already mentioned, when the

---

1 On these events, see Lilie (1993), pp. 176–83; Harris (2022), pp. 116–9.
2 Thoros II was prince of Cilician Armenia from c.1145. Manuel marched into Cilicia in December 1158.
3 Raymond of Poitiers had been killed at the battle of Inab in 1149.

DOI: 10.4324/9781003015345-6

emperor dispatched Roger, the caesar,[4] so as to marry her, she changed her mind and joined in marriage with a certain Reynald, with the consent of all the Antiochenes, because they were anxious lest they become liable to pay tribute to the Romans if the woman ever married Roger.[5]

Since the emperor did not agree to what he requested, this Reynald alarmed him with many vile threats. When Reynald realised that he was in need of money, he acted in this way. Having constructed ships, he sailed against the island of Cyprus.[6] He attacked the locals like a pirate, and, in this manner, he acquired great profit for himself. Initially, John, the emperor's nephew, who was in charge of the region, as well as Michael Branas and the others who were appointed to defend the island, pushed Reynald back and inflicted losses on him. [179] Then, while Branas was conducting the pursuit towards Lefkosia more hastily than he ought to, John joined him and thus both were captured by Reynald.[7]

On account of this, the emperor marched to Cilicia. While he was marching near Phrygia Minor, he encountered the Turks. He defeated them in battle and inflicted heavy casualties on them. As he was heading towards Cilicia, he plundered the nearby district of the Turks, pretending that it was against them that he was supposedly waging war. In this way, he expected to catch the unsuspecting Thoros unawares. In fact, to appear before him even more unexpectedly, he did the following. He commanded Alexios Kasianos, who was the governor of Seleukeia at that time, to assemble the local army and have it at the ready.[8] Manuel picked the most well-mounted men of his army and hastened to Seleukeia. The rest of the Roman army, which remained in Attaleia, was commanded to take care of its horses. For some kind of disease, which customarily falls on equines, had afflicted their hooves and distressed them severely. When Manuel crossed the plains of Seleukeia, the [local] army was not available as he had commanded, for Alexios had neglected this matter, so he turned to another course of action, hoping to seize Thoros with all his forces.

He sent forth Alexios so that he might find a way to hold Thoros in check, after the latter had engaged him there. Manuel marched behind him in command of no more than five hundred troops. [180] The tyrant would have probably been ruined and fallen at the hands of the Romans, had fortune not delivered him unexpectedly. For one of the beggars, the common people of the Latins going to Palestine, wanderers who surround mountains and thickets, and thus leave nothing untrodden on account of their numbers, encountered the emperor. After he had received a gold coin from him, he went to Thoros as quickly as possible, and informed him about the emperor's impending arrival. When Thoros heard the news, he

---

4   John Roger was a mercenary in Byzantine service: PBW (2016): Ioannes 306.
5   Constance married Reynald of Châtillon in early 1153. William of Tyre (1943), ii. 224.
6   In the spring of 1156. Cf. William of Tyre (1943), ii. 253–4.
7   Lefkosia is also known as Nicosia. On John Komnenos and Michael Branas, see PBW (2016): Ioannes 17006 and Michael 17002.
8   On Kasianos, see PBW (2016): Alexios 17007. Seleukeia is modern Silifke.

was understandably astounded. He shared the news with nobody but Thomas and Korkes, men loyal to him. Choosing to become a fugitive, Thoros fled from one place to another.

The emperor marched into Cilicia the next day, but Thoros was nowhere to be found. He subdued the fortress of Lamos, which was strongly fortified, without battle. Then he captured Kistramos and the lofty city of Anazarbos. Marching forward, he conquered Longinias with all its environs after he had laid waste on them. From Longinias he marched to Tarsus, which is the capital city of these peoples, and he captured it without a blow. He also dispatched [some troops] to Tili, a very strong fort, and placed into under Roman rule. I will now explain how the emperor subdued Tarsus in a day, a city which could easily have withstood a siege from troops many tens of thousands strong. Since Manuel perceived that it was impregnable, he did not want to spend any time there. So, while he turned against other cities, he dispatched his brother-in-law, his sister's husband, Theodore surnamed Vatatzes, to Tarsus [181] so as to besiege it.[9] But Theodore had not yet arrived at the city, when the garrison on the walls, thinking that it was the emperor who was bearing down on them, was overwhelmed by a violent fear. These miserable people committed suicide by throwing themselves off the towers. That is how the city was captured so swiftly.

So, Tarsus was captured in the aforementioned way. Now Thoros and Prince Reynald observed these things and in no way dared to send envoys to the emperor, since they were aware of their great transgressions. Nevertheless, they dispatched some of their most noble men to the emperor to beg forgiveness. As their proposals were rejected, Reynald, who was hard pressed from every direction, agreed to surrender the citadel of Antioch to the emperor, provided that he be granted an amnesty.

For the emperor was aware of the business concerning the high priest of Antioch. He was a compatriot of theirs whom they had established over themselves supposedly calling him patriarch,[10] but he felt enmity and a grudge towards Reynald for the following reason. As I have already stated, since Reynald experienced extreme poverty, he decided to ravage Cyprus. He held a private meeting with the high priest and requested that he give money to him, because he knew that the high priest was very wealthy. As he was unable to persuade him, he initially removed the man's garments and inflicted many wounds on his body. Then, since summer was at its height, he anointed the wounds with honey and left him to be burned by sun. Thus, wasps, bees, flies and the rest of the blood-sucking insects settled all over his [182] naked body and sucked his blood. Exhausted by all these [tortures], the man was compelled to offer all his wealth to Reynald. The propitiated Reynald supposedly honoured him and led him on a horse through the city, as was the custom, Reynald walking of foot and holding the strap suspended from the saddle in his hand.[11] Even though he performed those things, the high priest was no less

9 Theodore was married to Manuel's sister Eudokia. PBW (2016): Theodoros 17002.
10 Aimery of Limoges had been Latin patriarch of Antioch since c.1140.
11 For another account of Reynald's treatment of the patriarch, see William of Tyre (1943), ii. 235–6.

enraged at Reynald and looked for any opportunity to avenge himself in some way. He, therefore, frequently corresponded with the emperor and promised to betray the man to him, although since the emperor did not agree on this (for he wanted to prevail by battle rather than by deceit), he held his desire in check.

Because Reynald had all these matters in mind, he made the aforementioned promises to the emperor. When the emperor declined his supplication, Reynald acted as follows. He uncovered his head, bared his arms up to the elbows, walked barefoot through the city with a crowd of monks and presented himself before the emperor. A noose had been fastened around his neck and in his other hand he held a sword. A splendid platform had been raised there for the occasion. Reynald stood in a place far away from the imperial tent, as if he did not dare to proceed. The group of the monks, who were not true monks, entered to meet the emperor, barefooted and with uncovered heads. They all knelt in supplication, shedding tears from their eyes and [183] raising their hands. At first, the emperor threw his head back in refusal, but later, after being entreated, he commanded the prince to enter. As Reynald entered in the aforementioned fashion, the emperor was moved to pity and forgave his unlawful behaviour. Reynald had earlier guaranteed his good faith by oaths in regard to many different matters. He openly complied with everything the emperor desired, including, of course, to have a high priest sent to Antioch from Byzantion, according to the old custom.[12] When the envoys who happened to be present there that day saw the above, they were amazed. They had come from the nations of Asia, from Chorasmia, Susa, Ecbatana, from all over Media and Babylon, whose ruler they call Great Sultan, from Nur al-Din, the governor of Aleppo, from Yaqub Arslan the chieftain of the Turks, from Abkhaz and Iberia, and even from Palestine and Armenia beyond Isauria.[13]

That is how events unfolded. Baldwin, the king of Palestine, sent a letter to the emperor and requested to meet him so as to discuss important matters.[14] That is what he professed although this initiative was a pretext. For he coveted the Principality of Antioch which lay on his borders but had no means to make it his own. Since he was unaware of what had taken place with Reynald, he advised the emperor never to release him. That way, with Reynald out of the picture, [Baldwin] would come as the saviour of the Antiochenes and would either be able to make them his subjects, or to exercise equal authority over them [184] in the event that they appealed for joint sovereignty.

Having contrived such plans, Baldwin arrived at Antioch.[15] He addressed the Antiochenes and cunningly mentioned to them that he had travelled there from Palestine for their own benefit and that, as matters stood, they were greatly obliged

---

12 Reynald of Châtillon probably made this act of submission to Manuel at Mamistra in March 1159. Cf. William of Tyre (1943), ii. 276–7.
13 The envoys present had come from Muhammad II, Great Seljukid sultan (1153–9), Nur al-Din, ruler of Aleppo and Damascus (1146–74), and probably Malik Yaghibasan, Danishmendid emir (1142–64).
14 Baldwin III, king of Jerusalem (1143–63).
15 In April 1159. William of Tyre (1943), ii. 277–8.

to him. With the Antiochenes agreeing with him, Baldwin once more requested that the emperor meet him. Since the emperor understood the man's plan, he initially stalled, claiming that, if the emperor held a meeting with him while he was still occupied with matters of war, he would not receive a fitting welcome and hospitality. Seeing that he was importunate, however, and that he beseeched him every day about the matter, he consented to his request and urged him to come. It is said that the Antiochenes surrounded [Baldwin] as he went out from the city and begged him to reconcile them with the emperor if he possibly could.

[. . .]

[185] When the emperor learned that the king was approaching, he dispatched first this man and then another from among those who held office to accompany him, and then in turns the most distinguished up to his nephews in-law to mediate with him and to honour him accordingly, until he reached the emperor himself. In this worthy manner, the emperor honoured and welcomed the man who held the throne of David. Baldwin, on the other hand, behaved arrogantly either because of the above, or because had within him a certain inherent haughtiness. When he arrived at the imperial tent, escorted by imperial staff-bearers and high-ranking Romans, he dismounted from his horse at the place where the emperor customarily does so. After the emperor had observed the man's arrogance on that point, he refrained from paying him many of the respects which would have honoured him even more. Nevertheless, he welcomed and addressed him. He provided a low seat for him to sit on, conversed with him on many occasions and invited him to a banquet.

The Antiochenes were displeased with the terms which Reynald had agreed upon: the forces with which they would join the emperor in battle, inasmuch as the city had lost its former might, and the fact that a Byzantine high priest would be dispatched to Antioch [186].[16] So, they came to implore the emperor on these matters as did Baldwin too. Since Baldwin perceived that his request was not strongly contested, he threw the envoys at the feet of the emperor. The latter, after considering which of the two contributed more to the glory of the Romans, immediately granted the request to provide a smaller force for military service since demanding something which exceeds one's capabilities brings the most transgressions, while where something less harsh is demanded, it suffices as a token of subjugation. He affirmed, however, that he would accept not a high priest from any other place other than Byzantion. The Antiochenes gladly accepted these terms and returned to the city.

The affairs of Reynald come to an end here and so the emperor considered marching against Thoros. At first, Thoros ran off to the wilderness and mountains of the Taurus. Then Baldwin beseeched the emperor on his behalf and Thoros came to the Roman camp as a pitiable supplicant. The emperor accepted him and enrolled him among the Roman subjects, thus bringing the war to an end.

---

16 i.e. the Byzantine emperor would have the right to appoint the patriarch of Antioch.

Manuel I and the Latin East 95

When the emperor was already on the move to enter Antioch, the Antiochenes seem to have feared that if the Roman forces were allowed inside, they would attempt to expel them from the city. Unable to thwart the emperor's march, they came up with some specious excuses and went out to meet him. They claimed that some daring men among them planned to employ some treachery against him, since he would enter the city completely unarmed for it would be improper to do otherwise. [187] The emperor, however, perceived their deceit and replied that what they had in mind would never transpire. He refuted the envoys, explaining why these things were impossible. Not least among many reasons was the fact that Baldwin would parade unarmed a long way from the imperial regiment, while Reynald and the others would be occupied with holding the trappings and the straps of the horse's saddle, proceeding on foot, and completely unarmed. The emperor, on the other hand, would be guarded by a numerous band of axe-bearing barbarians, as it was customary. That is how he confounded the aforementioned arguments.

When he was about to enter the city, the emperor put on double breastplates, induced by the inexhaustible strength of his body. In addition, he wore a surcoat covered in precious gems, which was no less heavy than the armour underneath, a crown and all the other things that emperors customarily wear. I can say the following with astonishment. When the triumphal ceremony had been concluded, in the same manner that is the custom in Byzantion, he arrived at the church of the Apostle Peter and dismounted nimbly from his horse. Then he leaped over to remount his horse with a bound, just like some unarmoured and unarmed man. At that time, the high priest of the city came to meet him, clad in his priestly robe, along with all the clerical host. They made the sign of the cross and uttered the holy words so that all the aliens and foreigners were amazed. They also witnessed Reynald and the Antiochene aristocracy accompanying the imperial horse [188] on both sides on foot, as well as Baldwin, a crowned man, riding far behind on horse, but with no kind of insignia.[17]

After the triumph had been concluded in this manner, the emperor remained in the city for eight days and then departed. The Antiochenes demonstrated such servility towards him that, during his stay in Reynald's palace, all those who had disputes pleaded their cases to a Roman for judgement rather than to their compatriots.

Having accomplished the above, the emperor prepared to move against Nur al-Din. He, however, informed of the attack, released two prominent men, an Italian, the son of St Gilles, and the commander of the knights in Palestine, which the Latins call the Master of the Temple, as well as many well-born men.[18] In addition, [he set free] about six thousand men of the common and ordinary populace who happened to have been taken captive by him from the German and Frankish army, when they campaigned in Asia.[19] These were Nur al-Din's actions, and

---

17 Manuel entered Antioch on 12 April 1159. William of Tyre (1943), ii. 279.
18 Bertram of Toulouse, grandson of Raymond of St Gilles, and Bertrand of Blancfort, Grand Master of the Templars.
19 i.e. during the Second Crusade in 1147–8.

96 *Manuel I and the Latin East*

additionally he agreed to assist the emperor in his battles in Asia. Having admitted him [as an ally] on these conditions, the emperor abandoned the project.[20]

Shortly afterwards [Manuel] was eager to annul the agreement, but he did not implement his intention, as it will become apparent from the following. A company of Saracens, completely without the knowledge of Nur al-Din, set an ambush and inflicted harm on some of the Romans who went to forage. When the emperor learned about this, he too set up ambushes at dawn in some suitable spots in the same area [189] and attacked them without them suspecting anything.

After he had put them to flight, he longed to go hunting and went out to the farthest plains of Syria to do so, which in the current circumstances was an unheard of, daring thing. Consequently, no more than six of his men went ahead whose task was to track the beasts' lairs. They had not advanced far though, when twenty-four enemy soldiers appeared in front of them. Their aim was to lure by trickery some of the Romans to their army which was laid in ambush behind them. When the trackers perceived this, they immediately launched themselves into a nearby river-stream. After they had swum across, they came to the emperor and reported to him what had took place.

Unperturbed by what he heard, the emperor said 'Let us go! Tell us where the enemy is'. Although the soldiers were very reluctant, the emperor gave his horse full rein and charged the enemy. Then, out of nowhere, a countless Saracen army appeared, emerging from the heights nearby. Displaying no hesitation whatsoever, the emperor rushed with great force against the many soldiers in the centre. He put them to flight and did not cease the pursuit until the field was filled with corpses and the fleeing enemy had sought refuge inside the forts which had been built there. That is why then, when he returned to camp, the emperor wanted to annul the agreement, as I have said. Some rumours, however, which came from the West, reported that [190] things were in turmoil there, and prevented him from the task.

At that time, Baldwin broke his hand in the following way. While the emperor was hunting, Baldwin was present and joined him in the exercise. Since he was amazed at the emperor in every other respect, he desired to know whether the emperor was distinguished at this activity as well. Aspiring to match the emperor's dashes, for he engaged in the chase in a marvellous sort of way, he accidentally slipped and fell along with his horse, and, as I said, he injured his hand. At once, the emperor bound it up, took care of it in an appropriate manner, and after a few days he took the bandage off.[21]

For he surpassed in medical matters many of the doctors who had practiced medicine all their lives. For instance, I have seen him, when there was a lack of practitioners, cutting veins open and administering drugs to patients. He had already made many contributions to medical science, things which remained unknown to

---

20 Manuel concluded his treaty with Nur al-Din in May 1159. Cf. William of Tyre (1943), ii. 280–1.
21 According to William of Tyre (1943), ii. 280, the accident took place on 21 May 1159.

everybody for centuries, such as which natural [drugs] are good for anointing and which for drinking, as well as those which can be taken from the public hospitals, which are customarily called *xenones*, by whoever wants them. But so much for that.

35. Niketas Choniates: Manuel I, Antioch and Jerusalem (1158–9)

Choniates' account of the events of 1158–9 is considerably shorter than that of Kinnamos. Much of it is given over to a detail absent in the latter's account: a tournament organised by Manuel outside Antioch after his triumphal entry. The campaign against Nur al-Din and the subsequent treaty with him are not mentioned.

Choniates (1975), pp. 108–10:

[108] At first, the Antiochenes did not receive the emperor's arrival well. On the contrary, they viewed it with hostility and considered how to stave it off. Since they were completely unable either to hinder him or to change his mind, they poured out the gates to meet him with a servile spirit and appearance. They also made ready for him a magnificent entry procession, adorning the boulevards and the streets with cloths and carpets and embellishing them with freshly-cut sprays from trees. In the centre of the city, they transplanted the delights of plants and flowers, and, in this manner, they prepared for him a lavish procession. There were not only distinguished people present, but almost all of the inhabitants, so that one could see the Syrian epicure, the Isaurian bandit, the Cilician pirate, the lance-bearing Italian knight along with his haughty steed, putting aside its haughty spirit and marching in step as part of the triumph.[22]

Seeing the Latin troops priding themselves in their prowess in arms and bragging about their skilful spear thrusts, Manuel arranged a day for a tournament with blunted spears. When the appointed date arrived, the emperor chose, according to merit, those from the Roman military lists who were skilful in wielding lances, as well as his relatives who volunteered. The emperor himself participated as well. He grinned a little then wore his usual relaxed smile and rode out gently to a field which could accommodate two opposing drawn up cavalry contingents. [109] He ordered his kin and those who had been selected to compete with the Italians to wear the most splendid equipment possible. He himself held his spear straight and was clothed in a very elegant military cloak, which buckled onto his right shoulder and left the hand under the brooch unhindered. He rivalled the splendour of his steed, since he was mounted on a war horse with a beautiful mane and golden trappings. It bowed its neck gently and flexed its feet slightly as if it were looking forward to galloping off.

Prince Reynald also participated, mounted on a horse whiter than snow, dressed in a slashed tunic which reached his feet and wearing on his head a

---

22 12 April 1159. William of Tyre (1943), ii. 279.

cap embroidered in gold which resembled a tilted tiara. His knights, all tall in stature and distinguished in arms, went out with him. Since the battle which bristled with spears witnessed no bloodshed, both teams clashed bravely, skilfully thrusting at one another with the spear and evading the spears thrown at them. At that time, during this mock battle, one could see a rider thrown on his head and overturned on his shoulders in one place, elsewhere a knight knocked from his saddle, another headlong to the ground, another lying on his back, and still another showing his back and fleeing hastily. One man, pale with fear, completely buried himself behind his shield, intimidated by his opponent throwing at him, while the other was exuberant since he noticed his rival's cowardice. The rush of the wind, cut off by the speed of the horses, fluttered the standards and produced a shrill whistle. Seeing this kind of melée, one would put it gracefully if he said that Aphrodite had united with Ares, or that the Graces had embraced Enyo. That contest, therefore, turned out to be a mixture of divers beautiful events, deeds and sights. The desire to surpass the Italians even in tilting with the spears and the eyes of emperor which were the judges of the contest made the Romans compete with extraordinary eagerness. For the Latins, on the other hand, it was their perpetual haughtiness, their arrogant mentality and their inability to tolerate the Romans getting the upper hand in an engagement with spears. [110] The emperor himself unhorsed two knights with one blow, charging against the first with spear in hand and due to the force of the thrust unhorsing the second who was nearby. After he had filled the Antiochenes with wonder on account of his manly courage, and they had witnessed with their eyes the rumours they had earlier heard with their ears, he determined to celebrate again and to return to Constantinople.

36. John Kinnamos: Manuel's search for a bride from the Latin East (1160–1)

Following his triumph at Antioch in 1159, Manuel sought to enhance his influence in the Latin East still further by making a marriage alliance with one of the Christian rulers there. John Kinnamos describes the despatch of three embassies to the area and the eventual choice.[23]

Kinnamos (1836), pp. 208–11:

[208] Since empress Irene had already passed away, and the emperor had not up to that point become the father of a male child, he considered a second marriage.[24] For there was a certain maiden in Tripoli of Phoenicia, Latin by birth and extremely beautiful to [behold].[25]

---

23 On these events, see Lilie (1993), pp. 183–7.
24 Manuel's first wife, Bertha of Sulzbach, had died in 1160, leaving him with a daughter, Maria the Porphyrogenita.
25 Melisend, daughter of Raymond III, Count of Tripoli (1152–87).

Manuel dispatched the Sebastos John Kontostephanos and an Italian, Theophylact, whom people called Exoubitos, to fetch her from Tripoli.26 [209] The men saw the maiden and admired her beauty. Since at that time no obstacle whatsoever was manifest, they embarked on the trireme without delay.

But as soon as they were about to lift anchor from there, the maiden was afflicted by a severe disease, and she was in a dangerous situation. On account of this, they kept postponing the voyage until the next day, and they spent their time in vain. For even though she had been relieved from pain for a short time and been deemed fit to travel by ship, she was afflicted by suffering once again, as if by some providence. When she lay down on a bed, her body shivered and shook quite violently, then fevers struck her, and, by that time, mortification and consumption were already evident. The graceful bloom of her appearance, which had formerly gleamed, was quickly corrupted and darkened. Anybody who happened to see so beautiful a meadow fading away before its time, would have burst into tears. That is how badly the maiden suffered when she was staying at home. Whenever she embarked on the ship and departed a short distance from Tripoli, the waves doubled in height and noise. Once more, the ship docked in Tripoli, and the maiden fell into a more severe illness which hardly ever left her.

Since the same thing was happening repeatedly, it led Kontostephanos to constant reflection. Feeling understandably distressed on that account and turning one idea after the other over in his mind, he finally visited one of the local churches and requested that he might learn whether the emperor was destined to betroth the maiden. From the priests of the church he received the oracle 'the wedding is ready, but those summoned were not worthy to be present'.27 [210] When he heard these words, he perceived [the meaning] of the oracular response because a certain rumour had already oppressed them that the maiden might not have been conceived in lawful wedlock, surely a matter of everlasting shame. At once, he aborted the mission, and, departing from there, he arrived at Byzantion.28

Raymond, Prince of Antioch, had daughters who were at that time distinguished in beauty.29 The emperor dispatched an order to Basil Kamateros, who was at that time commander of the imperial guard, to [go and] see them.30 As soon as he

---

26 John Kontostephanos, who was a nephew of Emperor Manuel I. See PBW (2016): Ioannes 392. On Theophylact, who acted as interpreter, see PBW (2016); Theophylaktos 20139. Constantine Manasses was another member of the delegation, which probably set out for the Latin East in late 1160 and his account of it is given in [37]. Kinnamos omits to mention that Kontostephanos and Theophylact went to Jerusalem first to discuss the project with King Baldwin III: William of Tyre (1943), ii. 287–8.
27 See Matthew 22:8.
28 Kinnamos' account of Melisend's illness and the oracle might be treated with some caution. William of Tyre (1943), ii. 289–90, has a very different account, suggesting that the Byzantine ambassadors dragged out negotiations and then lost interest, probably because a more advantageous match was on offer in Antioch.
29 Raymond of Poitiers and his wife Constance had had two daughters Maria (or Marguerite-Constance) and Philippa.
30 On Basil Kamateros, see PBW (2016): Basileios 17005.

arrived at Antioch, he saw that both were handsome, but it appeared to him that Maria was the most beautiful. The observation of our ambassador proved to be accurate. For such a beauty, the Byzantines used to say, was previously unknown to our era. These events took place later, however. Now, after Basil Kamateros had favoured Maria, the emperor was informed of it and dispatched dignitaries to Antioch in order to betroth the maiden to him. These were: the grandson of Alexios I, Alexios, who was then Grand Duke, Nikephoros Bryennios, who had already become sebastos and was the emperor's son in law through his niece, and Andronikos Kamateros, who then held the office of Eparch and had been honoured with the dignity of sebastos, also the emperor's relative.[31] The men saw [Maria] and were amazed. They embarked her on a trireme and magnificently escorted her to Byzantion.

Thus, on the twenty-fifth of the month Apellaios, [211] which is called December by those who speak the Roman tongue, she was led splendidly into Hagia Sophia, the renowned house of God. She was married there, with Luke, who had then been appointed patriarch of Constantinople, Sophronios of Alexandria and Athanasios of Antioch, laying their hands on them, and proclaiming her Augusta, according to the Christian custom.[32] [After the ceremony], she returned to the palace. [The emperor] invited the dignitaries to magnificent banquets as his guests and arranged public feasts all over the byways of the city. The next day, he invited the patriarchs to dine with him. After he had honoured each of them with abundant gold, he dismissed them. But most importantly, above all else, he bestowed a hundred pounds of gold on the church as a gift. Shortly afterwards, he entertained the public with horse races, and took care not to neglect anything that brings joy.

37. Constantine Manasses: Poem about his journey to Jerusalem (1161–2)

Constantine Manasses (c.1130–c.1187) was a well-known man of letters at the court of Manuel I. At the request of the emperor's sister-in-law, Irene the Sebastokratorissa, he wrote a chronicle of events from Creation to the accession of Alexios I in 1081, as well as an erotic novel entitled *Aristandros and Kallithea*. Early in 1161, he was selected as one of the members of the delegation led by John Kontostephanos to Jerusalem and Tripoli that is described by Kinnamos above [36]. He described his experiences in a poem written shortly after his return. His personality comes out very clearly in this work, especially in his waspish insistence that most

---

31 Alexios Bryennios Komnenos was the son of Nikephoros Bryennios and the historian Anna Komnene: PBW (2016): 17005. Nikephoros Bryennios had married Manuel I's niece Irene: PBW (2016): Nikephoros 17004. On Andronikos Doukas Kamateros, see PBW (2016): Andronikos 112.
32 The marriage took place on Christmas day 1161, presided over by the patriarch of Constantinople Luke Chryoberges, Sophronios III, patriarch of Alexandria and Athanasios I Manasses, patriarch of Antioch. See PBW (2016): Loukas 11, Sophronios 17001, Athanasios 112.

of the towns of the Holy Land would not be worth visiting, were it not for their association with Christ.[33]

Manasses (2017), pp. 4–190:

Lord Constantine Manasses on his journey to Jerusalem.

I
Having just escaped from the roar of the terrifying waves
and from the foaming sea of troubles,
which my naive nature imposed upon me
and my ignorance of human wickedness,
[5] I just managed to enter a tranquil port
full of the delightful breeze of calmness
and so, having found the plentiful charms of the books
I imitated the labour of the bees.
One night I was weary and exhausted
[10] holding *Naukratites* in my hands[34]
when sleep came to me, drew my eyelids together
and surrendered me to wild dreams.
In my dream I think I saw
the shrewd Pansebastos John,
[15] descended from the Kontostephanos family,[35]
boarding on a trireme with eager steps
and forcibly dragging me behind him.
Then, [I saw him] as a general, making the assembly,
light and heavy infantry, slingers, knights
[20] and another multitude of men, marines and seafarers,
so as, if the winds happened to be light,
to sail directly to Sicily,
for in my dream I thought I saw him,
to have been appointed as general and admiral.
[25] How to bewail and interpret the rest?
Conquered by various crafty coercions,
I embarked with him on the sail-winged vessel,
and voyaged on the salty sea.
In the beginning, though, I was sailing smoothly,
[30] as the wind was blowing gently
and the open sea welcomed the ship.

---

33 On Manasses, see PBW (2016): Konstantinos 302; Aerts (2003), pp. 165–221; Treadgold (2013), pp. 399–403; Neville (2018), pp. 200–4.
34 This is probably a reference to Athenaeus of Naukratis, who compiled his *Deipnosophistae* in the second century CE. For an alternative interpretation which envisages this word as wordplay see Manasses (2017), pp. 157–8.
35 i.e. John Kontostephanos.

Then a harsh north wind raged,
it shook the ship like a light pile of leaves,
raised roaring noises of tumultuous waves,
[35] and enraged the water with contrary gusts.
Growling, it wrenched the vessel up and down,
as if the ship were using scales wrongly and dishonestly
making it sail up and down erratically and with great speed.
It grounded on underwater rocks which were hard to escape from
[40] and the danger from the turmoil was manifest.
There was no harbour with good mooring-places, no fair weather,
no haven for ships to save the vessel.
All around there was noise, whirlwind, and a storm of adverse winds.
We were, therefore, afraid and seasick,
[45] our chests were heaving, and our hearts were restless,
until the contrary wind subsided
and with some difficulty we ran ashore in peaceful havens.
After it had fabricated and arranged such things,
the sleep which had unfortunately seized me that night
[50] quickly flew and soon disappeared.
When I recovered my senses and reflected on the matter,
I brought up many sunken groans,
fearing that the bitter vision of my dreams,
predicted and foretold evils.
[55] I was trying to fight off that interpretation,
considering the vision worthless and a mere illusion
which troubled me falsely with empty fears.
It was, however, true and foretold
the sea and storms of my troubles.
[60] Why should I gabble on?
The light of the day had just begun to shine with a bright hue
and the light-bringer and torch-bearing master of the stars,
having risen from the earth, was conversing with those in the heavens.
At once, at the spur of the moment, there arrived at once
[65] an unfortunate message, full of bitterness.
It read: 'Along with the sebastos you will go
to Jerusalem and Palestine'.[36]
I was stricken by these words as if by a goad.
I did not curse, I did not begin to weep,
[70] nor did I release a drop from my eyelids.
Because when bitter words fall into the ears
they mortify the soul and make the heart grow cold,
and the flow of tears is cut off.

---

36 i.e. with John Kontostephanos.

Lamentations [become] runaways and deserters,
[75] gone is the sigh and the mouth speechless.
But why do I vainly wrap up my words so much?
After I had departed from the dearest royal [city],
I saw Nicaea which boasts of the beauty of its location,
I saw a sea of fruitful plains,
[80] the city of the Ikonians, of countless men.
I saw the region of Cilicia
and its very productive cities,
beautiful to behold, and even more beautifully sited.
The city of Antiochenes appeared before [my] eyes,
[85] the splendour, delight and decorum
of all the districts located in Asia.
I also gazed upon the beauty of Daphne,[37]
enjoyed the springs of Kastalia,[38]
which are like nectar and sweet to drink,
[90] but cold to touch and appear transparent.
Why should I describe all of the cities,
Sidon, Tyre, the ports of the Berytans,
Ptolemais, the murderous city?[39]
Ptolemais deserves to be ruined.
[95] Jesus! Light of ever-pouring brightness,
please obliterate the solar flame for Ptolemais
and shadow the all-seeing pupil,
in order for the hated city to be completely unseen.
I reached Samaria, I saw a district
[100] adorned with many charming beauties,
elegant to see, well situated.
The atmosphere [was] clean, the waters flowed
delicate, transparent, uncorrupted, ever on the move.
The land [was] fertile, fecund, rich, yielding grapes and fruits of all kinds,
[105] producing wheat,
planted with olives and vegetables.
The plain [was] suitable for horses, the roads easy to travel on.
The meadows [are] famous for their fragrant roses.
The setting [is] delightful, naturally suited to the town.
[110] If you were to see it, you would compare it to a child-loving woman
embracing a breastfeeding baby.
Thence, a hill is raised, hard to climb,
hard to transverse, unconquerable, pathless,
steep, rough, stretching in great size.

---

37 A suburb of Antioch.
38 A spring and town in Cilicia.
39 i.e. Beirut and Acre, which were known for their unhealthy climate.

[115] On the other side, another reaches up to the heavens,
projecting wild, steep rocks,
a steep, precipitous, straight hill.
The town lies in the middle of the two [hills],
like a baby wrapped in swaddling clothes by its mother,
[120] like a very beautiful girl being watched over
by a child-loving woman in charge of raising the young.
This is how well-ordered everything about that place was.
Our journey was coming to an end
and its secret [purpose] begun to reveal itself.
[125] For the sebastos strictly believed
that excellent is he who shares
the emperor's secret with himself alone.[40]
[128] He disclosed [the emperor's] intentions to nobody,
[140][41] even though many people begged quite often
and asked for a disclosure
[142] of the reason we travelled in a hurry and of our destination.
[129] The whole intention of the emperor
[130] and the secret which the sebastos kept from us,
as I realised too late and after a period of time,
was, after the empress had passed away,[42]
the idea of another, new, marriage.
Since he had two daughters,
[135] and saw his second one in the darkness of tomb,
when [she was] still an infant,[43]
and much grief was caused by a desire for male children,
who are much needed by states so as to command,
[139] he sought a second legal marriage.
[143] As it was impossible to remain hidden till the end,
the affair for the sake of which we arrived in Palestine
[145] and in the well-watered region of the Samaritans,
I desired to see the beauty of the young girl,
she who the aforementioned man was secretly commanded
to dress as a bride and to escort her so as to wed
the born-in-purple Lord Manuel.[44]
[150] In Samaria, in the small suburb,

---

40 i.e. Manuel I's intention of seeking a bride in the Latin East was not revealed to most members of the delegation.
41 In the Manasses (2017) edition the text is rearranged. The odd numbering reveals the order in which the poem used to be.
42 i.e. first wife, Bertha of Sulzbach, who had died in 1160.
43 Manuel and Bertha's older daughter, Maria, had been born around 1150. The name of the younger daughter, who died in infancy, is not recorded.
44 Maria, daughter of daughter of Raymond of Poitiers, prince of Antioch.

she happened to live at that time.[45]
And then I noticed her, but how can I even give a description?
There was a small dwelling with dim light,
boastful of its decoration but also reproachable
[155] for it was not rich in sunlight.
I visited it regularly and I often investigated it,
criticising its darkness.
Yet, I had entered the house, as was customary,
and all of a sudden, a snow-white young girl appeared.
[160] From the illuminating torch of her face
she gave forth a flash of light, sparkling like fire
and she lightened and drove the darkness away.
She illuminated me, she amazed me, she dazzled me.
I said to myself 'Perhaps a thunderbolt has struck,
[165] perhaps the lunar disk has fallen to earth'.
The young girl was unrivalled in beauty,
finer and whiter than milk,
charming, symmetrical, blonde, with a good complexion,
adorned with a beautiful physical stature,
[170] a date palm, one would say fittingly,
beautiful, freshly sprouted, upright.
Her hair was very thick and golden throughout,
her brows well-rounded, her eyelashes graceful.
Her gaze was kind, cheerful, gleaming with grace.
[175] Her mouth was well-defined and her lips beautiful,
fair lips, reddish, the colour of carmine.
Without a doubt, if something made the young girl smile a little,
and she let herself loosen up moderately,
Oh! I cannot describe her beauty!
[180] Her nose was well-rounded, [allowing her to] breathe without trouble.
Her movement was graceful, and her step rhythmical.
Her good manners were accompanied by calmness
and were fitting to so appropriate a young girl.
Her education was second to none and her family distinguished.
[185] For she was from the house of Julius Caesar
which reigns over the western countries.[46]
Frankly, the mass of all kinds of graces,
after they had been melted into one and very beautifully blended,
made a delightful mixture, the young girl,
[190] a statue made by nature, an adornment of her family.

---

45 Manasses may be referring here to Sebasteia (Samaria), although this town is some distance from Antioch. Kinnamos and William of Tyre say that the envoys saw Maria in Antioch itself.
46 Maria of Antioch was not literally descended from the Roman dictator Julius Caesar but from the dukes of Aquitaine, who were prominent and powerful rulers in the eleventh and twelfth centuries.

Momos himself would be at a loss for slander.[47]
For what is Helen's whiteness to hers,
whom legend fashioned to be a child of Zeus?[48]
Most distinguished her kin, sparkling like fire her appearance,
[195] the young girl was unrivalled, worthy of her high status,
with fine eyebrows, with a beautiful face, most seemly,
good-looking, with fine locks of hair, most noble,
with a young stature and a body shape
better than a plane tree, better than vines.
[200] Since she was as I have described, after I had seen and marvelled at her,
I judged that she was worthy of the emperor,
since she had a graceful face and a healthy complexion,
[and] I excited the sebastos concerning his hopes
that he would receive plenty of the greater rewards,
[205] if he offered such a rare gift
to the munificent emperor of the Romans.
I, the most unfortunate, imagined
that I would see the city of Constantine very soon.
After the north-east wind of misfortune, however, had blown contrary,
[210] it produced storms with tempest winds,
terrible mighty waves, squalls, seasickness,
doldrums and unexpected idleness.
Why do I, the unfortunate, vainly enumerate all these things,
which require Aeschylus' talent for the composition of dramatic stories
[215] or Phrynichus' mourning wordiness?[49]
For if one recounted everything in detail,
he would surpass the history of Thucydides.
After long time and great hardship,
leaving the city of the Neapolitans behind,[50]
[220] Jerusalem, the most blessed city,
we saw, which is well served by its fortified location.
For not even a small portion was exposed,
a deep valley, a steep ravine
surrounded the city all around.
[225] We paid homage at the holy sepulchre
where, for the sake of us sinners,
lies, like a lion cub,
He who shaped the soil into the form of Adam
and showered Adam's descendants with eternal life.

---

47 According to Greek mythology, Momos was the son of Night and he personified mockery and slander.
48 Helen of Troy, the wife of King Menelaus of Sparta, was renowned for her beauty.
49 Aeschylus and Phrynichus were Athenian tragedians of the sixth and fifth centuries BCE.
50 Neapolis was the ancient name for Nablus.

[230] I gazed at Golgotha, I saw the rocks
which were broken apart then and dissolved by awe
when my God and moulder of mankind,
after He had faced His world-saving suffering,
raised the children of Abraham from the stones,
[235] restoring their broken nature.
I saw the ground,
into which the God-slayers plunged into darkness
the blessed and holy wood, and I embraced it.
After I had departed from that place, I reached Zion[51]
[240] which beguiled me with her numerous charms.
Even though it is outside [of the city], it is located nearby
since it almost touches the walls.
There I gazed at the thrice-blessed site,
where He washed the disciple's feet,
[245] He who holds the resistless seas in check.
After I had walked for a while, I saw a small house
where the company of disciples concealed themselves
to escape the rage of the murderers,
just as the grazing sheep
[250] escape from the prowling of wild wolves
if the beast-killing shepherd is not present.
How could the fine room have escaped my notice,
in which the net-makers stayed inseparably,
and were richly supplied with foreign tongues,
[255] like fiery burning coals,
which the force of the Spirit forged
with the invisible unfiery flame throwers?[52]
There I gazed at another divine site
where the Purest Dwelling place of my God gave up her spirit
[260] into the hands of the Son.[53]
Shortly after, I descended into a dark place
where the dastard Peter had stood
and washed away his sin with his tears.[54]
Gethsemane indicated to me the most beloved tomb,
[265] of the maiden who bore the Divine Son,

---

51 Manasses is referring to Mount Zion here rather than to the city of Jerusalem itself.
52 The Cenacle or Upper Room on Mount Zion, which was identified as the location of the events of Pentecost, when the disciples, in hiding after the ascension of Christ, were inspired by the Holy Spirit in the shape of tongues of fire. See Acts 2:1–9.
53 Most probably an allusion to the Tomb of Mary at the foot of the Mount of Olives, which was said to be the site of dormition of the Virgin when she was assumed bodily into heaven.
54 A spot halfway down Mount Zion was identified as that where, after betraying Christ three times, Peter wept bitterly. See Matthew 26:75.

a poor and wretched place to look at,
but concealing inside an invaluable ruby
(it is audacious to say that, but may I be pardoned).
I said to myself 'This place [resembles] the hardness of a shellfish
[270] which conceals the imperial purple [dye],
or the shell of a rough sea oyster
which nourishes inside the brightness of a pearl,
or, to put it more accurately, the sharpness of thorns,
below which the golden rose springs forth'.[55]
[275] I ascended the celebrated hill,
where, He who arranged the mountains, had stood with a human body,
blessed the wise apostles
and was raised towards His Father, the source of light.[56]
I paid a visit to Bethlehem, I saw the manger.[57]
[280] I was scorched by the kilns of Jericho.
I saw a sultry sandy plain,
parched, waterless, deadly,
where the rays of the sun penetrate so deep
that they go in as far as the brain itself.
[285] On the one hand I want to say it, but again, I tremble with fear,
(all-observing eye! Don't be angry with me!)
may I not see Jericho [again] even when I am asleep.
I washed my body in the water of Jordan.
I saw its waters which were totally mixed with mud,
[290] neither transparent, nor fit for drinking.
Its colour was the same as that of milk,
for its flow was in slow motion.
One might say that the river's course was drowsy.
Christ, light [which shone] prior to the creation of daylight, why
    are things like that?
[295] How did you live for such a long time in places [so]
dry, stifling, burning and deadly?
When I bring to mind the stifling heat of Nazareth,
Christ, I am amazed by Your humility!
You rightly confirmed that,
[300] Nathanael's words about Nazareth were true:
'Can any good thing come out of Nazareth?'[58]
It seems, however, that only You truly understand,

---

55 The Garden of Gethsemane is at the foot of the Mount of Olives.
56 The Mount of Olives, from which Jesus was believed to have ascended into heaven. See Luke 24:50; Act 1:4–12.
57 The stone manger in which the infant Jesus was supposedly laid was displayed in the church of the Nativity in Bethlehem.
58 The words of the apostle Nathanael in John 1:46.

in all Your corporeal [life] You chose
all that is poor and common,
[305] from all the rivers, You chose the stream of Jordan
which is not even reckoned among rivers,
from all the towns, You chose Palestine's
most poor and rugged,
Capernaum the hateful
[310] and Nazareth the charred.
Of course, all the holy places in which
the Saviour lived as a human are sacred.
On the other hand, if one fearlessly removed
the sweet-scented miracles of the Lord,
[315] he would compare these places with harsh thorny plants.
For what thing worthy of mention do they have?
The air is dreadful, scorching, fiery,
insubordinate, unreliable, never-ending,
it brings an excessive and unbearable heat.
[320] Intemperate air, deprived of water.
Whenever dew pours out from above
and drops run out of the clouds,
it is bottled like a sweet-smelling wine, like a perfume.
If one is parched by burning thirst
[325] he drinks stinking and filthy water,
and this he has to pay for (curse the drought!).
The soil
on which the ploughing ox and harvesting hands suffer unbearable toil
and endure the heaviest labours,
[330] is hard, rugged, parched.
Land of Byzantion, city founded by God!
You that have shown me the light and nourished me,
if only I could come to you and gaze upon your beauties.
Oh yes, I wish I were in your lap,
[335] Oh yes, I wish that I were under your wing
And that you protected me like a sparrow.

II

After I had enjoyed these beautiful sights,
I expected to achieve a quick return
and to discard my responsibilities.
Once again, however,
[5] the bad luck which accompanies me everywhere arrived swiftly.
Once again it seized and disturbed me.
I had barely embarked on a fast-sailing trireme
and we were voyaging with a fair wind to the hated Tyre,
which lacks even so much as a cup of water.
[10] Oh Tyre, most spiteful and hated by everybody!

How would the tongues of rhetors describe
your violent and stifling air
and your sun's scorching flame?
From this time on, the time of sickness began for me.
[15] A deadly, calamitous disease,
A burning fever, kindled in me
like a bright flame, replete with firewood,
burned my insides, fed on my body.
It cremated, exhausted me.
[20] It burned and roasted me.
It darkened my head with thick steam
and with it, the pupils of my reasoning.
My hair fell like a dead man's,
unable to bear the fire's heat.
[25] Alas! I, the wretched, the woeful,
a frail, easily-wilted man,
who had an emaciated and gloomy flesh,
or, to put it better, just the skin of the flesh.
Christ, creator of the world and God the life-giving,
[30] such was the emptying from my guts
and such from my mouth that burned like a slow fire,
reminding me of that ancient
forbidden fruit
which I, the most wretched, having been deceived and deluded
[35] exchanged for bitter misfortune.
Judging from the bitterness of my bile,
I believed that death was certain.
My hands were numb, my legs were shaking.
The latter, lacking a firm step
[40] dropped me down into the ground, like a spiritless corpse.
I was eager to swallow every single drop in the sea,
I desired to drink every river out,
for the fierce fire which resided in me
dried all my body up.
[45] Alas the human race, full of groans,
an abyss of evils, deep water of misfortunes!
Alas ever-whirling, agitating life,
fickle, thrice-accursed, duplicitous,
unjust, mingled, without order!
[50] You are a bitter worm which devours the heart,
a stormy sea of myriad evils,
a wild open sea of endless perils.
Now the sebastos, perceiving that I was half dead,
made a fuss about it, worried compassionately
[55] and deemed me worthy of abundant care.

Alexios the renowned, of the Doukas family,
the ruler of the Cypriots at that time,[59]
also took pity on me for suffering so badly,
a munificent man, the personification of gentleness,
[60] who derived from a royal family.
To cut a long story short,
by the order, will and judgment of both,
I was shipped to the celebrated Cyprus
so that I might enjoy its cleaner air
[65] and beat my disease away.
As I was saying, with so many and so great benefits
did he shower me with his munificent and wealthy hand
the offspring of the Doukas family, the gentle character,
that it would be impossible to describe with words.
[70] The murderous disease, however, attacked me once more
like a boar from a thicket, like a lion cub from its mother.
It ground its teeth, opened its mouth,
rushed headlong with unlimited boldness to devour me.
It dried the skin of my flesh,
[75] burned the soil of my bodily mixture,
and deprived the flux of my entrails.
Wretched body, made of earth!
Had you, Father, gardener of mankind,
not rained down a refreshment of reviving dew,
[80] since I had already fallen down, dried up and dehydrated,
I would have quickly been reduced to ashes and reached the point of no return.
Having escaped for now, as a roe deer from a trap,
I began to flap my wings freely.
And now I lived in celebrated Cyprus,
[85] in this fertile land that bears many fruits
which is aromatic to others, but to me filthy.[60]
For how can the dimness of mere feldspar
be compared with the sun's flame which nourishes the whole world?
Or rather, how can it be compared to the city of Constantine,
[90] Cyprus as a whole, and all that pertains to it?
Oh, the labour, the learning, the books of wise men
on which I foolishly broke my neck studying since childhood!
Oh, the bodily suffering, the course of one night after another
which I spent reading books,
[95] sleepless, without closing my eyelids to repose,
as a sparrow which stays alone on the roof top,

---

59 This Alexios Doukas, governor of Cyprus, is not attested elsewhere.
60 A wordplay on Κύπρον = Cyprus, κύπειρον = aromatic and κόπρον = filthy.

or to put it better, as long-eared owl in the darkness!
I dwell in a land where learning is scarce,
having bonded my lips together, I lie idle,
[100] doing nothing, motionless as a prisoner,
an ineloquent rhetor lacking the courage to speak up,
a speechless orator lacking training.
In the same way that a waterless garden
is consumed away by the scarcity of water,
[105] dries up due to the lack of rain
and the beauty of the trees falls like their leaves,
I myself have suffered the same, I have been ruined
and I lost the beauty which abounded in me.
I am idle, nurtured by hopes,
[110] or waiting for the water to move,
like the lame man of old, so as to be healed.[61]
Roman city, jewel of the whole earth,
my eyelids have fallen looking for you!
Alas, I sigh deeply, I long for you and I breathe you,
[115] most virtuous uncle, the jewel of kinfolks!
I am separated from your beloved sight,
golden crown, most pious among the monks!
I am frozen, done, doomed.
The very thing which dew-feeding cicadas suffer from,
[120] who sing harmonious songs during the summer,
but drop dead when cold arrives.
For the ever-worried human race,
when it is warmed by the splendid sun of insouciance,
raises its voice higher than that of Stentor,[62]
[125] brings forth the lyre on its chest
and composes a harmonious and elegant tune.
If, however, it freezes from the cold of affliction,
alas, it expires, unable to bear the frost.
Yet the munificent Doukas, the golden,
[130] the Nile of favours, the gold-flowing,
filled me with abundant mouthfuls
and rained down for me the dew of mount Hermon,
without expecting anything from me in return,
(for how can the bright shining lunar disk
[135] borrow light from a glow-worm?)
but solely moved by kindness.
Whenever I thought of the city of Byzantion though,

---

61 Alluding to the cure of a paralysed man in John 5:1–15.
62 A character in the *Iliad* distinguished by his loud voice. See Homer (1924), i. 264–5 (*Iliad* V. 785–6).

the delicacies of the table tasted like bile to me,
everything bitter, even if I had been offered nectar to drink,
[140] even if I had been invited to eat the food of the Gods.
For when a fine-tweeting sparrow is caged,
even if fed persistently, more than needed,
it [still] longs to fly free
and, unable to endure life with humans,
[145] it seeks a hidden way out.
Because nothing is so pleasant and desirable
as the day of deliverance, a carefree life.
Christ, please allow me to experience a good death.
Make it true, make it true, moulder of mankind!
[150] Make it true, make it true, gardener of the mortal creation
so that we will dedicate hymns to you as a reward for our deliverance
and drink the wine of the eucharist.
Land of Byzantion, thrice fortunate city,
eye of the earth, jewel of the world,
[155] far-shining star, lamp of the earthly world,
I wish I dwelt in you, I wish I enjoyed you!
And I yearn for you to cherish and support me
and never to exclude me from your motherly embrace!

III
It would seem that it had been destined for me to move my hand again
and to describe my misfortunes,
for my sufferings have by no means disappeared,
always pouring on me and afflicting me.
[5] And I thought that even as far as the dregs
I had drunk all the bitterness of fortune,
the goblets of calamity and the cups of diseases.
These were, however, like a bowl which fills with bile anew
and pours fourth a never-ending stream of troubles.
[10] I thought that the tree of my misfortunes,
would decay in winter, even if it blossomed in the summer,
but it is evergreen, fruitful, abundant
in all seasons, surely not only in summer.
Alas blind, wretched, human race,
[15] your eyes are blind as to what the future holds!
For after I had fallen into an open sea of diseases
and my body had been shattered by all kinds of harm,
I had been brought into the great island of Cyprus
so as to throw out the load of my misfortunes,
[20] I was once more troubled by the same dangers
and the roughness of the waves played a joke on me,
like one who, having been lifted up on a steep hill,
then plummets supinely down again.

I wish the wickedness of that day were erased,
[25] the day which I departed from Byzantion!
I wish it were not included in the days of the year,
the time when, after I had left the blessed city behind,
I wandered about over precipitous places.
But why on earth do I accuse the days in vain,
[30] since I dealt a sword blow to myself?
Once more, I will open my mouth wide
and I will speak of the sufferings which troubled me.
A severe pain wakes me up
from the kidneys down to the back parts of my body,
[35] rightly so, Christ, and in accordance with a just law,
for I did not restrain my kidneys reasonably,
trampling on your laws, I did not gird up my loins.[63]
Alas the unbearable feeling, the pain's severance,
it even reaches the brain itself!
[40] Moving was impossible, standing up was difficult,
lying in bed even more unpleasant.
One would think that he saw the paralyzed man,[64]
looking at me lying in bed lifeless.
I was, therefore, in pain, disheartened, feeling ill,
[45] screaming, distressed, disturbed, struggling.
Sun, may your light never see
a man enduring such a load.
For even if one happened to be a giant or made of stone,
even if he matched the cedar trees of Lebanon,
[50] he would, alas, prove to be as weak as a reed,
he would, alas, bend as the wagon's wheels!
Oh, the tree which causes bitterness and spouts bile,[65]
the council of the most evil Satan
and the unfortunate greed of our first ancestors,[66]
[55] because of whom, seas of myriad sufferings
the miserable human race has drunk.
I was like that, like a half-breathing corpse,
for not being able to move my leg,
I was drying up as a halfdead tree.
[60] Since the circulation of my heart was defective,
reasonably so, my movement suffered.
I was without food; I was not taking water.
The length of my entrails became contracted,
for the nails of bitter pain

---

63 Probably an allusion to Proverbs 31:17.
64 Most probably an allusion to the paralysed man lying in bed in Capernaum, see Mark 2:1–12.
65 A reference to the apple tree.
66 i.e. Adam and Eve.

[65] drove away hunger and thirst.
Christ, let it never happen to me, even to my sleep
to see the bitterness of this suffering,
for, should the illusion of dreams linger
and not dissolve and fly away quickly,
[70] may Hades' voracious mouth devour me!
After I had experienced the disease for a long time
and understood that the wise art of the physicians
is not capable of more
than wasting time and chatting vainly and incessantly,
[75] I was compelled to turn to another path
and I said to myself 'the die should be cast'.
I began to wash my body in hot baths.
Bath, source of my strength,
you that bring much refreshment to the sufferers
[80] kindly restored to health the functions of my body as well!
I want to speak out loud and to proclaim
the abundant stream of your benefits,
but the sound of my voice is still weak,
dried up by the flame of suffering.
[85] The sun and the moon know how to set,
but the quick foot, the fast-flying wing
of the grievous fate which grasps me closely
know no rest, no pause.
How happy I would have been, if for a short time
[90] I [had] the tongue of Jeremiah who suffered in the same way
so as to wail the befalling of my troubles![67]
Alas my many dangers and calamities
and darts of envious fate!
Bitter fortune, for how long will I put up with you!?
[95] Why do you oppress and afflict me so much?
You drained my flow of blood dry,
you ate up the flesh of my body,
you burned up my entrails almost completely.
Why then do you strike the deathblow on me, why do you choke me?
[100] Sun and daylight, and the company of stars,
seeing all this happening, how could you not conceal yourselves?
Golden city of Byzantion,
sun of the earth, beautiful beyond measure,
for how long will I see you in my sleep!?
[105] I wish I saw, your coveted brilliance!
I wish I saw your fair-lighted features!

---

67 The Biblical prophet Jeremiah proclaimed volubly to his people the punishments which God had in store for them, only to be persecuted for his pains.

IV
Hands be strong and move,
legs stand up and leap for me,
tongue cry aloud the hymn of gratitude,
and you, thrice wretched heart, rejoice!
[5] For behold! I clearly see in front of me
the coveted, the blessed city of Byzantion!
But how can that be!? Perhaps I am once more deluded?
Perhaps I am [really] in Cyprus, the ill-smelling bitterness,
or in the stifling city of Ptolemy,[68]
[10] or Nazareth which is anything but dear to me?
Have I created a mirage of you in my eyes, golden city?
Is this a dream of mine and a trick of night,
or did I clearly gaze upon you awake, and not in a dream?
Those [I see], however, are neither Paphos, nor the district of Kition,
[15] nor the poor city of Thremithos.[69]
There is no hot flow of foul-smelling air,
nor the carrying of dead bodies
moved in piles for burial,
things which those who live in the city of Ptolemy
[20] can often see on a daily basis.
But it is the highly honoured, the renowned city,
I see the breathless horseman up high in the sky,[70]
I see the harbour which shelters myriad ships,
and the very house of God,
[25] the flaming ruddy marble,
mighty, like the sun, bringing light.
Alas what has happened to me? When was I driven from the course of reason?
How did the many deceitful dreams
remove my trust in what I see?
[30] That place is indeed the dear one,
the island of the blessed, the golden city.[71]
And since all fear has gone,
as well as the illusion of nightly dreams,
and I clearly saw Constantine's city,
[35] I will resume the orderly description of events again.
While we were returning through Isauria,

---

68 i.e. Acre.
69 Paphos and Kition (Larnaca) are on the southern coast of Cyprus, while Thremithos is probably Tremithousa in the interior.
70 A reference to the equestrian statue of Emperor Justinian I, which stood on a tall column outside the cathedral of Hagia Sophia in Constantinople.
71 In Greek literature the islands of the blessed were a paradise where heroes and virtuous men went to live after their death.

leaving behind the whirlpools of Drakon,
which is a river in Isauria,[72]
and above all bypassing the wild Syke,
[40] the all-hateful, abominable, city
(for I do not wish to include the details),[73]
we found out that Cyprus was dismayed
by many disquietudes and wild horrors.
For the ruler of Tripoli was bubbling in rage,
[45] because his hopes had failed him, the wretch.[74]
Since the woman who was chosen to unite in marriage
with my emperor, the great general,
although she had been born from seeds related in blood
with the ruler of Tripoli, who has a hard time restraining his arrogance,
[50] was deprived of the imperial wedding.[75]
For the golden city of Antioch
nurtured the offspring of the Graces,[76]
worthy to fulfil such a marriage,
a maiden with graceful eyes, a comely virgin,
[55] who sprouted from royal roots.
The ruler of Tripoli, therefore, boiling in anger,
a reckless man who breathed out insolence,
(for what was he but an arrogant young Latin?),
massed a fleet, prepared his naval commanders
[60] and anchored himself in the island of the Cypriots so as to plunder it,
an irrational man who did not know
that he could never prevail over imperial territory.[77]
For the unfeathered bald sparrow
how could it approach the eaglet's nest?
[65] How could the small young deer scare the mighty
loud-bellowing lion, the king of the beasts?
The wretch was arrogant for a while,
but his rush and his arrogance were checked.
All of us were perplexed,
[70] since worn out by many such miseries,
we did not experience an auspicious outcome
until the pansebastos came to Cyprus,

---

72 Modern Anamur Hayi.
73 'Syke' literally means a fig tree so it is unclear which city Manasses is referring to.
74 Manasses is referring to Count Raymond III of Tripoli.
75 A reference to the decision of Manuel to marry Maria of Antioch rather than Melisend, daughter of Raymond III discussed by Kinnamos in [34].
76 According to Greek mythology, the three Graces (Aglaea, Euphrosyne and Thaleia) were minor deities of beauty, fertility and creativity.
77 Raymond launched an attack on Cyprus in 1162. William of Tyre (1943), ii. 291–2.

after he had escaped from many perils and deaths,
and then, the storm of distress
[75] transformed for us to tranquillity, to spring.
Even if one doubts that joy is very powerful,
let him hear me, and having heard, let him believe!
For the very thing which shattered me,
the burning fire of the quartan cycle,[78]
[80] once it perceived the presence of the sebastos,
ran away from me immediately.
The sebastos then, brought us all together in a group,
just as a bird which sings
the melodious harmony,
[85] chirps to its children and gathers them one by one
so as to avoid nets and traps.
He proclaimed the signal of return
and we all rushed to meet him.
It is neither novel, nor contrary to the rules of the art
[90] to introduce comedy to the discourse,
For [matters which are] distressing and full of suffering
should be mixed with beautiful ones
and in gloomy stories
one should introduce amusements which bring laughter.
[95] It was the day of the awe-inspiring festival
– it is customary to call it Pentecost –[79]
and we were all gathered at the temples,
performing the evening offering.
By chance I was standing next to the courtyard.
[100] Another man came in, Cypriot by birth,
who surpassed all other Cypriots in lack of sense.
He approached, came and stooped near me.
He smelled of wine mixed with garlic.
I, who experienced the bad smell in my nose
[105] (for I abhor this foul smell
as the stinking manure of my misfortunes,
as the very image of Satan himself),
became dizzy. I began to faint,
darkness fell upon my eyes,
[110] and almost razed me to the ground half-breathing.
Gazing upon him gently, I said to him
'Man, stand away from me, do not come near me.

---

78 The quartan fever is a type of malaria; the patient exhibits fever every four days.
79 Pentecost or Whit Sunday fell on 27 May 1162.

You stink of garlic, so go away,
for I am unable to bear this misfortune!'
[115] He did not take notice though, he did not move from his place.
I talked to him again with a harsher tone.
'Man, stand away, do not suffocate me,
for your mouth smells like mire!'
But having plugged his ears, he was like a cobra,
[120] for he cared for me as much
as the boar does for the mosquito, or as the lion for the fly.
Realising, therefore, that my words were useless
and that it was necessary to discipline the man with my hands,
I stretched out my hand manfully and boldly
[125] struck the man in his jaw and cheek
with a blow full of my wildest anger
and so much noise did the blow produce
that it was noticed more than the strain of the hymns.
Thus, the dung-eater went away by force.
[130] That was the case, even if it is deemed wrong.
The excellent and good in everything Doukas,
after he had filled everybody with abundant presents,
dispatched us home, wishing us well.
Son, imprint and hand and of the Father,
[135] king of all, sun of justice,
you delivered us from Palestine
like Israel from the hands of the Egyptians in past times!
Word of God, among the gods there is no other like You,
the living mightiest God, the highest, the unique,
[140] the King of the Heavens who created the universe.
You freed us from Latin arrogance,
just like Daniel, the great prophet, in past times,
whom you delivered from the mouth of the lions!
(For which race is more insolent than of the Latins?)
[145] He, who dispatched in the land of Babylon,
the remarkable ferryman, Habbakuk through the air,
so as to feed Daniel the prophet,[80]
rendered my path free from difficulties, beyond hope,
and turned me into an aerial horseman.
[150] You freed me from the all-devouring heat
of Ptolemais which murdered myriads,
you delivered me from the town in Tripoli

---

80 According to *Bel and the Dragon*, one of the deuterocanonical additions to the Book of Daniel, verses 33–9, the prophet Habbakuk was transported through the air by an angel to take stew to Daniel when he was in the Lion's den.

and from the land of the Cypriots the wretched fortress.
For truly, the island of Cyprus is a fierce fortress,
[155] a wall stubborn as iron, a cage made of stone,
an irrevocable Hades, admitting no escape.
He who is unlucky to be trapped in Cyprus
shall not come out from there easily,
because if one follows the earthly roads,
[160] he shall surely fall into the hands of the barbarians,
unless God supports and rescues him from danger,
for where would he flit, where would he hide to escape?
If he sails on the surface of the seas,
alas, among how in many dangers shall he find himself!?
[165] From above, the noise of strong-blowing winds,
from below, the crashing of waves, speaking in alien tongues.
The wave dashes with a roaring sound, the mighty wind blusters.
About the terror of the pirates on the sea,
which tongue and mouth will speak?
[170] For it is better to throw yourself into the fire or to the beasts
than to the harmful pirates of the sea.
Woe to the miserable man, full of groaning,
who is captured, God forbid, in their fishnets!
They do not value human beings, even if manna rained down
    on them,
[175] even if fire burned upside down, even if kilns spread dewdrops,
even if lions' molars broke to pieces.
They demand swollen sacks of gold.
And if one does not deliver (for where to find so many?),
they hang him upside down from the testicles and strike
    him with beams
[180] they fetter him in the masts and lower him in the water
until he gives up the ghost violently.
I think that anyone who has been caught in their traps
shall not be handed over to other eager [tormenters],
when the time of the awful and last judgement comes,
[185] even if he surpassed the tax-collectors in wicked deeds,
for the pirates' tortures are fair recompense for him.
Thus, having escaped from so many misfortunes,
with God's will, providence and judgment,
should I ever think to travel again
[190] to the arid lands of Palestine,
unless one dragged me there violently,
may I fall to the hands of the barbarians!
Glory to Christ for supporting me
and for delivering me from such great perils!

38. Ephraim of Ainos: Manuel I and the Latin East (1158–61)

Ephraim's account of Manuel's expedition to Antioch is clearly derived from Choniates, who supplied the detail that the emperor participated in a tournament during his stay in the area.

Ephraim of Ainos (1990), p. 155.

And so he campaigned against Cilicia.
He reached Adana and Tarsus
and invigorated, as was fitting, the nearby fortresses
[4220] which were subject to Roman rule
and had up to that point been experiencing harm from Thoros.
He marched as far as illustrious Antioch
and entered in triumphal procession with bodyguards
and imperial insignia, as its ruler.
[4225] The inhabitants poured out of the gates
and ably arranged an escorting procession with
cheers and applause.
Emperor Manuel remained in the city
[4230] and exhibited feats of bravery and strength in sporting competitions.
True to his heroic and noble nature,
he prevailed in lance tournaments over the
Italian knights who take pride in their [handling of] the spear.
Thus, he demonstrated the might of his courage
[4235] and his shrewd practice in battle.
Having filled everybody with wonder,
the emperor returned home to Constantinople.
He married a maiden most glorious in beauty,
as a sharer in authority and in marriage bed,
[4240] the daughter of the ruler of Antioch,
Raymond, an Italian knight.
Manuel had been divorced from his first wife due to death.
She was from a noble German family.

39. John Kinnamos: Manuel I and the expedition to Egypt (1169)

In the late tenth century, the Byzantines had fought a series of wars against the Fatimid rulers of Egypt in northern Syra, but from 1027 the two powers had established a treaty and their relations were generally peaceful. By the 1150s, however, the regime in Cairo was visibly ailing, torn apart by internal power struggles. Both the ruler of Damascus, Nur al-Din, and King Amalric of Jerusalem were eager to move in and take over Egypt, which was one of the most fertile and productive lands in the region. In these circumstances, Manuel could hardly stand aloof, and in the summer of 1168 he entered into discussions with Amalric about possible joint action.[81] Kinnamos' account of the campaign places the blame for its failure on King Amalric. The Latin chronicler William of Tyre not surprisingly has a different version of events, criticising Manuel for failing to fund the expedition properly so that the Byzantines ran short of supplies during the siege of Damietta.[82]

Kinnamos (1836), pp. 278–80:

[278] Around the same time, Egypt came close to being conquered by the Romans but managed to survive in the following way. A long time ago, Egypt was subject to Roman rule and contributed a very great amount of annual tax revenue.[83] When Asia had already been badly afflicted and the Arabs were constantly prevailing, Egypt was also conquered and submitted to them.

Emperor Manuel, however, having already recovered much of the East for the Romans, eagerly resolved to claim Egypt as well. So he dispatched envoys there and ordered them to remind the Egyptians of the former custom and the past taxes which, weighing many talents, had reached us, but to warn them that war would soon be waged against them, in the event of their refusal. Such was the task of the embassy. When the Egyptians strongly opposed the proposition, the emperor built a fleet of cavalry-transports and war ships, embarked a great number of troops on them, and dispatched them to Egypt.

The commander of the fleet was Andronikos Kontostephanos, whom I have mentioned many times, for, as I have said, he had already been appointed as grand duke at that time.[84] Having sailed with all speed, he reached the shore of Egypt. Then he sent word to Palestine and [279] summoned its king, so as for him to support the Romans in their struggle, as had been agreed.[85]

While the king was delaying, Andronikos realised that the army ought to march forward into the land, so that time would not be spent there in vain. Thus, he captured the city of Tenesion without bloodshed and often went out from there and ravaged the countryside.[86] Since the king was reported to be approaching by that time, they directed hostilities towards Damietta, a city exceedingly rich in inhabitants and wealth.[87] The Romans fought many bruising battles there, but to no avail, for the reason I am going to relate. There was an agreement between the emperor and the Palestinians that, after they had fought as allies in the war against Egypt, half of the captured region would go to the Romans and the other half to the Palestinians. Since the Romans had arrived in Egypt earlier, the king had treacherously first planned to delay his participation in the struggle and to acquire his share of the

---

81 On these events, see Lilie (1993), pp. 198–202; Harris (2022), pp. 121–2.
82 William of Tyre (1943), ii. 366, 369–70.
83 Egypt had been part of the Byzantine empire until 642 when the Arabs had captured Alexandria.
84 Andronikos Kontostephanos (d.1182) was the brother of John Kontostephanos. See PBW (2016): Andronikos 17004. William of Tyre (1943), ii. 367, pays tribute to his courage during the campaign.
85 Amalric set out from Ascalon on 16 August 1169. William of Tyre (1943), ii. 362.
86 Tenesion may be either Tinnis or Pelusium.
87 Amalric and his army reached Damietta on 27 October 1169. William of Tyre (1943), ii. 363.

region effortlessly after the Romans had run all the risks. When he arrived, after much delay, he kept postponing battle and advised the Romans to do the same, even if the latter undertook heroic struggles every day, paying little heed to king's words. Whether [the Palestinians] did so because they intended for the Romans to face the risks so that they might obtain an easy victory, as I have already said, or because they were altogether envious of the emperor's lordship over Egypt, I cannot prove which holds true. Some say that the besieged corrupted the king with money [280] and induced him to such actions.

Since the Romans realised that they were insufficient for this war by themselves, they withdrew and sailed back to Byzantion. When a storm spread, however, many of the ships were destroyed. That was the conclusion of the Roman expedition against Egypt. The people of Egypt, to avoid a second Roman invasion against them, dispatched ambassadors to the emperor and promised to furnish the Romans annually with some fixed amount of gold from that time onwards. They were dismissed without having achieved anything, the emperor rejecting the embassy with a view to overrunning all of Egypt's regions sometime in the future. Around the same time the king of Palestine also arrived in Byzantion to petition for the matters he required. He obtained what he needed and in return he committed himself to many things including his servitude to the emperor.[88]

40. Niketas Choniates: Manuel I and the expedition to Egypt (1169)

Choniates also places the blames for the failure of the expedition on Amalric. Unlike Kinnamos he accepts that the Byzantine fleet was not adequately supplied, but the resulting shortages were the fault of Amalric who set out from Ascalon rather late in the year. He also gives numerous details missed out in Kinnamos' brief account, such as Andronikos Kontostephanos' decision to travel back overland rather than with the fleet.

Choniates (1975), pp. 159–68:

[159] What happened afterwards? Manuel longed for a military expedition abroad. Having heard of Egypt's richly fertile land, and of the many things that the fruitful and grain-rich Nile nourishes, and the richness [of the crops] which is measured by cubits, he determined to put his left hand into the sea and his right into the rivers so as to see the desired blessings of Egypt, of which he had heard, with his penetrating eyes and to render them [160] within reach of his grasp. This somewhat ill-timed ambition made him dream of these things, flying beyond everyday matters which kept on multiplying, and even though they were cut and burned, they were not wiped out and destroyed, but kept on reviving like the Hydra.[89] It was also a somehow inopportune quest for renown to vie with emperors whose glory was great, and

---

88 Amalric visited Constantinople in the spring of 1171. See William of Tyre (1943), ii. 377.
89 In Greek mythology, the Hydra was a gigantic water-snake with many heads and when one was cut off, a new head would grow in its place.

whose lands had extended for centuries not only from sea to sea, but stretched from the limits of the East to the pillars of the West.

And so, when Manuel had shared his plan with Amalric, king of Jerusalem, had found him receptive to the idea and had received his promise to support the expedition, he prepared a strong fleet against Damietta. It consisted of over two hundred warships, ten of which were launched from Dyrrachion and six, manned by the men of Euboea, were of the swiftest type. He appointed as admiral the grand duke Andronikos Kontostephanos. While the fleet was being assembled, he entrusted sixty of the triremes to Theodore Mavrozomes90 and dispatched him to the king to announce in advance the impending departure of the rest of the fleet and the arrival of Kontostephanos in Egypt. That way the king would be prepared for the expedition and would levy supplies for the knights of Jerusalem, those who were to march out along with the king who was about to participate in the war and to begin the march against Egypt.

Shortly after, Kontostephanos himself also departed (it was the eighth of July). He disembarked at Meliboton, where the emperor arrived to inspect the fleet and give precepts about the campaign. Two days later he departed, sailed south towards Koila which [161] is situated between Sestos and Abydos,[91] and embarked in the triremes those of the army who were dispatched and assigned to him, both of Roman and foreign companies. Later, when the wind was fair and favourable, he loosened the stern cables, spread the sails and ordered a course to be set via Cyprus. During this voyage, he encountered six ships which were sent by the emir of Egypt for reconnaissance. He managed to capture two of them, but the others had been sailing warily and they escaped due to their superior speed.

After he had reached the shores of Cyprus, he informed the king of his arrival and inquired as to how to proceed, whether to wait for him in Cyprus or to sail towards Jerusalem. The king, in the manner of Epimetheus, for whom there is the saying that when planning and forethought are absent much regret is present,[92] was troubled deep in his heart that he had promised to support the emperor in the first place and had encouraged the expedition against the Egyptians when the latter had been thinking about it. He thought it best to delay and to ponder endlessly over what ought to be done. Late in the day, he dispatched a message to Andronikos to hasten to Jerusalem in order to meet there and to discuss which joint undertaking they would conduct.

Kontostephanos came to Palestine but once more delay and the burden of regret vexed Amalric's soul from within. He put forward the pretext of Patroclus along with various other [excuses] and among the more usual was the mustering of his

---

90 On Mavrozomes, see PBW (2016): Theodoros 262.
91 Meliboton and Koila were both ports on the Dardanelles.
92 In Greek mythology, Epimetheus was the brother of the Titan Prometheus, his foolishness contrasting with the latter's wisdom.

troops.[93] After these [developments], Andronikos was troubled about the waste of precious time which could not be reclaimed anew since it does not flow backwards. He was particularly worried about the supplies of the naval crews which were being consumed in vain, because the emperor had rationed the fleet with grain for three months, starting from August and it was already the end of September.

[162] When he decided to depart, the king preferred an overland march instead of sailing by sea. He advised Andronikos to do the same, arguing that he was certain that the land route was much more convenient and safer to choose, and that in this manner, it would also be possible for them to capture Tounion and Tenesion along the way at the first assault.[94] The latter two were villages subject to the emir of Egypt, neither inaccessible nor impregnable, situated on a flat plain, with most of their inhabitants being Christians. Since Andronikos believed the king's advice to be sound, he changed his course [and] followed that of the king. In the meantime, they completed their march without trouble, attacked the aforementioned forts, and received their surrender, since the defenders did not possess sufficient garrisons or the strength to march out against the enemy divisions. Then they marched on.

When they joined up with the fleet, which was already anchored at Damietta and assaulting it, they immediately dashed against the Saracens who had poured out in front of the city and opposed them with their arms. Thus, the Romans took them so much by surprise and threw them into such confusion by their undaunted charge, that they were forced back inside the gates, unable even to look the [Romans] in the face. This took place the day on which the triremes ran ashore on the Nile and the king arrived by land. The following day the Saracens assembled once more to engage in battle with the Romans in front of the winding and slightly convex encircling wall of the city. Once again, however, they did not hold out against the Romans. And so, having moved a short distance away from the gates and permanently taking positions behind the curtain wall, they mounted hostilities in this manner. When the [163] Romans alone rushed against them, they continually turned to flight and streamed into the gates so as to keep themselves safe, lacking the courage to lead their battleline straight against the enemy. The same thing occurred for many days. It is clear that their strategy could accomplish nothing but to deceive the Romans so as to waste their time vainly and to be carried away by their impossible hopes.

Shortly after, Andronikos moved forward the siege engines and inflicted blows against the wall, but not without toil and risk. For the barbarians were shooting at the operators of the engines from above and hindered the operation by releasing missiles more thickly than snowflakes and taking measures in turn for the safety of their walls. In this way, he nevertheless, managed to destroy the battlement of one of the walls, behind which was an incense-exuding church dedicated to the Mother

---

93 Patroclus gave his friend Achilles a pretext for remaining in his tent rather than fighting the Trojans by suggesting that he might fear some prophecy of his own death. See Homer (1924), ii. 164–5 (*Iliad* XVI. 36–45).
94 Choniates may be referring to Tinnis here.

of God.[95] The citizens claim that the Virgin Mother along with her spouse Joseph took a rest from their wandering near this place at the time when they were hastening to Egypt to escape Herod the slayer of children.[96] The Saracens, therefore, jeered at the Romans and showered Andronikos with insults for paying no heed to the church in which the Christians used to gather, performing rites and chanting prayers and thank-offerings.

Since Andronikos had not accomplished his plans with his earlier actions, he decided to challenge the defenders with a more powerful assault. He discussed it with the king and, with great forcefulness, he convinced him to lead the army out and to encircle the whole perimeter of the walls, and if the operation succeeded to employ ladders and command his climbers to attack. On the one hand, Amalric agreed with the proposition and lauded Andronikos for his tactical thinking, but on the other, he took an oath on Christ's tomb, and he affirmed and insisted that he would not undertake the operation unless wooden towers were first constructed and then brought up against the walls. Having spoken in this manner, he ordered the surrounding palm trees be cut down and fashioned as storeys for the towers.

[164] The lofty leafy-crowned palm trees were cut down, the groves were emptied of trees, and all the gardens were stripped bare, but the fitting and arrangement of the timberwork of the towers had still not been completed. For the king extended the work over many days, ever putting it off until the morrow and never implementing what had been discussed. Andronikos saw these things and became vexed. For he was neglected and felt pity for the army which was already in need of provisions and in danger of dying from famine. Some did not possess enough money to buy the necessities of life, while others were distressed because they did not have their own market, and even though they paid a large sum of money to the king's food merchants, they barely had enough food available. Furthermore, the agreed-upon time for the campaign had long since been exceeded and, more than anything else, the pointless and unprofitable siege which had lasted more than 50 days prompted complaints and anger.

Since Andronikos could not consider any other course of action, for the emperor's letters clearly forbade him to undertake actions which would be contrary to the king's wishes, he sat and waited for the king's initiative. Nevertheless, since he realised, from his actions, that king was planning nothing helpful and appropriate, and was neither assisting nor sharing in the struggles of combat, he ceased talking into the ear of a dead man. Moreover, he saw that the army was in danger of falling into great hardships and perils. So haggard and so greatly consumed by famine was it that some troops laid their hands on forbidden animal fodder, while all ate roots and cut the foliage of the palm trees, boiled them, and served them as meals. What is more, there were the rumours which arrived that mercenaries would soon arrive from the sultan of Egypt in support of the besieged and that a regiment of horsemen which the eastern Arabs and the Assyrians had hired would shortly approach.

---

95 On the church, see William of Tyre (1943), ii. 365.
96 According to Matthew 2:13–16, Joseph, Mary and the infant Jesus fled to Egypt to avoid the massacre of children ordered by King Herod the Great of Judaea.

Manuel I and the Latin East 127

He grew tired of dealing with Latin drivel and took his own decisions about the conflicts of the campaign. Thus, he assembled the troops and said:

'To remain here for a long time would be detrimental and to return empty-handed without inflicting any harm upon those we have attacked would be utterly shameful. Nevertheless, the burden of relying on a man whose disposition is in complete disagreement with [165] the Romans and thus no better disposed towards us than our enemy, is worse than those two alternatives and contrary to any rational thought. Can you not see how the king pitched his camp far from ours and never advances from there, how our comrade and ally is to be perceived not as one who strives for the deeds of Ares, but as a spectator at a holiday show? Do not our enemies even act in the same manner when they postpone battle and come forth from the gates without fighting? And so, from now on it is not the following that worries me, that we should not return unless we have achieved something valiant, but whether we would be unable to preserve our own lives. Nor do I care and think about how the king shall fight along with us, but how we might escape his guile, because he no longer conceals his true intentions nor veils them with a curtain, [and how] having evaded the danger before our eyes, we might depart from this place unharmed.

Perhaps the contemporary Egyptians have devised stronger drugs than their ancestors: ones which cannot merely quench grief and heal the soul's sorrow with joy, but also have the power to make warlike men effeminate and forgetful of valour, just like the ancient drug that removes all sorrow [and] dissolves all kinds of harm which the wife of Thon gave to the Laconian woman.[97] I surmise that the Egyptians offered a cup of this kind of drug to Amalric. He seems to have been fascinated by the drink and, having drunk deeply from a wine cup, fell into a long torpor. His shield hangs from a peg, his sword sleeps in its scabbard and his spear is planted in the earth by its butt-spike. Alternatively, he was hypnotised by silver to make him change his mind, and his ears were plugged with gold, and affected by this, he became hard of hearing.

And now, the treaty of alliance which was agreed with the Roman emperor is broken, because he honoured him only with his lips and turned his heart into the opposite direction. We are surrounded by such great dangers, [166] for surely we are worn out by both war and famine. In addition, the pride of the Romans has abandoned us and glorious deeds have vanished. Even though we crossed vast and boundless seas, it would have been better not to have brought our ships into this basin, than to disembark, achieve nothing and then sail back. Now we will not be able to put our ships to motion with white sails, with which we voyaged from Byzantion, but only with grey ones on account of our blot of shame.

---

97 Polydamna, wife of Thon, the warden of the Nile, gave a drug that quieted all pain and strife to Helen of Troy. See Homer (1919), i. 134 (*Odyssey* IV. 220–34).

We at least, comrades and countrymen, and all the foreigners who are here, must attack the barbarians and deploy for battle against their walls, having separated ourselves from the knights of Palestine, who have proved to be arrogant, haughty and treacherous to the Romans. Let us fight as if the city is about to be seized and strive eagerly as if the riches within are now within our grasp! If the problem is the wall of the barbarians and the missiles they loose from the height of their ramparts, we have our shields, which are not easily raised by men (for they are better than the seven-layered bull hide shield of Ajax),[98] but are put forward like towers, unshaken by arrows, invulnerable to strikes inflicted by hand, and certainly greatly fortified against the siege-engines' shots. After we have erected these shields like fortified towers a short distance from the wall, we shall take care of its defenders.

So, if you decide to do what is right, it is time to trust in me, because along with you, I will gladly endure whatever is required. For nobody will be able to claim that Andronikos leads by word and is adept at inciting others to martial deeds but is a leader unfit for war who does not know to beat the enemy. Instead, the enemy shall see the face of my helmet before yours. I will fight in the front ranks, if it is necessary to do so, and I shall be your file-closer, if the occasion requires it. May God fulfil our plans and deflect all calamities onto the heads of those whose land we are ravaging'.

After he spoke those words, he armed himself and the army broke up the assembly and put on their armour. The day was progressing until it reached the third hour and the battalions marched out [for battle]. Andronikos departed from the camp and advanced in an orderly fashion, standing in front of the whole army. The Saracens [167] secured the gates with bars and bolts, deployed some war engines at intervals for their protection and remained on top of the walls. They repulsed those who approached with every kind of weapon, rendering the entire area within missile range impassable by hurling stones from the battlements and releasing arrows from bows. Even though the garrison defended itself in this manner from within, Andronikos charged with his horse and pierced the gate with his spear. Then the archers and the rest of the troops proved themselves in action, while the trumpets were sounded frequently to convey the command for battle, and the cymbals were struck loudly so as for the enemy within the walls and the towers to lose heart at the continuous noise and assaults of the troops, and at the missiles of all the war engines.

As soon as the ladders had been brought forward and had been fixed on many sections of the wall, the news of what was happening struck the king like a piercing wound. He acted as if he had suffered some great and inconsolable calamity or as if his mind had been struck by a hurricane and he was unable to speak properly. Once he recovered from his daze, he called for a horse, leaped onto it and came before the Roman army with picked men under his command. He checked all the assaults and advised them to stop fighting with men who had recently offered to surrender themselves and their city to the emperor without bloodshed.

---

98 Ajax was a Greek hero of the Trojan War. See Homer (1924), i. 330 (*Iliad* VII. 219).

Manuel I and the Latin East 129

These words slackened the hands of the Romans like some kind of numbness and stopped those who were by that time close to conquering the city from doing so. The king gave his attention to pleasing agreements which gave more honour to the Arabs than to the Romans and negotiated the treaties. The soldiers now paid no heed to the terms of peace. Instead, when they heard about it, the only thing in their minds was returning home. [168] They proved by their actions that naval incompetence is a thing more destructive than fire, and, at once, they filled the camps with disorder. They set the siege engines on fire without orders from the general; they divested themselves of most of their arms and armour, and headed towards the oars, looking at the restless sea. They rushed onto the ships with so much frenzy that they did not even consider the stormy weather and the untimely occasion for a voyage (for it was the fourth day of December).

And so, one could see that numerous fleet as a whole and its landing in the havens, and then its putting to sea again scattered into thousands of parts. Some favoured this or that direction and everybody steered the ships towards their homelands, so that no more than six which were to carry Andronikos back remained at anchor. The latter marched on the road to Jerusalem along with the king.[99] From there, suitably escorted, he bypassed Ikonion and arrived at Constantinople. From the aforementioned numerous ships, some fell into contrary winds and were sunk into the sea along with all their crew, whereas others were scattered by the choppy waters of the sea and returned to the docks of the City later, when spring came. Some of the ships, after they had reached the land and had been emptied of their crews, were left to be borne by the ebb and flow of the waters, without ballast, like boats of Charon.[100] And so, they survived both the tides at the coast and the negligence of the sailors.

As they had plainly demonstrated, the Saracens were terrified of the Roman invasion in their lands. In order to prevent a future naval expedition, they dispatched envoys to the emperor, sent gifts which they considered rich, and confirmed the treaty of peace.

41. John Phokas: Description of the Holy Land (1177–85)

Some manuscripts specifically name the author of this text as John Phokas, an otherwise unknown former soldier and monk of Patmos. A case can be made, however, for identifying him with John Doukas who held the office of grand hetairiarch and was active in the service of Manuel I in the 1150s to 1180s. Doukas was certainly a soldier of wide experience, as the author clearly was, and he was sent on a mission to the Kingdom of Jerusalem in 1177. Whoever wrote this text, he was well travelled as he refers to places in the Balkans and Asia Minor that he had visited. He was also very well read, referring directly to both classical and religious texts. His description reflects Byzantine preoccupations, notably his frequent references to the largesse of Manuel I and his interest in saints of the Greek Orthodox

---

99 Amalric's army reached Ascalon on 21 December 1169. See William of Tyre (1943), ii. 368.
100 In Greek mythology, Charon was the boatman who ferried the souls of the dead across the River Styx to the underworld.

130 *Manuel I and the Latin East*

tradition.[101] It also gives an intriguing glimpse of the Latin East in the years running up to the battle of Hattin and the loss of Jerusalem in 1187.

Phokas (2008), pp. 39–61:

A synoptic description of the fortified settlements and regions of Syria and Phoenicia, and of the holy places in Palestine, from Antioch to Jerusalem, by John Phokas. Written by John Phokas, most pious priest, son of Matthew, who practiced the monastic habit in the island of Patmos and saw the holy places at his time, in the year 6685.[102]

1. Preface

[p. 39] We have enjoyed the holy sites and seen the places in which God was at work in ancient times, when, through Moses, He led His fugitive people out of Egypt with wonders, signs and a mighty hand, and smote the gentiles and their rulers, Sihon, the king of the Amorites, and Og, king of Basan,[103] and all the kingdoms of Canaan. With His mighty arm He settled the chosen people there and multiplied them as greatly as the holy scriptures state. In more recent times He sanctified these regions through the holy incarnation of His only begotten Son and accomplished the wondrous task of our renewal. Should we be the only ones to partake of this benefit, acting in the manner in which gluttons do at dinner time? How would fellowship with and care for our fellows, through which the acts of love shine and can be labelled as distinct traits of our nature, manifest themselves? Therefore, we ought to attempt, as best as we can, to make a map with words, as if it were a drawing, and, through our writing, to describe to devout souls what we witnessed at first-hand. Those who have seen these places will probably think I am doing something unnecessary. For if my aim is to imitate vision with my writing, and every imitation seems to fall short of precision, it is obvious that I will provide less pleasure than the actual sensation which is drawn from the eyes. So, what is the reason? I believe that those who have not perceived these magnificent places with their eyes, but have, at some time and to some degree, gained a certain familiarity of them by words, will be taught more vividly than by those who have attempted the task without due care and examination. It will probably also bring some pleasure to those who have beheld them, for if the sight of them is delightful, hearing about them is pleasant [too].

---

101 On John Doukas, see PBW (2016): Ioannes 20185; Chryssogelos (2021), pp. 285–304.
102 i.e. 1177. The author is using the Byzantine reckoning from the creation of the world which supposedly occurred on 1 September 5509 BCE. However, a post-1180 date may be more likely. See Chryssogelos (2021), pp. 286–90.
103 Numbers 21:21–35.

2. Antioch the city of God, the Springs of Kastalia, Mauron Mountain and Skopelos, Caucasus, river Orontes

[p. 40] There was truly a time when the city of God,[104] Antioch on the Orontes, was adorned by the size of its theatres, the beauties of its porticoes, the images of its churches, the multitude of its citizens, and the great extent of its wealth. It used to greatly surpass almost every other city in the East. Time, however, and the hands of the barbarians have removed its bliss. Yet it is still brilliant with its towers, the might of its battlements, the splendour of the flowers in its meadows, and the babbling of the waters with which it is surrounded. As the river gently runs through the city and surrounds it, it embraces its towers with watery caresses. In addition, it is excellently irrigated with running water from the springs of Kastalia. The river gushes like a spring and, via the stream of Kastalia and its many irrigation conduits, it pours all over the city and fills it with its streams, thanks to the generosity of the city's magnanimous founder who diverted the running water, from the springs through the mountains and up to the city.

Towards that direction, there is the famous suburb of Daphne which is encircled with all kinds of flourishing plants, and also the Wondrous Mountain, where the marvellous Symeon lived.[105] Next to these lies the Mauron and Skopelos mountains, places in which, in ancient times, many god-loving men sought God and found Him. Even now there are such men who will achieve salvation. They live in the thickets of these same mountains, longing for the beauty of God. As regards the springs of Kastalia, they emerge between two hills from the foot of the hill which is nearest to the sea. The water which flows there abundantly is of the highest quality. In this place one can see a huge portico roofing the water of the spring. The water pours from the spring abundantly and is divided into two streams. The first is conveyed in channels high above the ground and the water turns into an aerial river, coming round to the high ground on the right side of the city. The second overflows the plain on the left side of the spring, floods the marsh-meadows, irrigates the whole meadow of Daphne, and joins the streams of Orontes on the left side. The Wondrous Mountain is raised between the city and the sea; it is a remarkable thing, and it is perceived as a splendour of the eyes by those who come across it, for it forms a boundary for Antioch and Roso and on both its sides it has the Skopelos Mountain and the so-called Caucasus. The river Orontes flows round the feet of the mountain, revolving around it with infinite bends, and pours out into the waters of the sea. On the summit of this mountain [p. 41] that great man lived a life of contemplation. Having achieved the lifting up of his heart, he also became elevated in his body, and strove to become heavenly while still in the flesh, and to be half-way between men and God. I will explain how this miracle was accomplished by this God-loving man. He dug deep into the summit of the Wondrous Mountain with the help of masons, and then built a monastery out of one solid rock and summit. In

---

104 Antioch was renamed Theoupolis, the city of God, during the sixth century.
105 Symeon Stylites the Younger founded a monastery on Mount Kasion (Jebel Akra, Kel Dağı) during the sixth century.

the centre of the monastery, he hewed out a natural pillar and put steps in it, setting his feet upon the rock as in the Scriptures. Towards the rising sun, he built a very beautiful church for God. In it, he gathered his disciples and, he being out in the open air and they inside the church, they remained standing all night long, offering to God the worship which befits his holy ones.

3. Laodikeia, Gabala or Zebel, Antarada or Tortosa, Hasysioi

After Antioch and all these places, comes Laodikeia, a large and populous city, but the passage of time has damaged its splendour. After Laodikeia comes Gabala or Zebel. Then comes the castle of Antarada or Tortosa, and in the same manner there are various forts along the coast as far as Tripoli. Along the interior, however, stretches a great mountain range, where the so-called Hasysioi live. It is a Saracen nation which is neither Christian nor Muslim, but worships God according to its own heresy. They call their leader the ambassador of God, by his command, they are dispatched to the rulers of great countries, and they slay them with daggers. They rush upon their targets unexpectedly and they also perish in the enterprise since the few are killed by the many after the execution of their plot. They consider this a martyrdom and a bid for immortality.[106]

4. Mount Lebanon, Tripoli

After this mountain range, comes the all-beautiful Mount Lebanon, worthy of its renown in the Scriptures. It is a huge mountain range, covered, from its foot up to the summit, by snowdrifts as if they were locks of hair. It is overgrown with pine, cedar and cypress and adorned with many other fruit-bearing trees. The Christians live on its coastal regions, while the Saracens possess the districts towards Damascus and Arabia [p. 42]. Rivers flow from its clefts and valleys and into the sea, beautiful and very cold when the snow is melting, and makes the rivers flow cold as ice. Near the foot of Mount Lebanon lies Tripoli, whose founder established it on a peninsula. Since a thin ridge comes out from Mount Lebanon and is fixed on the sea like a tongue, the ridge becoming elevated at its eastern end, the founder of the city established it in that place. Although it is very small in circumference, it gains in beauty in terms of the height of its walls and the beauty of its buildings.

5. Gibelet, Beirut

After Tripoli lies Gibelet, and then Beirut, a large and populous city, surrounded by many meadows, and adorned by the beauty of its harbour. For the harbour is not natural, but artificial. It curves into the city in the shape of a crescent, and in accordance with the crescent shape, two great towers are set as horns. A chain is

---

106 The author is describing the Assassins or Nizaris, a sect of the Isma'ili branch of Shi'a Islam, who were notorious for murdering enemy political leaders.

stretched from one tower to the other and encloses the ships into the harbour. Beirut is the border between Syria and Phoenicia.

6. Sidon, the Twin [Harbour], the stone on which the Saviour stood and taught the masses

Next comes Sidon and its celebrated twin harbour, whose description has been excellently expressed by the author of *Leucippe*.[107] For if you visit the place, you will see the true appearance of the harbour and the outer harbour matching the written description. Outside of the city, at a distance of about three bowshots, there is a church surrounded by an extensive colonnade. A square stone is placed in the apse of the Church, on which, according to the testimony of the common people, Christ, the Saviour of the world, stood and taught the masses.

7. Sarepta, the Church of Prophet Elijah

After Sidon comes the castle of Sarepta founded on the sea shore, and the Church of Prophet Elijah established in the middle of the town, upon the house of the widow who received him as a guest.[108]

8. Tyre, the stone on which Christ sat and dispatched Peter and John to the city for bread, the fountain in which Christ rested with the Apostles

[p. 43] Next lies the city of Tyre which is probably the most beautiful of all the cities of Phoenicia. For it too has been founded on a peninsula, like Tripoli, but it is much more famous than the latter for its size, allure and beauty of its buildings. Its outer harbour is similar to the harbour of Beirut, even though that of Tyre far exceeds that of Beirut in size and beauty, and the height of its towers is greater. Outside of the city, at a distance of two bowshots, is a huge stone upon which, according to the tradition, Christ leaned to rest and dispatched Peter and John, the holy Apostles, to the city so as to look for bread. After the Apostles had gone and brought it, they, along with the Saviour, departed for a neighbouring fountain, a mile away, where the Saviour sat down, ate with the Apostles, drank from the water and blessed it.[109] Indeed, up to this day, this fountain is a spectacle for the eyes difficult to describe. For it emerges in the midst of the meadows there, and it is truly something wonderful and heart-warming for travellers. Rumour has it that it is bottomless. The construction around it and its shape is as follows. Those who first devoted their labour to the fountain, built around it an octagonal tower. They raised the tower to a considerable height and shaped its ends in every corner like

---

107 *The Adventures of Leucippe and Clitophon* was a romance written by Achilles Tatius in the second century CE.
108 Sarepta was also known as Zaraphath. See I Kings 17:19.
109 This story does not appear in the New Testament.

a bowl. At the same height, across the meadows, they constructed channels on top of arches. They made the pressurised water pour forth like in a spring, making a gurgling sound. It irrigates the meadows around the fountain with constant streams. If one stands upon the tower, it is possible [to see] from afar the thick foliage moving, and, in high noon, all the plants of the meadow are constantly watered.[110]

9. Ptolemais, Carmel

Next comes Ptolemais or Acre. This city is large and populous, surpassing all the others. It receives all kinds of merchant ships, and all the people who go abroad for the sake of Christ arrive there, by land and by sea. Since the air here is corrupted by the presence of numerous travellers, constant diseases occur and cause death among them. The air carries with it the stench of their death, and that is the unbearable evil of this city.[111] On its right lies Carmel and the seashore of all the regions of Palestine. The regions on its left include Galilee and Samaria.

10. Sepphoris, Cana, Nazareth, the Church of Archangel Gabriel, the fountain from which the Mother of God drew [water], the house of Joseph and the place of the Annunciation, the chamber in which the Lord lived after his return from Egypt, the crag

The first site after Ptolemais is Sepphoris. A city of Galilee which is almost totally uninhabited and does not even manifest a trace of its former prosperity. After Sepphoris is Cana. Today it can be seen as a very small castle. Here the Saviour turned water to wine.[112] And next, between various hills, at the bottom of the latter's ravine, the city of Nazareth has been founded. Here, through the Archangel Gabriel, the Virgin Mother of God, was informed about the great mystery, about the great and abundant mercy of Christ our God who was incarnated for our salvation. At the entrance of the main gate of this town, there is a church of the Archangel Gabriel. On the left of the church's altar one can see a small cave in which emerges a fountain which pours forth clean water. The all-immaculate Mother of God used to come here every day to draw water, when she had been given by the priests to the righteous Joseph and was under his care. Six months after the conception of John the Baptist, as she was about to draw water as usual, she received the first greeting from Gabriel. She was thrown into confusion and returned to the house of Joseph trembling. There she heard the angel say the phrase 'Hail blessed one', and she replied to him 'Behold the handmaid of the Lord, be it unto me according to your word',[113] and from that moment she received the Word of God in her

---

110 This is probably a description of the Roman Aqueduct of Tyre.
111 Constantine Manasses says much the same about Acre in [37].
112 John 2:1–11.
113 Luke 1:28–38.

all-immaculate womb. After all these events, this same house of Joseph was turned into a very beautiful church, on the left side of which, near the altar, there is a cave. The latter has not been made deep in the earth, its end is shallow and visible, and its mouth has been decorated all-around with white marble. Above it, there is, by the hand of a painter, a winged angel descending towards her who became a mother without yet having a husband. He salutes her with the good news, having found her seemly, spinning wool finely. The angel is painted as if he is addressing her, but the latter, shocked at this unexpected sight, turns the other way quickly in a state of confusion and almost drops some purple cloth from her hands. The Virgin leaves the room in fear, meets a beloved relative, and embraces her with friendly salutations. Having entered within the mouth of the cave, you descend a few steps and then you see the very ancient house of Joseph itself, in which the archangel gave the good news to the Virgin, after her return from the fountain. On the spot where the Annunciation took place there is a cross carved out of black stone [fixed] upon white marble and beyond it the altar. On the right side of this same altar, there is a small chamber in which the Eternal Virgin used to sleep. On the left side of the place of the Annunciation one can see another dark chamber. It is said that Christ our Lord lived there, after his return from Egypt and until the beheading of John the Baptist. For, according to the holy scriptures, when Jesus heard that John had been arrested, he left Nazareth and resided in Capernaum.[114] After that comes a range composed of various hills, and there is a crag in it from which the Jews planned to throw down the Lord. He passed through them and walked towards Capernaum.[115]

11. Mount Tabor, the two monasteries, the small cave in which the Lord entered after the Transfiguration, the cave of Melchizedek, Damascus, the Sea of Galilee, the mound where the Saviour blessed the loaves, Nain, Endor, torrent Kishon

After the range comes a great plain, wherein, near the range, lies Mount Tabor, that heaven on earth, the delight of the soul and the joy for the eyes of orthodox people. For there is a divine grace that covers the mountain, and the latter exudes spiritual gladness. The mountain is round and moderate in height. There are two monasteries on its summit in which Christian monks propitiate God with hymns in foreign tongues. In the monastery near which the salvific Transfiguration of Christ took place there is a multitude of Latin monks, but in the one on the left-hand side, the orthodox Nazirites purify this holy place with their prayers. For the saving Transfiguration of Christ occurred in the summit of the mountain, where the Latin monastery stands. In the holy altar of its [church] lies the place where the Lord was transfigured in the presence of Elijah and Moses as well as of his three chosen disciples, Peter, John and James.[116] This place is enclosed with bronze railings. At the spot where the feet of the Lord stood, one can see a completely white round navel, in the middle of which is carved the holy

---

114 Matthew 4:12–13.
115 Luke 4:29–31.
116 Matthew 17:1–8; Mark 9:2–8; Luke 9:28–36.

cross. The carved cross exudes an inexpressible fragrance that delights the nostrils of those who approach it. Outside of the monastery, at a distance of a stone-shot, there is a small cave which Christ entered after his awe-inspiring transfiguration and ordered his disciples not to speak of what they had seen to anyone, until he rose from the dead. On the northern side of the mountain lies the cave of Melchizedek which is worth seeing. For it has been divided with various holes and there are upper and lower chambers in it and various dwellings and cells serving as hermitages for the ascetics. In these dwellings many of the great saints followed the ascetic path. Near this cave there is a church on the very spot where Melchisedek met, blessed and received Abraham as a guest, after the latter had returned from battle.[117] If you gaze from this holy mountain towards the first dawn, you will see the marshes and the gorge of Jordan, the holiest of rivers. If you extend your sight further, you will see the eastern regions of Lebanon and two great hills between which Damascus is situated. Turning your eyes slightly more towards the left parts of Jordan, you perceive the Sea of Galilee very clearly and without any obstacles. On the opposite side of the sea, one can see a small mound where the Saviour blessed the loaves and fed with them five thousand people.[118] [On the same spot], after the resurrection, He shared dinner with his disciples out of the catch of 153 fish.[119] On the north side of Mount Tabor, another range encircles the plain at a distance of 12 stades approximately, or even more. On its slopes is the city of Nain where the Lord raised the widow's son from the dead.[120] From the eastern parts of this city, one can see the village of Endor. Between Tabor, Nain and Endor flows the torrent Kishon, of which David says, 'Do to them as you did to the Midianites, to Sisera and to Jabin at the torrent Kishon who were utterly defeated at Endor'.[121]

12. The city of Sebasteia, the prison of John the Baptist in which there is a small chest containing the body of St Zacharias and a small chest containing that of St Elizabeth, the church in which is the dust of the burned body of the venerated Baptist, the body of prophet Elisha and the left hand of the venerable Baptist, the Roman monastery over Herod's palace, the spot where the head of the Baptist was first found

After a day's journey lies the city of Sebasteia, which Herod the Tetrarch restored in Caesar's honour.[122] In Sebasteia, at his banquet, Herod the Lesser [promised to] cut off the dear head of John the Baptist, the greatest of mortal men.[123] In the middle

---

117 Genesis 14:18–20.
118 Matthew 14:13–21; Mark 6:31–44; Luke 9:12–17; John 6:1–14.
119 John 21:1–14.
120 Luke 7:11.
121 Psalms 82:10–11.
122 Sebasteia was rebuilt in 27 BCE by Herod the Great, in honour of the Roman emperor Augustus (*Sebastos* in Greek).
123 Herod Antipas, tetrarch of Galilee and son of Herod the Great, was entertained at a banquet by the dancing of Salome, the daughter of his second wife, Herodias. As her reward, she demanded the head of John the Baptist. See Matthew 14:6–11 and Mark 6:21–8.

of this city there is a prison into which the Baptist was thrown because of his reproaches against Herodias and was decapitated. This prison is underground with 20 steps from top to bottom. In the centre of it there is an altar on the spot where he was beheaded by the executioner. On the right of the same altar is a small chest in which is stored the body of St Zacharias, the Baptist's father, and on the left, there is another chest in which lays the body of St Elizabeth, his mother. On both sides of the prison are deposited the relics of various saints and those of the disciples of the Baptist. Above the prison there is a church in which lie two chests hewn out of white marble. The one on the right contains the dust of the burned body of the venerable Baptist, and the other the body of prophet Elisha. Above this relic, in a golden chest, lies the left hand of the Baptist, which is also completely covered by gold. Near the middle of the city, in its most elevated part, is a hill where in ancient times stood the palace of Herod. There took place the banquet where that wretched girl danced and received as prize for her dancing the holy head of the Baptist. This place, however, is now a Roman monastery. The church of this monastery is domed. On the left of the altar there is a small chamber, in the middle of which one can see a small marble boss, lying in a very deep pit where the first discovery of the venerable head of the Baptist, who is revered by the angels, took place. The head had been buried there by Herodias.

13. Sychar, the mountain where God requested Isaac's sacrifice according to the Samaritans, the well of Jacob

Next, after a journey of approximately 15 stades, is Sychar, the metropolis of the Samaritans, which was named Neapolis in later times. It is situated between two mountains and its foundations are united lengthwise with the feet of both. The one on the right is the mountain where, according to the Samaritans, God discussed with Abraham and requested the sacrifice of Isaac.[124] They argue that the leader of the family made the sacrifice there, but they have no idea what they are talking about. For that holy mountain is the pavement of Golgotha, where the Saviour of the World endured the passion which brought salvation. At the foot of this mountain is the site which Jacob gave to his son, Joseph, and there is also in it the well of Jacob himself. Tired, the Lord sat down there and discussed with the Samaritan woman those matters which the holy gospel records. It was with regard to this very mountain that the woman said to the Lord 'our fathers worshipped in this mountain' and, through his discussion with her, the Lord taught everybody how those worshippers in spirit and truth should give adoration.[125]

---

124 Genesis 22:1–19.
125 John 4:5–20.

14. The Holy City, the stoning of Stephen the first martyr, the Mount of Olives, Holy Sion, house of John the Theologian, the site of the Lord's Supper and of the descent of the Holy Spirit, the place of the Washing and the entry of Jesus through locked doors, the site of the Stephen's burial, the Tower of David, the parish dependency of Holy Sabas, the Church of the Lord's Sepulchre, the site of Golgotha, the underground church where the cross was found, the Holy of Holies, cave in which prophet Zechariah was buried, the Church of Joachim and Anna

The distance between Samaria and the Holy City is 84 stades. The road between them is paved with stone throughout, and although the entire region there is very dry and parched, it is full of vineyards and trees. The Holy City is situated between various ravines and mountains and the sight of it is amazing. For the city appears both as high up and as low down, because it is situated higher than the countryside of Judea, but lower than the mountains which enclose it. This holy place is divided into two parts. The Holy City lies on the lower part of the mountain on the right and its walls meet the ravine. All of the ground above is covered with vineyards which is where the stoning of St Stephen, the first martyr, took place. On the left, beyond the ravine, lies the Mount of Olives. The Lord frequented the place and sanctified it through his prayers, his teaching and ultimately his holy Ascension to the Father. In front of the Holy City lies Holy Sion, situated towards its right parts. The appearance of Sion is as follows. There is a stronghold in which lies Holy Sion, the mother of churches. This church is huge with an arched roof. When you enter its beautiful gates, on your left is the house of St John the Theologian, where the supremely holy Mother of God dwelt after the Resurrection and gave up her soul. There is a small chamber in that place, surrounded by iron bars, and two navels on the spot where the All-Holy one delivered her soul to the Son and to God. On the right side of the church, towards the far right of the altar, is the upper story with a staircase of 61 steps leading to it. The church has four arches and a dome. On the left side of the upper story, one can see the place where the Lord's supper took place, and in the apse of the altar where the Holy Spirit descended upon the Apostles. In the lower part of the church took place the washing of the feet.[126] Opposite is a church where once stood the house where Christ visited the Apostles, even though the door was closed.[127] The protomartyr Stephen was buried in the same place after his stoning, and Gamaliel transferred him to another place.[128] In the north part of the city lies the, so-called, tower of David, an enormous tower. Although everybody in Jerusalem recognised it as David's, I have my doubts and for good reason. For Josephus reports that the Tower of David and the temple, as well as the more recent two towers erected by Herod in dedication to Phasael and Mariamme, had been

---

126 Mark 14:14–15; Luke 24:33, 36; John 20:19, 26; Acts 1:13.
127 John 20:26.
128 The martyrdom of St Stephen is described in Acts 7:57–60 and 8:1–2. However, the text only says that devout men buried Stephen rather than specifically mentioning the Pharisee Gamaliel.

built with polished white stone.[129] One can see, however, that this tower was built with common stone, perhaps the tower which we presently see was erected on the foundations of the very ancient one. After the tower is the gate which leads towards the city. You enter through it, and you walk along a broad street. On its right, near the royal palace, stands the parish dependency of our holy father Sabas. If you walk along the street for about an arrow-shot, you will find the celebrated Church of the Lord's Sepulchre the appearance of which has often been described. The cave which serves as a sepulchre for the Lord's body is double. In the first part lies the stone which was rolled away, cased on all sides by white marble. In the second part, towards the north, the stone has been hewn to rise about one cubit above the level floor. On it was laid, dead and naked, the Giver of Life. One sees it overlaid with pure gold by the desire and faith of my master and emperor, Manuel Komnenos the Purple-Born. Near the sepulchre is the site of Golgotha, containing the Place of the Skull, the hewn base of the cross and the crack of the stone which was shattered during the suffering of the crucifixion. Beneath the crack, there is a slightly concave spot in the rock in which is the skull of Adam and the streams of the Lord's blood which were shed onto it. The church [built] over Golgotha has four arches and a dome, and near this church is another, which is immense and underground. The venerable and life-giving cross of Lord Christ was found in this place. In the eastern part of the city there is a church, the Holy of Holies. This church is altogether extremely beautiful, with a domed roof. It is believed to [stand] on the ancient floor of the renowned Temple of Solomon, and is decorated inside and out with various marbles and mosaics. There are two arches on the left side of the church on which are depicted the following. On the first, the Presentation of the Lord Christ because on this very spot the righteous Simeon received Christ the Lord in his arms, and on the second, the wondrous ladder which Jacob saw reaching up to the heavens and the angels of God ascending and descending it.[130] Beneath the depicted ladder, one can see the very stone on which Jacob laid his head. On the right hand side is an opening leading down to some kind of cavern beneath the church. This is the place where prophet Zechariah is buried, whom the Jews slew, according to the Gospel 'between the temple and the altar'.[131] Outside of the church there is a great paved forecourt, probably the ancient floor of the great temple. Near the gate which leads towards Holy Gethsemane is the church of St Joachim and St Anna, where the Nativity of the immaculate Mother of God took place. Close to this church spring forth the waters of the Sheep Pool.[132]

---

129 Herod the Great dedicated the towers to his brother and his first wife. See Josephus (1928–9), i. 196–7, 338–41, 494–5 (i. 418, ii. 46, 439).
130 Luke 2:25–35; Genesis 28:10–19.
131 Matthew 23:35.
132 Joachim and Anna were the parents of the Virgin Mary.

15. Gethsemane, the tomb of the Mother of God, the cave of the prayer and the sleep of the apostles, the temple which stands where the Lord prayed and his sweat dripped down like drops of blood, the place of the betrayal, the cave where Peter wept, the Mount of Olives, the place of the Ascension, the cave of Pelagia, the place where the Lord's Prayer was taught, the Roman monastery on the foundations of the monastery of the devout Melania, the monastery holding the relics of Stephen, the Kedron torrent, the Ruba desert

Outside of the city from that direction, towards its eastern part, lies the village of Gethsemane in the midst of the great torrent-like chasm which divides the Mount of Olives from the Holy City. Gethsemane contains the tomb of our most holy Lady the Mother of God, and the garden where our Saviour often rested with His disciples. The same place also contains three churches. The one furthest to the left stands around the underground excavated site and contains the holy tomb of the Mother of God. This church is oblong, arched and domed throughout. In the middle stands her tomb, like a pulpit, hewn out of rock in a four-arched shape. On its eastern side, it is hewn in the shape of a bed from the same stone and covered by white marble. The Holy Apostles laid the immaculate body of the Most Holy Mother of God there, after it had been brought from Sion. The other church above is the cave where the Lord made his prayer and the Apostles felt drowsy and were overcome by sleep. Near the foot of the Mount of Olives, a stone's throw away, according to the Gospel, stands the third church at the place where the Lord, after he had reproached the Apostles for their indolence, left and prayed again, the same occasion when his sweat dripped down like drops of blood.[133] The betrayal took place in this garden too. Judas kissed the Lord treacherously and the throng of the Jews seized him.[134] On the opposite side of the garden, on its higher part, the one towards Sion, there is a church with a cave underneath. In the latter Peter entered after his denial, sat down and wept bitterly.[135] In the church the apostle is depicted in his grief. Above Gethsemane and the church of The Prayer, one can see the Mount of Olives, separated, as I said, from the Holy City by the Valley of Jehosaphat and the torrent of the Valley of Weeping. It is basically a mountain which stands a little higher than the city. On account of this, it does not appear very large when looking from the city, whereas from the side of Jordan and Bethany it is extremely lofty, for its slope descends right into the desert. On its summit is the place where the Saviour often addressed His disciples after the Resurrection and performed the most awesome mystery of the Ascension.[136] Near the summit, slightly lower, is the cave where St Pelagia accomplished her ascetic labours. Her holy body lies there

---

133 Luke 22:44.
134 Matthew 26:48–9; Mark 14:44–5.
135 Luke 22:62.
136 Luke 24:51.

in a stone coffin.[137] Near the cave is another church on the spot where Our Saviour taught the disciples the Lord's Prayer. On the left part of the city is a Roman monastery, erected, as they say, on top of the foundations of the old monastery built by the celebrated Melania.[138] Opposite this mountain, to the rear of the city, in the direction of Samaria, is a monastery on the spot where, after the stoning of the holy protomartyr Stephen and his burial in the place we have mentioned, his holy and saintly body was transferred by Gamaliel. The torrent which comes from Gethsemane continues as far as the Lavra of St Sabas and the desert of Ruba, which lies near the Dead Sea of Sodom.

16. The jar, the caves of the virgins, the Valley of Lamentations, the Potter's Field, the Pool of Siloam, the Lavra of St Sabas, the tomb of St Sabas, the monuments of the poets Kosmas and John

Right beyond Gethsemane, about a bowshot away, stands the so-called jar, built into the rock in the shape of a square. It is two spears tall, I reckon, and from its lower parts right up to the top it becomes acute in the shape of a pyramid. A Georgian monk has shut himself in there and is working on his salvation. After Gethsemane and the jar is a great barrow where various artificial caves have been made, named the caves of the virgins. Armenian and Jacobite monks mostly live there, but also a few orthodox ones. Then the chasm widens at the place of the Valley of Lamentations, and after it is the Potter's Field, bought for the burial of strangers with the money paid for [the betrayal] of the Lord.[139] Next is the Pool of Siloam whose waters irrigate this very dry location. After it one can also see meadows of average size, full of trees, across the width of the valley. The spring is surrounded and adorned by arches and many columns, and in the manner that we have described the valley spreads out for 11 miles, until the Lavra of St Sabas.[140] At that point the valley widens into a great and rough chasm where one can see the lavra, the church and the tomb of the saint. In front of the lavra, on both sides of the canyon's banks, there are caves and small towers inhabited by those who detest the world and its luxury, and endure, for the sake of the Kingdom of Heaven, the unbearable burning of the sun there, quenching fire with fire, through the quenchable, the unquenchable.[141] At the site of the church and the tomb of the divine holy father Sabas, the canyon is divided into three parts and the chasm becomes much deeper. The saint built towers on its summit, between the lofty towers he founded the church, and all around it he constructed the most humble ascetic cells which are described in the account of his miraculous life. The church itself is very delightful in many ways.

---

137 Pelagia of Antioch was a fourth-century ascetic who abandoned her previous life as a courtesan and went to live in a cell on the Mount of Olives.
138 St Melania the Younger founded her convent in around 417 and a monastery for men in around 420.
139 According to Acts 1:18, Judas purchased a field with the thirty pieces of silver which he was paid for betraying Christ.
140 Sabas was a sixth-century Palestinian monk. His monastery of Mar Saba still stands.
141 i.e. by temporary suffering in this life, avoiding the eternal torments of Hell.

It is huge, long and full of light. Its floor is decorated with chips of marble which, even though they are inexpensive and from the desert, have been skilfully worked. There is a paved court in front of the church and in the middle of it the tomb of our father Sabas. It is about a span in height, and it is covered by a very bright white slab of marble. Close to the tomb and all around it, and even underground, one can see the monuments of the Holy Fathers who became renowned in the desert, including the monuments of the ancient poets, St Kosmas and St John.[142] Close by are monuments of 40 God-bearing men who were distinguished from the others, six of whom spoke directly with God. They are known as follows: Stephen, Theodore, Paul, the fourth he who came from the great city, the fifth the Georgian, the sixth, well-known to everybody for his clear-sightedness, John the Stylite.

17. The monastery of Theodosios the Cenobiarch

Returning towards the Holy City, not via the valley, but by via the neighbouring mountain pass, you will find, at a distance of six miles, the monastery of our holy father Theodosios the Cenobiarch. This monastery is protected by many towers. In front of it, at a distance of a bowshot, is an arch at the place where, as the *Life* of the saint reports, the quenched coals generated smoke in his hand.[143] In the middle of the monastery stands the church at an elevated position. It has a circular roof and beneath it is a cave, the tomb of the saint. Near it are a number of vaulted structures which contain the relics of various great saints. Descending the steps of the cave, you will find the mouth of another cave on the side. Basil, a disciple of the saint, entered it and restored his own tomb, at the request of the saint, as reported in the *Lives of the Fathers*. And for 40 days, at the time of the service, one could see [the resurrected] Basil, singing hymns along with the saint and his brothers.

18. The monastery of St Euthymios

Opposite the monastery of Theodosios the Cenobiarch, on the right side, at the extremity of the Jordan desert, is the monastery of St Euthymios the Great. It is also fortified with towers and great ramparts. In the middle stands the church also with an arched roof. Beneath it is a cave, and in the middle of it the tomb of Euthymios the Great.[144] The monument resembles that of the God-bearing Sabas since it also covered by white marble. In the same place along with the saint, rest also the relics of the holy fathers Pasarion and Domitian.

---

142 Kosmas the hymnographer and John of Damascus were both monks in the monastery of Mar Saba during the eighth century.
143 The life of Theodosios the Cenobiarch, who died in around 529, was written by Theodore of Petra.
144 Euthymius died in 473.

19. The Choziba Monastery

After the monastery of St Euthymios is an interval of 12 miles. Then there is a great ravine and in the middle of it runs a torrent. On the opposite side of the ravine is the monastery Choziba. It is a thing which reading about it causes disbelief, and gazing upon it, amazement. For the monk's cells are cave openings and the cemetery as well as the church itself have been founded in the chasm of the rock. They are so much scorched by the burning heat of the sun so that one can see tongues of fire emitted by the stones in the shape of pyramids. The water drunk by the monks is the kind [that comes] from stagnant pools when the sun appears above them in midsummer and heats them to boiling point with its fiery rays. We saw several blessed men in this monastery. One of them was a performer of miracles and spoke directly to God. The name of this old man is Luke. It was dangerous to ascend and descend from this monastery due to the steepness of the place and the excessive heat of the sun.

20. The road to the end of the desert and the road leading to Jericho

After the monastery is a long and narrow very rough road, leading at the opposite side of the desert until you see two rocky edges on the path, between the latter two, the road meets the track leading to Jericho. On this track, there is not even a stone foundation and its outline is barely visible. That is because the whole area is very well watered and presently serves as a garden for the monasteries founded in the desert. And so, the land has been divided and parcelled among these holy monasteries and has become full of trees and vines. On account of this, the monks have set up towers on the shares of each monastery and reap abundant harvests from them. To my mind, the whole of the desert, the Jordan and the Dead Sea of Sodom have a shape like the arrangement of the site of Ohrid.[145] The only difference seems to be that from the lake of Ohrid the water flows out and waters many ravines of the land, which the locals call *stroungai*, whereas in this case Jordan flows into the lake. In addition, the width of the desert is infinitely more extended than the plain of Ohrid.

21. The side of the Dead Sea, Segor, the desert of Ruba, the Mountain of the Forty [Days' Fast], the church on the spot where the Archangel Michael conversed with Joshua

On the right of the aforementioned double rock edges is the shore of the Dead Sea and beyond it Segor. From this place, beyond this desert, the great desert of Ruba can be seen, after crossing to the two monasteries, namely those of Euthymios and the Lavra. On the left of the rock edges and the road, one can see the mountain where, after the 40-day fast of the Saviour, the Tempter presented him with two

---

145 Ohrid and its lake, now in the Republic of North Macedonia, were Byzantine territory in the late twelfth century.

temptations, but retired in disgrace, defeated.[146] Opposite this mountain, there is another one, six miles away I think, and in this mountain there is a church on the spot where the Archangel Michael conversed with Joshua.[147]

22. The Monasteries of John the Baptist, of Chrysostom [and of Kalamon], the Jordan

Three monasteries have been founded near the Jordan, of John the Baptist, of Chrysostom [and of Kalamon]. The monastery of the Baptist was completely destroyed by an earthquake. Now it has been built anew by the wealth-giving right hand of our God-crowned emperor, the Purple-born Manuel Komnenos, after its abbot had spoken passionately to him about rebuilding it. About two bowshots away flows the Jordan, the holiest of rivers where my Jesus humbled himself and performed the great mystery of my renewal through baptism. On the bank, about a stone-shot away, there is a square domed [building]. On that spot, where the Jordan flows backwards near its bend, the river received naked Him who filled the sky with clouds, the shaking right hand of John the Baptist touched His head, the Spirit joined its kindred Logos in the form of a dove, and the voice of the Father affirmed to the Redeemer that he was truly his Son.[148]

23. The hill of Hermionim, the monastery of St Gerasimos, the hermit pillar where the old man lived

Between the Monastery of John the Baptist and the Jordan is the very small hill of Hermionim, where, as the Saviour stood there, John pointed to him and declared to the crowd, he is the one 'who takes away the sin of the world'.[149] Between the monasteries of the Baptist and of Kalamon is the monastery of St Gerasimos which has been terribly damaged by the flow of the Jordan. Almost nothing is to be seen of it but some small remains of the church, two caves and a pillar for recluses. A great Georgian old man has secluded himself on the latter, a very charismatic and remarkable individual. We met him and we benefited greatly by our conversation, for some divine grace adorns this old man. We feel compelled to tell the story of his miracle which took place a few days before we arrived there, in an engaging way for those who eagerly enjoy divine things. In the meandering and curving stretches of the Jordan, some pieces of land adjunct to the river are enclosed by it, as one would expect. A great mass of reeds grows naturally in this place and prides of lions usually live there. Two of them came to the old man's cell one Sunday, and pushing their heads against the pillar, asked by the expression of their eyes for food. They were given it and readily and happily returned to their habitat at the curves of the river. The food was legumes soaked in water and pieces of either rye bread or barley. When they continued to come to him and to ask for their customary food

---

146 Matthew 4:1–11, although three temptations are described there rather than two.
147 See Joshua 5:13–15.
148 Matthew 3:13–17; Mark 1:9–11; Luke 3:21–3.
149 John 1:29.

by nodding with their eyes, the old man, had not the means to satisfy the beasts' appetite. For it happened that for 20 days that holy man had had nothing whatsoever to eat. So, the old man said to them 'Beasts, since for the past twenty days we have been unable to comfort the weakness of our nature with any kind of food, and we have no supply of the usual necessities, it seems to me that the providence of God and his words will show us how to remedy that ingeniously. You should go to the streams of Jordan and bring to us some small pieces of wood. We will make crosses and give them as a blessing to pilgrims. We will receive from them in return a small amount of money, each as he pleases, and we shall be able to buy both my food and yours'. He spoke these words and the beasts heard him, as if they were rational beings, and they proceeded, running and walking, to the streams of Jordan. After a while, what a miracle, they brought under their necks two pieces of wood. They left them in the base of the pillar and eagerly returned to the marshes of Jordan. But enough with the stories, we continue with the description of sites.

24. The Monastery of Kalamon, the Monastery of Chrysostom

The monastery of Kalamon is also built with towers and curtain walls out of square hewn rocks. The church in the middle has been erected solid and domed resting on barrel vaults. Another domed church, a tiny one, is attached to the first, to the latter's right-hand side. It is said that it was built in the time of the Apostles. An image of the Mother of God is depicted in its apse, bearing the Saviour Christ in her arms. Its appearance, colour and size resemble that of the most holy icon of the Hodegetria in the imperial city. The ancient tradition reports that the icon was painted by the very hand of the Apostle and Evangelist St Luke.[150] The frequent miracles and the most awe-inspiring fragrance that is exuded from the icon, persuade one to believe that. At a distance of five stades from the tiny church, the monastery of Chrysostom has been established. About a bow shot away stands a pillar for hermits. The great man of Georgian origin stood on it. He was of simple ways [and] venerable words. Previously, for many years, he had undertaken the labours of asceticism on a stone fixed near the sea at Attaleia. While we were campaigning along with the glorious Manuel, emperor and purple-born, we ourselves met the man.[151]

25. The cave of John the Baptist, the cave of the prophet Elijah, the desert where Zosimas saw Maria the Egyptian, the desert leading to the mountain of Sinai and the Red Sea

Across the Jordan, opposite the site of the Baptism, are various bushes and in the midst of them, at a distance of a stade, is the cave of John the Baptist. It is very small and cannot accommodate a tall man standing. There is another cave, sitting [across] the other, towards the depths of the desert, where the prophet Elijah

---

150 The icon of the Hodegetria ('She who shows the way') was housed in the Hodegon monastery in Constantinople. It showed the Virgin pointing at the infant Christ.
151 The author may have been in Manuel I entourage when the emperor marched east in December 1158 for his campaign in Cilicia and Syria.

lived and was carried off by the chariot of fire.[152] Beyond these caves, towards the course of the Jordan, is said to be the desert where the remarkable Zosimas was deemed worthy to see the Egyptian woman who was equal to the angels.[153] Beyond the mountains stretches the desert leading to Sinai, Raithu and the Red Sea. My account of the desert should end at this point.

26. The monastery of the Georgians, the mountainous region, the house of the prophet Zacharias, the cave where John the Baptist was born, the rock which received the fleeing Elizabeth along with her baby

On the right edge of the holy city of Jerusalem, on the side of the tower of prophet David, is a ridge completely covered with vines, and the monastery of the Georgians has been erected in its lower parts. It is said that on the land on which it stands the venerable cross was cut. Beyond the monastery, one finds the region called 'mountainous', and rightly so because for a distance of many stades it is the most alpine of all the mountains. Around 14 stades from the Holy City is the house of the prophet Zechariah. After the Annunciation, the all-immaculate Mother of God arose and walked there in haste. She embraced Elizabeth and the baby in her belly leaped for joy, as if it was welcoming the Lord. Then the Virgin uttered that remarkable prophetic song.[154] There is also a castle at this place and a church built over a cave. The birth of John the Baptist took place inside the recesses of this cave. Near the cave, where the mountain gets higher, about two bow shots away, is the rock which split and received the mother of the Baptist. She had been running away, with the baby Baptist in her arms, during Herod's massacre of the Innocents.

27. The road that leads to Bethlehem, the Monastery of Prophet Elijah, the tomb of Rachel, the city of Bethlehem, the cave in the field where the shepherds heard the 'glory to God in the highest', the holy cave and the manger, the well from which David desired to drink

Outside of Jerusalem, between the two roads, one leading to the 'mountainous' and the other to the Monastery of the Cenobiarch and the Lavra, is a ridge with a road on it which takes you from Holy Sion to Bethlehem. The city of Bethlehem is about six miles away from the Holy City. Half way between the two is the Monastery of the holy prophet Elijah. It had been erected by god-loving men in quite ancient times, but completely collapsed in an earthquake. Nevertheless, the universal benefactor, my lord and emperor, built it from scratch through [the oversight] of its abbot, a Syrian. And so, the area between the monastery and Bethlehem forms

---

152 2 Kings 2:11.
153 Mary of Egypt was a former Alexandrian courtesan who in c.400 went to live as a hermit in the Palestinian desert, where Zosimas encountered her.
154 The Virgin sang 'My Soul doth Magnify the Lord', later known as the Magnificat. Luke 1:40–55.

a triangle due to the tomb of Rachel which is sheltered by a four-vaulted domed building. On the left edge of holy Bethlehem, between the latter and the Monastery of the Cenobiarch, one sees a field and in it a cave. This is where the blessed shepherds rested with their herd and heard the angelic hymn, as the angles sang 'Glory to God in the highest, peace on earth and salvation to the world', on the birth of my God from the Virgin Mother of God.[155] As regards Holy Bethlehem, it was founded on a paved ridge. It contains the sacred cave, the manger and the well from which David longed to drink. A church sits upon the wide surface of the cave; one can see that it is of great size and length. It is roofed by imperishable wood in the shape of a cross, save for the altar's roof which is an artificial stone vault. This most beautiful and immense church was also built by the world-saving and munificent hand of my emperor and had it decorated all over with golden mosaics. The Latin pastor in charge of this region forthwith rewarded the emperor for his generosity by setting up his fair portrait in many places in the church and on the very altar which is above the holy cave. The layout of the cave, the manger and the well is as follows. On the left of the sacrarium is the entrance of the holy cave and close to it is that well from which David, the forefather, desired to drink both literally and spiritually. Two men, who were invested with great authority by him, cut through the enemy lines, drew water in a small pitcher and offered it to David who was burning with thirst. He spilled it to the ground as an offering to God, and he is still praised today for having accomplished a renowned feat of temperance.[156] From the cave's entrance to its bottom is a descent of 16 steps. Towards the north part of the cave is the holy lodging where the Virgin gave birth to Christ the Saviour, and the whole creation saw God in flesh, the whole world was renewed, and I, a mortal man, am enriched from the divinity of my God and Creator, the one who impoverished himself to [the level of] my [mortal] deficiency. Descending a step, one can see the manger of the animals, square in shape. The people of more distant times covered it with white marble and made a navel-shaped aperture in the middle, from which a part of that same manger is visible. It contained the Infinite One, who was wider than the sky, and much more spacious than the earth, the sea and the subterranean regions. For even though all the latter could not contain Him, the manger comfortably accommodated him when he was an infant.[157] I am overjoyed as I write, and in my mind I am actually inside this holy cave. I see the veil of the birth of Lord, He who became an infant lying in the manger, and I am astonished by the love of Christ for me, and by the wretched poverty of the manger, through which he deemed me worthy of the kingdom of heaven. On the other hand, I think of the cave as a palace, of the Lord sitting on the Virgin's lap as if on a throne. I also see choirs of angels surrounding the cave and the magi bearing gifts for the Lord. I am filled with every kind of joy, and I delight in my understanding of the magnitude of the grace of which I have been deemed worthy. In this cave, the craftsman has

---

155 Luke 2:14.
156 2 Samuel 23:15–17; 1 Chronicles 11:17.
157 A recurring theme in Byzantine theology was the paradox of Almighty God allowing himself to be contained in the narrow compass of human flesh and, in this case, an animal's feeding trough.

painted with an artistic hand the mysteries which took place in here. For in the apse, of this cave where the great mystery of the world [occurred], the Virgin has been drawn reclining on a bed. She places her left hand below her right elbow, inclines on her cheek with her right, and looks towards the baby. She manifests her inner chastity by her seemly smile and the fresh colour of her cheeks. For her face is not altered for the worse, like that of an ordinary woman who has just given birth and becomes pale, especially with her first child, because she who was deemed worthy to give birth in a way that surpasses the natural, should also have been spared the usual pains. Next to her are the donkey, the ox, the manger, the baby, and the flock of the shepherds. The ears of the latter had been filled by some kind of noise from the heavens which led them away from their sheep. Indeed, they leave them to consume the grass and the running water, entrusting the dog with guarding the flock. They raise their heads towards the heavens, turning their ears towards the direction of the sound. Each draws himself up in a different way, in a manner each thinks easier and less demanding. Some consider their staffs useless, because drawing back their right hands in the throwing position, they extend their hearing [here and there] in shock, while others fix their gaze towards the sky. Nevertheless, they need not listen twice, for eyes are more reliable than ears and because the angel meets them and shows them the baby lying in the manger. The sheep do not turn round towards the spectacle but in their simplicity move back and forth, some dropping their heads to the grass, the rest running off to the aforementioned spring. The dog, however, which is an animal hot-tempered towards strangers, appears to stare fixedly at the unusual sight. The Magi leap from their horses, bearing the gifts in their hands. They bend the knee and offer them reverently to the Virgin.

28. The cave in the Monastery of the Cenobiarch where the Magi received a divine message and returned home via another road, the Monastery of St Chariton, the double tomb of Abraham in Hebron, the oak of Mamre

Approximately two miles outside holy Bethlehem, in the Monastery of the Cenobiarch, is the cave where the Magi received a divine message not to return to Herod, and went back to their country by another road.[158] Twelve miles beyond this Lavra, near the desert of Ruba, is the Monastery of St Chariton. A considerable distance away from the latter, is the double tomb of Abraham in Hebron and the oak of Mamre where the patriarch Abraham received the all-holy trio.[159] And so much for the description of sites from Acre, through Galilee, to the holy city of Jerusalem, and of the Jordan and the holy desert. The sites of the coastland are as follows.

---

158 Matthew 2:12.
159 According to Genesis 18:1–2, Abraham was visited by three angels.

29. The city of Arimathea, Emmaus, the region of Ramla, the Church of the Great Martyr George

Approximately six miles from the holy city of Jerusalem is the city of Arimathea where the great prophet Samuel was born.[160] Beyond the latter, about seven miles or farther away is Emmaus, a large city, situated in the midst of a valley, on a projecting ridge. Next, at a distance of twenty-four miles extends the region of Ramla. In it one can see a very great church of the great martyr St George. He was born in this area and competed in the greatest struggles of devotion to God. His holy tomb is in this place too. The church is rectangular and in the apse of the bema, under the floor of the holy table, one can see the small opening of his tomb sealed with white marble. It is also important to recount the things we heard from the priests of the church that took place at the holy tomb several years ago. For they affirmed that the present Latin bishop, who was wrongly appointed, attempted to open the mouth of the tomb secretly.[161] When the slab which sealed it had been removed, a great cave was discovered, on the inner part of which the tomb of the saint was found. Then, when he attempted to open secretly this as well, fire was seen leaping out from the tomb. It left one of the Latins half burned, and the other was burned to death instantly.

30. Caesarea Philippi

After this region comes Caesarea Philippi, a large and populous city which has been founded on the seashore. There is a harbour in it, wonderful in every way, constructed by human craft. The munificent hand of Herod [paid] for its construction with an abundance of money.[162] In this city, Christ asked the Apostles 'Who do people say the Son of Man is?' and Peter replied to him 'You are the Messiah, the Son of God', demonstrating in this way his ardent love.[163]

31. Mount Carmel, the Cave of Prophet Elijah

After these regions is Mount Carmel which is often talked about in the Old and New Testament. It is a mountain range which begins from the very bay of Acre and Haifa and extends as far as the boundaries of Galilee. Near the far end of the range, the one towards the sea, is the cave of prophet Elijah, where that marvellous man spent his life in accordance with the instructions of the angels and was raised to Heaven. In the past, there used to be a large monastery in this place, as one can deduce from the ruins of the building which are still visible. Nevertheless, it has

---

160 According to I Samuel 1:1, the prophet was born in Ramathaim-Zophim, which was later identified with Arimathea.
161 Presumably Bernard, former abbot of Mount Tabor, who was bishop of Lydda and Ramla from 1168 to c.1190.
162 Caesarea Philippi (modern Baniyas) is in fact far inland and was not founded by Herod the Great but his son, Herod Philip II. The author may be confusing it with Caesarea Maritima.
163 Luke 9:18–20.

been utterly laid waste by time, by which everything grows old, and by the successive raids of the various infidel peoples. Some years ago, a Calabrian who was a monk, a priest in rank, with grey hair, came to reside here as a result of a vision he had had of the prophet. He fixed a small enclosure in this area, namely in the ruins of the monastery, built a tower and constructed a small church. He also gathered about ten brothers and now lives permanently in that holy place.

32. The End

I should end the book of my description here, now that I have completed the circuit of the holy places. If those who read this book truly find it useful, I shall regard this as a reward for my toil and a profitable prize. If otherwise, let my child return to me, its creator, and remind me of these holy places by its defective speech, so that we can gladly delight in remembering them.

V The Third Crusade

The death of Manuel I in 1180 was followed by a period of instability. His son Alexios II succeeded but as he was still a child, his mother Maria of Antioch headed a council of regency. In 1183, Manuel's cousin Andronikos seized power, murdering Alexios II, Maria of Antioch and numerous other prominent individuals. Andronikos was in turn overthrown in 1185 by Isaac Angelos, who was then crowned emperor as Isaac II.[1] Events in the Latin East were equally turbulent. In the summer of 1187 Saladin, sultan of Egypt and Syria, destroyed the army of the kingdom of Jerusalem at Hattin. In the months that followed, he occupied the coast south of Tripoli and on 2 October secured the surrender of the Holy City. Of the kingdom of Jerusalem, only the port of Tyre now remained in Christian hands. In response to the news, on 29 October 1187 Pope Gregory VIII issued the crusading bull *Audita Tremendi*, calling for a concerted effort to retake Jerusalem. One of the first European monarchs to respond was the German emperor Frederick I Barbarossa who took the Cross at Mainz on 29 March 1188. Planning to take the same route to the Holy Land via Constantinople as the First and Second Crusades had, he entered into negotiations with Isaac II with a view to agreeing the route and supply arrangements. He crossed the River Sava into Byzantine territory with his army on 1 July 1189.[2]

42. Niketas Choniates: Frederick Barbarossa in the Balkans (1188–90)

As in his account of the Second Crusade, Choniates is critical of the way in which the Byzantines dealt with Barbarossa's army as it passed through the Balkans. In this case, however, he was much better informed because he was an eyewitness. As governor of the town of Philippopolis, modern Plovdiv in Bulgaria, he found himself in the path of the oncoming German army and in receipt of contradictory orders from the emperor in Constantinople.

---

1 On Isaac II Angelos (1185–1195), see PBW (2016): Isaakios 1. On the events leading to his accession, see Brand (1968a), pp. 31–75; Harris (2022), pp. 127–44.
2 On the events that followed, see Brand (1968a), pp. 176–88; Harris (2022), pp. 149–64.

DOI: 10.4324/9781003015345-7

152 *The Third Crusade*

Choniates (1975), pp. 401–17:

It was impossible for a single month to elapse without inflicting some kind of public evil upon us, as if God had destined days without peace to rush in on our people. For as if the fighting with the barbarians all around us was somehow not enough for a proper chastisement, another peril, beyond our boundaries, burst in upon us, Frederick, the king of the Germans. He sent an embassy to Emperor Isaac so as to request, for the sake of friendship, that he might march through Roman territory on his journey to Palestine, along with the entire army under his command. In addition, he requested food and drink to be made available for purchase and asked the emperor to communicate his views on the matter to him by dispatching his own ambassadors in reply.

[402] Thus, the logothete of the drome, John Doukas, was dispatched to him, giving and receiving assurances that if the king passed through Roman territory, without resorting to fighting and without inflicting any kind of harm to cities, villages, citadels or forts, then the Romans would make abundant supplies available to him, so that his army would experience no shortages. On the contrary, it would have everything with which humans and horses are provisioned, available to consume on the spot without any difficulty.3 Sometime later, the logothete returned and announced the agreement to the emperor. The emperor took measures for the gathering of supplies and by his command they were to be transported at once by the provincials to the locations through which the king was expected to pass.

As soon as Frederick reported that he had passed the Roman borders, he exchanged with the emperor by means of noble men letters which communicated his presence according to what had been agreed.[4] Once more, the same logothete was dispatched along with Andronikos Kantakouzenos to supervise the king's passage carefully. Being ignorant of their duties, however, and because of their indolence, they managed to enrage Frederick against the Romans and to demonstrate to the emperor misguidedly that Frederick should be considered as his enemy (for it is our duty to regard truth as more important and dear than these men, even though they are our friends). The oaths were, therefore, violated and the offering of supplies ceased. We who narrate these events experienced many grievous things since we were assigned with the administration and assessment of taxation of the *thema* of Philippopolis. One day, during these hard and perilous times, we were commanded by the emperor to rebuild the walls of Philippopolis as well as to dig a moat and we carried this out. Nonetheless, a few days later, we were warned by letters to destroy them so that Philippopolis could not be used as a base by Frederick.

Frederick, of course, secured supplies for himself by raiding, while the emperor did not allow the king's ambassadors to return to their master. He thought fit to block the narrow passes [403] by cutting down with axes those trees which were

---

3 John Doukas Kamateros, one of the emperor's closest advisers, met with Frederick at Nuremberg in late 1188. See Brand (1968a), pp. 100, 176–9, 183, 209.
4 Frederick's army crossed the River Sava into Byzantine territory in July 1189.

tall and deep-rooted and by piling them up as an impassable bulwark against Frederick. He also ordered his cousin, Manuel Kamytzes, for he was a protostrator, and the domestic of the West, Alexios Gidos,[5] to shadow the Germans and to attack unexpectedly those who collected fodder and searched for food. So much did the barriers in the defiles, made out of felled trees, hinder Frederick, that he bypassed them without trouble. Smartly enough, he marched along another road, reached Philippopolis and set up a fortified camp in front of the city. Since he passed on the opposite side, he escaped the notice of the Romans and appeared from the other side, occupying the places from which he was to be kept away and for the sake of which the passes had been blocked.

Entering Philippopolis, he found it emptied of most of its inhabitants and of [all] the most notable ones. If anybody was left behind, he was either a beggar, who owned no more than the clothes he stood up in, or an Armenian. For only the latter regarded the passing of the Germans, not as a barbarian raid, but as the arrival of allies, since Germans and Armenians are on friendly terms and in agreement with one another on most of their heresies. For the worship of holy icons is prohibited equally among the Armenians and the Germans and they both use unleavened bread in their religious ceremonies. Erroneous in their teachings, they uphold as lawful additional practices which orthodox Christians reject.[6]

Although Frederick had occupied Philippopolis, he did not cease sending letters to the protostrator, underlining that the Romans had impeded his passage for no good reason and that they should not hinder him from his urgent goal, because he had not planned anything unprofitable and unpleasant for the Romans, either in the past, or now, [404] and that he had kept his side of the agreement intact. When the protostrator revealed the content of the letters to the emperor and received his orders as to the correct course of action, he was never told anything about concluding a peace treaty. Instead the emperor urged him to prove himself as a man in an engagement against Frederick and reproached him for his laziness, because hitherto he heard no reports about the destruction and defeat of the Germans who roamed in companies of a few hundred men in search of provisions and who spread out in broad herds here and there with as much boldness as possible. He had written such things because he believed in the [words] of Patriarch Dositheos as if they were divine prophesies, namely that Frederick never intended to capture Palestine, but that he nurtured the desire and the impulse to attack the Queen of Cities. Supposedly, Frederick was destined, beyond doubt, to enter the city through the so called Xylokerkos postern gate.[7] He would do abominable things at first, but then we would suffer equally through the righteous judgement of God. Influenced by such false opinions, the emperor accordingly barricaded the Xylokerkos with lime and baked bricks, and holding newly forged arrows in his hands, he would often

---

5 See PBW (2016): Manuel 20114 and Alexios 20103.
6 Choniates is in error here: neither the western nor the Armenian Church forbade the veneration of icons, though both used unleavened bread in communion.
7 Also known as the First Civil Gate or the Gate of Belgrade, the Xylokerkos lay to the north of the Golden Gate in Constantinople's Land Walls.

154   *The Third Crusade*

say that he would sharpen them so as to fix them in the hearts of the Germans. He also pointed to a side door in the Blachernae palace, from which one could see the plains located in Philopation which are just outside of the walls and suitable for horsemanship, and claimed that he would release his missiles from that place so as to shoot and knock down the Germans. All who heard the aforementioned words were moved to laughter.

[Choniates now digresses to tell the story of how Dositheos, formerly patriarch of Jerusalem, came to be patriarch of Constantinople in 1189–91. The translation resumes when he returns to the Third Crusade.]

[408] The protostrator followed the imperial orders and distrusted the words which Frederick wrote to him.[8] He wholly devoted himself to inflicting continuous harm on the Germans while they were wandering around for the gathering of firewood. On one occasion, in fact, having picked about two thousand men, with good horses, arms and amour, he resolved to march by night to the vicinity of Philippopolis, to lie in ambush in the nearby hills and to attack the enemy detachments which were out for supplies early in the morning. He himself proceeded to implement this course of action, but, as if inspired by God, he commanded that the pack animals, the army servants and the rest of the army which was with him should come with us. The daylight had not yet dawned and the Germans were informed about the protostrator's plans by the Armenians in the fortress of Prousenos (where the imperial army was stationed). The very same night, they detached more than five thousand heavily armoured men from Philippopolis and made haste to attack us. They were not detected by our army's scouts and advance guards, nor did they encounter the protostrator's picked men. Since the protostrator had marched to the areas near the mountains, where there were villages still full of provisions, he had taken cover in the hills, to avoid being spotted by his prey. The Germans marched confidently along the level road leading to the Roman camp. [409] Since the enemy found no adversary, they inquired and learned that the army's baggage train would return that very afternoon and that the protostrator, along with his best men, would attack those of the Germans who carried food back to their barracks. Without awaiting orders, they turned their horses, resolving to be found by those who were seeking them.

Therefore, while the Germans were descending the nearby hill, which rises near the fortress of Prousenos, our men were ascending it and they came to close quarters with each other unexpectedly. When they engaged in battle, almost all the Alans, under the command of Theodore Branas, son of Alexios,[9] fell, since they were the first and the only ones to hold their ground against the Germans. The Romans, on the other hand, ran away headlong and ignobly, unable even to face the enemy directly. Since the protostrator retreated by another route, his whereabouts were unknown to us for some time. Not until the third day, did he manage to return.

---

8   i.e. Manuel Kamytzes.
9   Theodore's father, Alexios Branas, had rebelled against Isaac II in 1187 and been killed in a confrontation with troops led by Conrad of Montferrat. The Alans were a nomadic people from the northern Caucasus who were occasionally recruited as mercenaries for the Byzantine armies.

He was very thankful and delighted for having barely escaped from the hands of the enemy, as if he had returned to port from a distant open sea, still spitting out the bitterness of battle and still hearing, fresh in his memory, the piercing cries of the Germans, who had been sent forth so as to capture him. Many men returned to the camp without their horses and weapons, since their animals could not bear the intensity of the flight.[10]

After these events, Germans and Romans became separated from each other, moving away a distance of more than 60 stades. For the Germans still remained in Philippopolis, while we, having reached the boundaries of Ohrid, remained quiet, thinking only of how to save ourselves. I will confess this as well: we acquired food by plundering imperial territory.

When this news was announced before the emperor, it hardly convinced him to give way without second thought. Shortly after, we arrived at the court and described in detail everything which had taken place. [410] We also explained that, according to the Germans, the Roman emperor had decided to neglect his vows to western Christians only because he had concluded a treaty with the ruler of the Saracens and both had slit a vein in their chests, offering one another to drink the blood which shed from there, in accordance with their prevailing custom of friendship.[11] We were able to overcome his opposition.

Consequently, the emperor reversed his former intention and longed for Frederick's crossing to the east. Perceiving, however, that Frederick had postponed his crossing until the spring because the season was turning into winter (for it was November when these events took place), the emperor, in turn, persisted in his former mindset. Sending a letter to Frederick, he predicted that he would be dead before the days of Easter, an action which is unbecoming in an emperor.

I am not referring to the events that occurred in the meantime, for they merit more blame than praise to say and to do them. With great difficulty, the emperor was persuaded to permit the ambassadors to return to Frederick. When Frederick met his ambassadors, he learned that the emperor had not provided them with seats. On the contrary, they had stood before him being perceived as subordinate as the Romans.[12] In addition, the emperor had not deemed them worthy of any other special benefit, even though they were bishops and Frederick's relatives. Because of that, Frederick was clearly vexed and infuriated. Therefore, when our ambassadors arrived before him, he asked both them and their servants to take a seat beside him, leaving not even the cooks, grooms and bakers standing. When our ambassadors pointed out that it was improper for the almighty emperor to sit along with servants (for it is sufficient if their masters sit in council), Frederick did not trim back even a little on his intention, but even though they were unwilling, he sat them down along

10 The battle took place on 29 August 1189.
11 This passage is sometimes read literally as a reference to an undertaking supposedly given by Isaac II to Saladin that he would impede the progress of Frederick's army. However, Choniates makes it clear that he is reporting only a rumour among the Germans. See Harris (2022), pp. 149–56.
12 The released ambassador reached the German camp on 28 October 1189. It was a Byzantine custom that everyone should remain standing in the presence of the emperor.

156 *The Third Crusade*

with their masters. He followed this course of action so as to mock the Romans and to demonstrate that there was no distinction of virtue and birth among them, since the Romans kept everybody standing, just as the swineherds drive their sows into the sty all at once, without separating for slaughter the ones which are fat and can yield more in return.

[411] After a short time had passed, Frederick was compelled by the shortage of supplies to divide his army. Consequently, he marched to Adrianople but left his son and his bishops behind in Philippopolis along with a considerable number of troops with the following words. 'You should rest here until you recover your legs and knees which were paralyzed and weakened by standing before the emperor of the Greeks'.[13]

When winter had passed and the flowers had begun to give off their scent, the emperor and the king renewed their vows. On their side, Frederick's lords and dignitaries confirmed by oath that the king would march through Roman land by following the imperial road, neither passing through farms and vineyards, nor deviating to the right or to the left, until he crossed the Roman borders. The emperor, for his part, offered some of his relatives as hostages. Inside the Great Church, five hundred notaries and imperial courtiers swore that the emperor would keep the treaty inviolable and that he would provide the Germans with guides and supplies.[14]

At that time, some of the judges of the velum, who were to be dispatched to Frederick as hostages, did not comply and, being unable to resist the emperor and to remain in their homes, they secreted themselves, without second thought, in some obscure corner of other people's houses until Frederick had crossed to the east. The emperor was furious because of this and instead of the judges of the velum, he dispatched notaries as hostages. He granted the estates and the dwellings of those who had disobeyed him to whoever he preferred and nominated other judges. Later, when he realised that their deeds were caused not by disobedience but by reasonable apprehension, he restored their properties and deemed them worthy of their previous judicial rank. After the agreements had been concluded, the emperor sent to Frederick four hundred pounds of silver coins and splendid gold-woven fabrics, [412] and Frederick matched the emperor's gifts with presents of his own. Afterwards, a great many cavalry-transport ships were brought to Gallipoli, since both the emperor and Frederick agreed that the latter would be ferried over with all his men in two voyages. For he feared that the Romans would violate the treaty and attack those who crossed over on the opposite side in frequent intervals. Thus, Frederick arrived at the East in no more than four days.[15]

When he approached Philadelphia, Frederick did not even pass through the city but while he was departing from their district, the boastful inhabitants changed their stance to a hostile one and attacked a division of his army so as to plunder it. Because their intentions did not succeed, since they recognised that they engaged with bronze statues or giants, they turned their assault into a flight. The Germans

---

13 Frederick entered Adrianople on 22 November 1189.
14 The treaty was concluded on 8/9 February 1190.
15 The crossing in fact took rather longer, 22–28 March 1190.

marched through the area called Aetos and encamped in Laodikeia in Phrygia.[16] There, they were most warmly welcomed and treated with honour as never before. The Germans, and especially Frederick, implored for all the people of Laodikeia all the benefits given by God. For he raised his hands towards the heavens, lifted his eyes upwards, bent his knee on to the ground, and begged God, the Protector and Father of all, to send down to the people of Laodikeia all that is useful for life and delivering for the soul. 'If the land of the Romans had an abundance of such Christians', he said, 'and welcomed the soldiers of Christ with such a friendly spirit, the latter would gladly have bestowed their riches on those who peacefully offered provisions and they would have crossed Roman borders long before, without tasting Christian blood but carrying their sleeping lances in their sheaths'.

When they undertook the march inland, they realised that the Turks were by no means kindly disposed towards them. They too kept away from a face to face battle and practiced robbery in every possible manner they could. Yet they had, just like the Romans, agreed that the Germans would pass through their country without battle, that they would provide everything, as much as the travellers would need, and that no harm would come to them if they preserved the treaty. [413] Now, the Germans, relieved of empty hopes, bestirred themselves for open battle. And so, near the castle of Philomelion, Frederick engaged in battle with the sons of the sultan of Ikonion. They had dismissed their father from his rule and deprived Ikonion of the prosperity it had once possessed, transforming it into miserable old age. Frederick turned them to flight easily, besieged Philomelion, and set fire to it.[17]

In addition, Frederick engaged the Turks at the place known as Ginklarion and prevailed once more. Since the Turks had occupied the mountain passes in advance and kept watch there for the arrival of the Germans, Frederick encamped on level ground, for he had perceived the enemy's plan. During the course of the night, he divided his troops into two parts. He ordered one division to wait at their tents, and commanded the other to prepare for a withdrawal by following a different road, as soon as daylight began to show itself. Thus, the Turks perceived this guile as a genuine course of action and, full of joy, they abandoned the defiles. They arrived at the plains and invaded the German camp, heedless and delighted, since the loot which they would get in that place, set as an unexpected gift of luck before their eyes, was abundant and precious. For every single barbarian is greedy for gain and for money he says and does many, or all things. When the Germans who had withdrawn returned, those in the tents came out to fight courageously. The Turks were surrounded and took the road which led to death.[18]

Frederick became famous and an object of awe among the eastern nations, not only because of the two aforementioned battles, but also because he inflicted to

---

16 Frederick arrived at Laodikeia on the Lykos on 29 April 1190.
17 The battle took place on 2 May 1190. Five years earlier, Kilij Arslan II, Seljuk sultan of Ikonion, had partitioned his sultanate between his ten sons to ensure that none of them was unprovided for when he died. The arrangement did not work well and in the winter of 1189–90, the sultan's oldest son, Kutb al Din Malikshah, ejected him from Ikonion.
18 The attempted Turkish ambush was foiled on 3 May 1190.

158   *The Third Crusade*

the Turks the same disasters at Ikonion. For, on the one hand, the sultan, who had earlier escaped at Taxara,[19] alleged in his defence that he knew nothing of what his sons did and that he was ejected from his office by one of them, Kotpatinos.[20] [414] On the other hand, the Turks slipped into the gardens' ditches and canals, which were everywhere throughout Ikonion, and surrounding their gardens with stones like a wall of defence, they expected to check the march of the Germans to the city. They were all excellent archers, assembled into one place, fighting lightly-armed against heavy cavalry on rough ground. Their plan, however, once more fell into the void. For the Germans, after they had seen the Turks entering the walls of their gardens and shooting their arrows, as if from a fort, did the following. Each cavalryman raised a heavily armed footman on his horse and, with their mounts as thresholds, placed the infantry on top of the enclosures where the Turks had drawn up in close order. From this place, they left them to engage in close fight with the Turks and they also came to their aid whenever it was possible to charge with the horses. And then, most of these evil men had perished in evil way, while the rest escaped harm by scattering. We are certain about the great number of casualties from an enemy testimony as well. A certain Muslim, who was present at this battle, went over to the emperor and, having taken an oath on his religion, reported that he had paid two hundred silver coins for the removal of the corpses of those who had been slain in his garden.[21]

After the Germans had seized Ikonion, they did not enter the city centre but encamped in the so-called suburbs pitching their tents on housetops. They took for themselves nothing but the absolute necessities of life and they departed from that place.

Rumour has it that during this expedition a certain German, huge in stature and irresistibly strong, was left a great distance behind from his compatriots. He took the road on his tireless feet, leading forward from the bridle his horse which had been worn out by the march. [415] More than 50 Muslims assembled around him, all excellent men who had broken their ranks. They trapped him in a circle and shot arrows at him. The German, however, took cover behind his broad shield and trusting in the impenetrability of his armour he advanced cheerfully proving to be as unshaken against the enemy missiles as a headland or a bulwark. Consequently, one of the Muslims announced that he would do something braver than the others. He put away his bow since it was ineffective, drew out his long dagger, allowed his horse to gallop and undertook to fight on equal terms. The Muslim inflicted to the German as much damage he would have inflicted to a mountain ridge or a bronze statue. The German drew his heavy, mighty and sturdy sword with his huge and courageous hand, and struck the horse across both its front legs and cut them off more easily than grass on a farm. The horse, therefore, fell on its knees still bearing the rider fixed on the saddle. The German stretched out his arm and struck with the sword on the middle of the Turk's head. The stoutness of the sword and the bravery

19 Modern Aksaray.
20 i.e. Kutb al Din Malikshah.
21 Frederick's army entered Ikonion on 18 May 1190.

of its bearer resulted into so wondrous a strike that the smitten man was cut in half. The horse too suffered harm, in its back, since the blow scattered the saddle away. The rest of the Turks were amazed at this sight and no longer had the courage to fight with him in single combat. So much for the Turks. The German, on the other hand, trusting as a lion in his own might,[22] did not accelerate his march but, walking on foot he joined up with his compatriots at noon, at the place where they had encamped.

They say that the Muslims were afraid that Frederick might remain in their country, since he had already prevailed over them. Consequently, they displayed false amiability toward him and considered how to appease him. [416] After Frederick had received from the Muslims the headmen's elder sons as hostages and had accepted many guides for the roads, he crossed the territory of the Turks. Shortly after, when he reached Armenia, he killed many by the sword and sent back the rest.

After he had received an honourable welcome by the Armenians and had remained with them for many days, he began his march to the city of Antioch. He acquired great fame for his shrewdness and his invincible army and encountered no resistance along his way. When, however, he reached a certain river (how unforeseen and unexpected fortune is, or rather God's judgments which are beyond human grasp!), he was drowned in its water's eddies.[23] He was a man worthy of a perpetual and blessed memory and of being considered worthy of a blessed end with good reason by sensible men. For not only did he come from a noble family and ruled many peoples as a third-generation heir, but he had a burning love for Christ greater than any other Christian monarch of his time. Quitting his homeland, royal luxury and leisure, and his blissful and splendid home life with his loved ones, he preferred to endure adversity with the Christians of Palestine in defence of the name of Christ and of the honour of the Life-Giving Tomb. Having chosen the foreign land over his own, he did not slacken his onrush with regard to the long march, consisting of many and difficult roads of all kinds, and to the danger from the various states, through which he was about to pass. Neither the scanty water nor the fixed ration of bread, which had to be bought and was sometimes harmful, slackened his will. Nor did his children's shedding of tears, their embraces and their last farewells trouble or soften his soul. Instead, just like the apostle Paul, without regarding his soul as of exceptional value, he pressed on, not only devoting himself to the name of Christ, but also dying for it. [417] The man's zeal was, therefore, apostolic; his goal was pleasing to God and his success more than perfect. Those who lift up their minds towards uphill way of life of the sublime Gospels and strive earnestly towards the latter all the way through, generally despise worldly matters as useless.

I am sure that this man met a blessed end. His son assumed the command of his father and entered Antioch.[24] From this place, he reached the more distant Coele

---

22 See Homer (1919), i. 228 (*Odyssey* VI. 130).
23 Frederick drowned in the River Saleph on 10 June 1190.
24 Frederick, duke of Swabia, Barbarossa's eldest son, reached Antioch with the army on 21 June.

160   *The Third Crusade*

Syria and captured Laodikeia since it had rebelled and gone over to the Muslims.[25] He forced terms on Beirut without trouble and subjugated many other Syrian cities which had formerly been subject to the Latins but had joined the Saracens at that time. When, however, he had reached Tyre and had laid siege to Acre, which was occupied by the Muslims, he suffered greatly for the name of Christ and died there.[26] The remainder of the army did not attempt to undertake its withdrawal by the landward route, because they had observed the distrust of the polities they had crossed. They gained possession of merchant-ships, which belonged to their fellow western peoples and which had put into the port of Tyre, and safely returned to their own countries.

43. Niketas Choniates: Epiphany speech to Isaac II (1190)

Choniates' account of the passage of Barbarossa's army in 1189–90 was written some years later and possibly revised after 1204. Doubtless, with Isaac II now dead, he would have felt free to voice criticism that he would have had to stifle at the time. The extract that follows, on the other hand, was written as these events were taking place: an encomium delivered in front of Isaac II on 6 January 1190 when the German army was still in the Balkans. That accounts for the laudatory tone although it is possible to discern some criticism of Isaac's policy under the surface.[27]

Choniates (1972), pp. 85–91:

By Niketas Choniates, speech to the emperor lord Isaac Angelos. It was written by Niketas Choniates when he was secretary to the logothete and read at the feast of the Epiphany since there was no rhetor. Frederick, the king of the Germans, was marching to Palestine at that time.

[85] Because it was unfitting, God proved that he did not deem it right to disregard Roman rule which, full of loose wrinkles, has long been aging, and to continue to ignore that it was bent down towards the earth. His most excellent deed of love towards humanity was to render Roman rule upright and young again and to restore it like that weak woman in the Gospel whom Satan had possessed for many years.[28] Thus, He married her to a young and valiant emperor and now behold, she blooms and rejuvenates, [86] stripping off old age like the trunk of a palm and a leafy tree when they catch the scent of water after having formerly shed their leaves and died back over the years!
  [. . .]

---

25 The town captured by Frederick of Swabia was Laodikeia on the Orontes, not Laodikeia on the Lykos in Asia Minor mentioned previously.
26 On 20 January 1191.
27 For a discussion of this speech, see Angelov (2006) although his assumption that Isaac II had a military alliance with Saladin should be treated with caution.
28 Luke 13:11–13.

[88] It would have been a true deliverance and to the benefit of all if you could have taken the crown earlier. Since, however, God did not approve of this, we had to go through fire and water first, namely through the calamities for which Andronikos was mostly responsible, so as to experience relief.[29] [89] We had to be content with this since you appeared before us at the most appropriate moment. You came like a beacon showing the way through the night and like a fair wind to the sailors who struggle manfully and sweat on the oars. As soon as you came, you subdued the great sea monster. This unapproachable and crooked little old man who mostly swam underwater and who proved that he focused on this ebbing life and on nothing beyond the visible. The Queen of Cities herself was in danger of being devoured by this monster, much like Andromeda with the mighty beast of the sea in the ancient times. The ruling metropolis would have sunk into water in these great jaws and nothing would be seen and heard of it, had you not came to our aid by God's will, just like [Perseus] did for that virgin girl,[30] had you not, like him, marvellously shielded yourself and attacked the abominable beast. Having ripped its unwelcoming belly open, you put it to death and saved the city from impending ruin.

[...]

You put the most beneficial sword in your mighty hands, and you fought so as to fall for all, laying down your life for us. Thus, just like Christ, you redeemed us with your own blood, and even though you did not fall, you fought like one is about to perish. Where is this sword which slew the tyrant? I want to see it and to embrace it![31]

Behold another tyrant! The ruler of the Germans, an old man, master of many evils, and as fond of perjury as the other tyrant. He is accustomed to say one thing and to hide another in his thinking,[32] and covering up his leopard skin with that of a lion, he disguises his grudge against us with the mask of piety. For donning all colours, just like the chameleon, he only avoids white and prefers not to reveal his innermost intention. Let the same sword come for him as well, [90] or rather, what is written with God's help be said: behold, here are two swords[33] one which ruins tyrants and the other perjurers. For I see that this sword originates from the heavens too and is slowly becoming a mighty, heavy and sturdy scythe.[34]

[...]

---

29 Choniates is referring to the brief and turbulent reign of Isaac's predecessor, Andronikos I (1183–5).
30 In Greek mythology the hero Perseus rescued Andromeda, daughter of the king of Ethiopia from the sea monster Cetus.
31 There are numerous Biblical allusions in this speech. These sentences echo John 10:11; 2 Corinthians 5:14; Revelation 5:9 in reference to Isaac II's dramatic seizure of power in September 1185. It began when he charged out of his house on horseback, brandishing a sword, and killed Stephen Hagiochristophorites, one of the henchmen of Andronikos I.
32 An echo of the words of Achilles in the *Iliad*. See Homer (1924), i. 416–7 (*Iliad* IX. 313).
33 Luke 22:38.
34 Choniates is probably referring here to the Byzantine eschatological tradition where the last Roman emperor initiates a period of peace and prosperity, transforming swords into scythes and sickles. See Kraft (2012), p. 241.

[91] As if you had made a covenant to have God as your ally in your battles and always to devise victory after victory for you, He has hitherto not ceased to march in line with your battle order. He begins from Constantinople, as it were from some kind of centre, and He shows forth the rays of your triumphs which spread equally in every direction. There is no cardinal point in this world which did not see you achieve brilliant victories.

For the South saw how the Sicilian triremes harmed us but suffered even more miserably themselves. Famine, thirst and raging battle emptied the ships of their sailors, and all the triremes were either destroyed by violent winds or sank to the bottom with all their crews.[35] The West witnessed how the well-armed Latin league was mown down like grass in a field. It saw how those who boasted that they would erase Roman cities from memory, much like an abandoned nest or forsaken eggs, were slaughtered like cattle. When the harvest was plentiful but the workers few,[36] a fine harvest naturally took place during the winter. Alexander the Macedonian desired to be a winter reaper when he crossed to Asia, inspired by Homer's poetry.[37] On that day, to put it subtly, one could experience the fulfilment of the prophetic words: every valley shall be filled up, and every hill be made low. For the valleys were filled by the dead and the hills sank from the lying corpses. If you were fond of barbarian bragging, it would have been possible for you to count by the bushel the rings of those who fell at that time, to bridge the river Strymon at Amphipolis with the bodies of the fallen, and to demonstrate all your good fortunes by such standards as the Egyptians measure the fruit- and wheat-giving Nile as well as the impending harvest by cubits.[38]

[. . .]

[93] Thus, in the blink of an eye you have been glorified through your remarkable deeds, because you achieved faster than a thought and largely by improvisation, victories which were accomplished by the ancients with effort and time. Many times, you prevailed just by appearing and on other occasions you struck down the enemy after you had terrified him with a simple report and written exposition of how things are. Is it not remarkable that through your triumphs, which my speech has celebrated in a summarised form, you have prevailed against all warlike peoples?

[. . .]

Who does not know that the fast-sailing Sicilian ships and the tens of thousands of the heavily armoured cavalry were called up from the very best of the western families throughout their lands? The Italian knight, skilled with his lance, the brave

---

35 A reference to the mauling of the Norman fleet that raided the coast of the Sea of Marmara in November 1185. See Brand (1968a), pp. 171–2.
36 Matthew 9:35–8.
37 Alexander the Great crossed the Dardanelles into Asia to begin his conquest of the Persian empire in May 334 BCE. Plutarch (1914–26), vii. 262–3 (*Life of Alexander*, XV), describes how after crossing Alexander made his way to Troy to lay a wreath on the tomb of Achilles.
38 Isaiah 10:14, 40:4 is quoted here in reference to the Byzantine victory over the Normans at the battle of the Strymon on 7 November 1185. See Brand (1968a), p. 171.

Celt, and the lofty Teutons were there, and so were those who drink from Arethusa and live in the Ionian gulf.[39] At that time, you were to us a gentle rain falling on grass, but to the enemy, a rushing stream bursting out and inundating the splendour of the nations. We washed off water with water, the briny ranks of the enemy with that which lives in you and wells up so as to give life.[40]

[94] I am persuaded that, since you have laid such solid foundations for the rule of the Romans, huge compared to those white stones with which Solomon once built his renowned temple, you will add to it the most appropriate crowning roof and that you will repeatedly repay sevenfold into the bosom of our wicked neighbours, the Persians. You will deal with them the hard way, as they had dealt with us so that it may be clearly proven that God has aided a man of might and exalted a chosen one from his people, and that the enemy shall not outwit you, nor shall the son of lawlessness inflict harm on you in any way. Then, dashing the children of the barbarians against the rock, you will reach the same blessedness as David.[41] A Nissaean and an Arab horse will carry the Roman knight. The centuries-old Roman phalanxes will draw water from the Euphrates, drink from the Tigris and dine between the rivers. As you bathe your hair with great joy in the Jordan, you will be toughened in manliness, like the dipping of a red-hot iron into the water, and you will not merely reconnoitre Palestine, but having expelled the barbarous nations from there, you will settle the Romans and divide its land among them, as Joshua once did with the people of Israel.[42] Because you, the soaring eagle, who turn all eyes to yourself, ought to spread your wings towards the place where Christ restored the fall of nature with his fall, and, flying down on them, scare away the Persians like on croaking ravens, just with the whirring of your wings.

[. . .]

[99] Emperor, brace yourself, prosper and rule! May your left hand seize all your enemies and your right all those you hate you! As you bathe in the streams of the Jordan, may you be spiritually renewed like the eagle,[43] and emerging more fair from there, much like this natural sun rises from a magnificent lake, may you emit more bright rays against the mass of clouds which overshadow your kingdom! The clouds had risen from the West and stood firm before us, flashing the lightning of war through their frequent agitation. May they be dispersed like smoke by the wind and like rime by a storm! Shatter their bows, smash their weapons and consume their shields by fire more adeptly than once Phaethon [burned] the land around the river Eridanus which is now inhabited by the Germans![44] [100] Or even better,

---

39 i.e. the Sicilian Normans. The nymph Arethusa gave her name to a spring on the island of Ortygia, near Syracuse.
40 These sentences echo Deuteronomy 32:2, Isaiah 66:12 and John 4:14.
41 Psalms 79:12, 89:19, 22, 137:9 and Lamentations 1:22 are referred to in this section.
42 Joshua 14:1–15.
43 Psalms 21:8, 45:3–4, 103:5.
44 Here Choniates employs a mixture of Biblical and mythological allusion: to Wisdom of Solomon 5:14 and to Psalms 46:10 as well as to the legend of Phaedon, son of the sun god Helios, who drove his chariot too close to the earth, scorched it and turned parts of it into desert. Zeus struck him down with a lightning bolt and he fell into the river Eridanus.

punish the pride of the arrogant, doing so in imitation of Christ! For when the Saviour had risen out of the water after baptism, he immediately hastened into the desert accompanied by the Holy Spirit, and he repulsed the temptations of Satan, who asked Him to turn the stones into bread and insisted that He fell down and worship him through this act of reverence.[45] In the same manner, after you have been cleansed by this sanctifying water (or if you prefer by the water of your tears, since you bathe in them every night as David did),[46] and after you have become a companion of God and spoken to him face to face, due to your way of life which is free of morbid emotions, uncover the deep hidden aspects of the leader of the German legions! He is darkness and pretends to be light. Being destructive and a murderer from the beginning, he asked in good faith that stones be transformed into bread. Through these, he longs for the unattainable, and exceeding every righteousness, he attempts to steal away the submission of your imperial majesty, like another act of reverence. He does not know that, after his first or second attempt, he will be repulsed and that he will return defeated and humiliated, having acknowledged by experience his master, whom he attempted to entrap. May you halt the present flood of enemies by thundering their waters which sweep over us or by stretching like a celestial bow. As soon as this sea and this Jordan river, which symbolize the enemy army and the man appointed to its command, see the remarkable things which God did for you, let the army avoid storming into battle (for the holy book explains that its chariots are like a whirlwind), and the commander turn about and refrain from his ruses. If otherwise, the waves of this sea, rising up to heaven will pour down to the deepest earth and the Jordan will flee punished, fearful of the sound of your thunder. If you have let God inside you due to your divine virtues, we may not merely say that He is with us through you and will subject [to us] barbarian and war-desiring peoples, but also that you may be called the son of God, as Jacob and David.[47] [101] If one is very pious like those two, [he is God's] son and beloved, and if he is the beloved one, God is pleased with him in every way. If this is the case, then he is certainly the heir to the earthly rule as well as to the immortal and pure one in the next world.[48] As far as possible, may you last as long as the sun, Godlike emperor, and be restored for eternity like the moon. May your throne be eternal ever-succeeded by your sons, and your empire long-living.

44. Niketas Choniates: Richard I's Conquest of Cyprus (1191)

As well as Frederick Barbarossa, the king of France, Philip II Augustus, and the king of England, Richard I, took the Cross in 1188–9. They chose to convey their armies to the Holy Land by sea rather than by following the land route via Constantinople.

---

45 See Matthew 4:3, 9.
46 See Psalms 6:6.
47 David is referred to as son of God in Psalm 89:26–8.
48 There are numerous Biblical allusions in this passage: Genesis 9:13; Job 12:22; Psalms 69:2, 104:7, 26–6; Jeremiah 4:13; Daniel 2:22; Matthew 3:17; John 8:44.

Nevertheless, they were to have an impact on Byzantium. In May 1191, Richard I landed with his army on the island of Cyprus, which was then being ruled by Isaac Komnenos, a rebel against the authority of Emperor Isaac II. The king proceeded to conquer the island, which was never again to form part of Byzantine territory.[49] Choniates gives only a very short account of these events.

Choniates (1975), pp. 417–8:

At that time, it was not only the Germans who campaigned against the Saracens that had occupied Palestine and pillaged Jerusalem. The king of France and the ruler of the axe-bearing Saxons, now called the English, assembled a very large number of ships from Sicily and the land of Italy, loaded them with grain and other supplies, and sailed to Tyre.[50] The Crusaders used this city as a harbour and a base for their campaign against the Saracens. Nevertheless, they were also unable to drive them out of the holy city, and leaving their assigned task unrealised, they took the sea route back to their own countries.[51]

[418] During his voyage, the king of the English disembarked in Cyprus and captured both the island and its despot, or rather its inhuman and irreconcilable destroyer, Isaac Komnenos. At first, when he had laid hold on him, he had put him in chains, but after a while he expelled the wicked man from the island and, like a spoil of war, he gave him as a gift to an Englishman.[52] The king then sailed to Palestine and by dispatching cargo ships into the island he levied supplies from there as a tribute. For he had already claimed Cyprus as his own and left an army there. When he was about to depart from Palestine, he gave the land of Cyprus, as if it belonged to him, to the king and ruler of Jerusalem, so that the king would establish his residence there, and continue to abstain from hostilities, due to the fact that he had lost his own principality.[53] The king of Jerusalem would rule the Cypriots as if the latter were attached by him to the tomb of Christ and the borders of the island were united with those of Palestine. That is how things took place.

45. Neophytos: On the calamities of Cyprus (1191)

A longer account of Richard's conquest of Cyprus is given by a hermit called Neophytos (1134–c.1220), who lived in a cave near Paphos and was a prolific author. The account takes the form of a letter to a spiritual son, someone to whom Neophytos was giving religious instruction, so not surprisingly, his main concern here

---

49 On the conquest of Cyprus, see Harris (2022), pp. 146–7, 160–4.
50 Philip II Augustus of France arrived in the Holy Land on 20 April 1191, Richard on 8 June.
51 Philip left the Holy Land in August 1191. Richard stayed longer and, after defeating Saladin at Arsuf, concluded the treaty of Jaffa with him in September 1192.
52 Neophytos in [45] is more informative about Isaac's fate.
53 Richard initially sold the island to the Knights Templar for 100,000 gold pieces, 40,000 of which were handed over. When the Templars withdrew from the island, Richard sold it again, this time to the king of Jerusalem, Guy of Lusignan.

is to draw out the moral lessons of the episode. It should be borne in mind too that Neophytos was not one of the classically educated courtiers of the capital, so his work is written in much simpler language than that of Choniates and lacks the latter's frequent references to mythology and ancient literature.[54]

Neophytos (2005), pp. 405–8:

1. A cloud covers the sun and a fog the hills and the mountains. Due to the latter two, the bright ray of the sun and its warmth has been kept away from us for some time now. Because for twelve years, a cloud and a fog of successive calamities which have taken place in our land has surrounded us. For after Jerusalem had been conquered by the ungodly Saladin and Cyprus by Isaac Komnenos, in addition to the cloud and the fog, the land which the aforementioned men ruled, was covered with battles and wars, upheavals and tumults, pillage and terrible events. For behold! On account of our sins, the life-giving tomb of our Lord and the other holy places were granted to the Muslim dogs. Every devout soul weeps for this calamity. As it is written, the peoples were in uproar and the kingdoms humbled.[55] I am referring to those of Germany and England and almost all nations that marched in defence of Jerusalem and accomplished nothing. For providence did not consent to the dogs being ousted and the wolves let in instead. And behold! For twelve years the waves have been swelling for the worse.
2. Our very spiritual son, namely the man to whom we wrote these words, could not bear to see and to hear of the calamites and in part to endure them. By God's intervention, he escaped along with all his people from murderous hands with intelligence and guile. Then he went and appeared before [Isaac II] Angelos, the emperor of Constantinople. He was welcomed with honour and received from him the tile of sebastos. I am fulfilling my promise and thus I write the rest, with the help of God. Since I promised to reveal to my readers the present commotion of our affairs. Perhaps no man on earth knows when this commotion will cease, only He who rebukes the sea and the winds, and they become calm.
3. Strange and terrible calamities have taken place in this land. So terrible that all the local rich men forgot about their abundance of wealth, splendid houses, kinsmen, house servants and slaves, their multitude of flocks, herds, horses, all kinds of cattle, grain-giving fields, highly fertile vineyards and various gardens, and in all haste, they secretly sailed away to foreign countries and to the Queen of Cities. Of those who were unable to escape, who is able to reveal their distress, condemnation, common imprisonments, the weight of money demanded [from them] which reached to thousands and thousands [of pounds]? This was allowed to take place by God's fair decree due to the burden of our sins so that having been humbled, we may be deemed worthy of forgiveness.

---

54 On Neophytos, see Galatariotou (1991).
55 Psalms 46:6.

The Third Crusade 167

4. England is a country far away from the land of the Romans towards the North. From that country, a cloud of English along with their ruler embarked on large ships called *nakkai* and reached Jerusalem by sea. The ruler of the Germans marched against Jerusalem at that time as well, with an army of 900,000 men, as it said. But as he passed the district of Ikonion and as he was marching through the Eastern regions, the divisions were ravaged by thirst, hunger and the length of the journey, while their king was drowned in a river as he was riding his horse. When the accursed Englishman crossed over to Cyprus, he found for himself in the island a nourishing mother. Had it not been so, he would have suffered the same fate as the German. I will also briefly recount how Cyprus was conquered.

5. When it became necessary for the pious emperor Manuel of blessed memory[56] to send somebody as a guardian of the imperial fortresses of Armenia, he dispatched one of his kinsmen, a very young man named Isaac. After he had guarded the strongholds for some years, he engaged the Armenians in battle. He was taken captive by the latter and was sold to the Latins. The Latins held him in chains for quite some time. For emperor Manuel, his uncle, had passed away and left the empire to his son Alexios, who was also a mere boy. On account of this, Andronikos, his uncle, reigned jointly with him. He killed the young boy so as to take control of the empire.[57] After being persuaded by the senate's counsel, he sent a large amount of ransom and redeemed the aforementioned Isaac from the Latins. Isaac went to Cyprus, conquered it, and was proclaimed king. He ruled the island for seven years. Not only did he maltreat the land and completely plunder the property of the rich, but every [day] he persecuted and oppressed his own governors as well. As a result, everybody lived in despair and looked for a way to get rid of him.

6. While things were in such a state, behold the Englishman invaded Cyprus and quickly everybody rallied to him! Then, the king, having been left without subjects, surrendered himself into the hands of [the king] of the English. After he had put Isaac in fetters, thoroughly plundered his quite vast treasures, and looted his land extensively, he sailed to Jerusalem, leaving behind him ships to collect taxes from the land and to bring them to him later. He imprisoned Isaac, the king of Cyprus, fettered in irons, in a fort called Markappon.[58] This sinful man accomplished nothing against his fellow-sinner Saladin. He managed only to sell our land to the Latins for two hundred thousand pounds of gold. Consequently, as I have previously mentioned, the lamentation which came from the North was great and the smoke unbearable. Should one wanted to describe them in detail, time would fail him.[59]

7. The affairs of our country are in no way different than a sea driven mad by great waves and great storms. Actually, to put it better, they are worse than a raging

---

56 i.e. Manuel I.
57 Manuel I's son and successor, Alexios II, was murdered in September 1183.
58 i.e. in the Hospitaller castle of Marqab, near Baniyas in northern Syria.
59 Hebrews 11:32.

sea. Because after the rage of the sea comes tranquillity. In our land, however, the turbulence increases day by day and its fury knows no end, unless perhaps it received the command thus far you shall come and no farther, and your waves shall be contained within you.[60] The calamities which have befallen our land are explicitly mentioned in the book of Leviticus, namely wars, defeats, [and] sowing devoid of produce. The food of the enemy is the produce of our toil, our might has turned into nothing, we have become few in our land while the foreigners have grown in numbers. God said: Act contrary to me, and I will act towards you in a hostile way.[61] And that is how things are. For unless a man is filled with black bile after falling sick, the doctor does not apply a cut with harshness and cauterising. It is, therefore, evident that if we did not flagrantly disobey our beneficent doctor and did not behave contrary to him, he would not have been ill-disposed towards us, bringing bitterness to us for our salvation.

46. Ephraim of Ainos: The Third Crusade in the Balkans and Cyprus (1188–91)

Writing over a century after these events, Ephraim has clearly derived most of his information on the Third Crusade from Choniates. For some reason, though, he presents the German crusade as a great success, in spite of the deaths of Frederick Barbarossa and his son the duke of Swabia.

Ephraim of Ainos (1990), pp. 213–5:

Around the same time, the king of the Germans
[5965] dispatched envoys requesting the emperor
to grant him and his army safe passage
within the limits of Roman territory,
because he was rushing towards the land of Palestine.
Thus, the emperor sent the logothete of the drome
[5970] to the king and prepared the terms.
After he had received and in turn granted pledges of good faith,
so that the affairs of friendship may be established on firm ground,
the logothete quickly returned to the emperor.
The king reached the Roman borders
[5975] and then arrived at Philippopolis.
After arrangements, contentious disputes
and battles with one another, between
the imperial troops and those of the king,
the army of the Germans crossed the straits
[5980] and arrived at the city of Philadelphia.
Through Phrygia and Laodikeia,
he marched very quickly to Philomelion

---

60 Job 38:11.
61 Leviticus 26:23–4.

where the king engaged in battle with the sultan.
The king worsted him and captured the town,
[5985] which he set on fire, after he had plundered it.
Then he reached the city of Ikonion
and he obtained it by the law of battle and weapons.
Afterwards, as he was marching on the path which lay ahead,
heading towards the city of Antioch,
[5990] he was drowned, trapped by the water's whirlpools,
Alas, from the judgments of God!
His son assumed his authority
and reached Antioch.
From there, he marched against the cities of Syria
[5995] and set them free from the sons of Hagar.
After he had accomplished many things in the name of God and for His sake,
he too passed away in Syria.
The Germans returned safe and sound
by ship to their country again.

[6000] In their turn, the king of Frankia and the ruler of the Germans[62]
campaigned against the sons of Hagar with ships and men at arms,
but they did not manage to drive them out
from Holy Zion and to allot it to the Christians,
and sailed back again to their homeland.
[6005] The king of the English disembarked on Cyprus
and took it by storm with weapons.
He detained and put in fetters the tyrant of Cyprus,
Isaac Komnenos, who was just like Echetus.[63]
When the king of the Germans, namely of the English,
[6010] sailed south towards Palestine,
he left an army of his in Cyprus
and ruled over it as if it were subject to him,
acquiring from it the resources for life.
As he was about to return to his homeland,
[6015] he offered Cyprus to the king of Palestine
to reside there whenever he took a rest from fighting
and to control and rule the land of the Cypriots,
as it was his wish that the island would be assigned
to the life-giving tomb of Christ
[6020] and united with the borders of Palestine.

---

62 i.e. Philip II Augustus of France and Richard I of England.
63 The mythical Echetus was a particularly cruel king of Epirus, described by Homer as a 'maimer of all men'. See Homer (1919), ii. 206–9, 332–3 (*Odyssey* XVIII. 85–7, 116 & XXI. 307).

47. Theodosios of Byzantion: Philip II Augustus visits Patmos (1191)

The monk Christodoulos (d.1093) founded the monastery of St John the Theologian on the Aegean island of Patmos during the reign of Alexios I and was subsequently venerated as a saint. This encomium was written in his praise sometime after 1191 by an otherwise unknown monk from Constantinople called Theodosios. In its account of the miracles performed by Christodoulos' corpse long after his death, it tells the story of a visit supposedly made by the French King Philip II Augustus to Patmos, when he was travelling back from the Holy Land in September 1191. That would have involved a slight diversion from Philip's route, which is known to have been via Rhodes, Crete and Corfu, but his fleet did encounter a storm off the coast of Asia Minor, which might have driven him north to Patmos. The king's attempt to steal some of Christodoulos' skin may seem farfetched but the practice of *furta sacra* or sacred theft was widespread and occurred on a huge scale in the aftermath of the capture of Constantinople in 1204.

Theodosios of Byzantion (1884), pp. 163–208:

By the Monk Theodosios of Byzantion, Laudatory Speech to our Pious Father Christodoulos, the founder of the Monastery on the island of Patmos, named after the favourite disciple of Christ our Saviour, a virgin and a theologian, and a narration of the miracles which Christ performed on Christodoulos' account in the reign of the devout emperor Lord Isaac Angelos.

39. And why should the Lord perform such great miracles against the Sicilians through the pious Christodoulos because they were sinners, but overlook the endeavours of others to inflict similar harm on us? Or to neglect to strip up the sea around the island against those who attempted to remove what should remain in place and to enrage it in our defence?[64] It is not in the least possible. Did anyone plan to harm the monks when attacking the island? Our champion was most eager, [the sea] was commanded to assist us at once, its rage was irresistible, its weapons were mighty, its threat caused fear sparing not even kings, as indeed happened. In the year 6696 Jerusalem was conquered by the Ishmaelites, by the judgment of God, its Latin ruler was driven away from there.[65] A league was put together consisting of the three strongest Latin nations so as to expel the slave and the apostate by arms and force from the inheritance of the Lord and Master of all. To pass over the events there since they do not contribute to the purpose of the present work, the leader of North France, I mean the Frank, who is customarily called the king, was in some sort of disagreement with the other one, namely of a more

---

64 Theodosios is referring to events in 1186, when the Aegean islands were being raided by a Sicilian Norman fleet until it was scattered by a storm. See Choniates (1984), pp. 200–1; Vranousi (1966), pp. 71–4, 142–8.
65 i.e. on 2 October 1187.

The Third Crusade   171

distant land who rules over towards the limits of the earth.[66] In addition, after he had been weakened by an illness, since he was marching over a foreign and unfamiliar land and was unaccustomed to such bodily conditions, he hastened to return to his customary habits and to his kingdom. Having left Palestine, he sailed towards the Ionian Sea and the islands of the Cyclades. After he had brought his ships to the port of Patmos, he disembarked and came up to the monastery so as to revere the esteemed church in it and the relic of Christodoulos, the servant of the Lord.[67] For the reports about the wonders of God against the Sicilians for the sake of the saint reached him too. It was September when these things took place, the tenth Roman indiction of the year 6700.[68]

40. And so, when the king arrived, as it has been said, he made an atonement towards God with prayers in the Latin manner, and worshipped the relic of the pious man according to the custom of his country. Then, he handed to the monks a silver vessel as a gift and thirty Saracen gold pieces. Through his interpreter he declared to the monks that he would give them many more gold coins, as many as they desired, if only they agreed to hand over a part of the blessed man's relic. For he argued that he had a very strong desire to acquire a piece of the relic of the pious man for blessing. The monks did not find his proposal acceptable even with the tips of their ears and they rejected both the presents that they had been given as well as those which had been promised. After the king had returned to his ships and sailors, he dispatched, under the pretext of veneration, one of his audacious men to cut off some part of the blessed venerable dead man with his ravenous teeth, even though the monks were against it. The daring man, in line with the instructions of his dispatcher, came up, performed this sacrilegious play acting, cut off the skin of a finger tip of the pious man, joyfully reunited with his gleeful dispatcher, and handed over the very small piece of stolen skin.

41. But justice was not likely to keep silent on account of this theft, nor was the Lord of all to neglect the defence of his devoted servant. And so, around the time of the second night watch, when men were finally overcome by limb-relaxing sleep, there was a dead calm. [Then took place] a most remarkable thing. Even though the sea was at a rest, or rather deep asleep, a turmoil fell upon the harbour and a whirlwind threw the ships into great confusion. It ended the aforementioned deep sleep of those who were resting. The disaster before their very eyes was about to cause them complete mental confusion, because it was huge; it burst in without anyone expecting it, and without cause to those who observed it. By that time, it threatened to crush all the ships and there was no contrivance to counter, calm and tame it. For the waves which came after the profound calm were most fierce; who of those in trouble would expect it to die down? Consequently, they remained stunned, expecting to suffer the very worst and to descend into the bottom of the sea on the spot. The king then, tried to find out the cause of so strange a storm (for

---

66 A reference to Philip's well-known antipathy to Richard I of England, which had led to the French king's premature departure from the Third Crusade.
67 St Christodoulos' tomb can still be seen in the church of St John the Theologian.
68 i.e. 1191.

sharp minds are quick to comprehend that which brings benefit), and realised that what produced the extraordinary character of the tempest was nothing other than the offence against God and His servant Christodoulos because of the removal of the skin which covered the holy bones of his fingers. He commanded the man who had done the deed to take with him immediately the part which was cut off, to travel on the road which led towards the monastery as fast as his feet allowed, and to confess his sin to the monks as soon as he arrived there. He was to place what he had despoiled on the same part of the body from which he had removed it, in the presence of all, and to beg the holy man to no longer be angry with them, who had committed this sin out of love for him and not out of contempt. After the king had given these instructions to that insolent man who had dared to act with hot-headed youthfulness against the saint, he commanded more of his men to ascend to the monastery as well. As soon as they took the road which led to the monastery, the strength of the waves out of nowhere began to decrease. When they entered the monastery and the daring man confessed his sin to the monks, the storm ceased, the harbour returned into its accustomed state and to the calm, neither roaring contrary to the laws of nature, nor threatening to sink the ships into the sea. In the presence of the monks and his company, the sinner opened the chest of the relics of the blessed man, and delivered the small piece of the despoiled finger back from where he had removed it, or rather snatched it away. At once everything came to a rest, the unnatural calm, the harbour, the ships, the hearts of the afflicted, the king who had ordered the man to steal, and the man himself who had dared to perform such an impossible and totally fruitless theft.

VI The Fourth Crusade

Isaac II was overthrown, blinded and imprisoned in April 1195 by his brother who replaced him as Alexios III. Three years later, on 15 August 1198, the Fourth Crusade was launched by Pope Innocent III, with a view to the recapture of Jerusalem. In the light of the experiences of the Third Crusade, the leaders of the new expedition decided to make Egypt their initial goal. Having conquered the country, they would use its resources to retake the Holy City. An agreement was made with the Italian city state of Venice to provide ships to transport the army and it began to assemble on the Venetian Lido in the spring and early summer of 1202. In the event, the plan was never put into effect and the expedition was to take a very different route.[1]

48. Niketas Choniates: The Fourth Crusade comes to Constantinople (1203)

Choniates takes up the story, displaying deep hostility to Emperor Alexios III Angelos. The historian also distrusted the Venetians and was clearly convinced that they were behind the plan to divert the crusade fleet to Constantinople.

Choniates (1975), pp. 538–66:

[538] The Venetians, however, recalled their old treaties with the Romans and [could] by no means bear to watch their privileges pass over to the Pisans. Little by little they clearly distanced themselves from the Romans and planned to take vengeance at an opportune moment, and even more so when they saw that Alexios [III], because of his stinginess, refused to pay them the two hundred pounds of gold that remained unpaid from the total debt of fifteen hundred which emperor Manuel had agreed to give to the Venetians since he had confiscated their money for the public treasury after he had arrested them.[2]

---

1 On these events see Phillips (2004), pp. 56–101; Harris (2022), pp. 173–5.
2 The Venetians had long enjoyed special privileges in the trade with Constantinople, including exemption from customs duties and their own commercial quarter alongside the Golden Horn. In March 1171, however, Emperor Manuel I had abruptly ordered the arrest of all Venetians in Byzantine territory and had their property confiscated. His successors, in need of Venetian naval and

DOI: 10.4324/9781003015345-8

174 *The Fourth Crusade*

In addition, the doge of the Venetians at that time, Enrico Dandolo, was a grave threat.³ Although he was a blind old man, he was a creature most treacherous and envious of the Romans. Even though he was a cunning cheat, he called himself wiser than the wise and was inspired by glory like no one else. He thought death his proper recompense, if the Romans did not pay for their insulting behaviour to his people, for he wondered and calculated in his mind how many evils the Venetians had been exposed to when the Angelos brothers were emperors, and before them Andronikos and earlier still, when Manuel held the sceptre of the Romans. He knew that he would undermine his authority if he practiced some kind of treachery against the Romans with his own people alone, so he thought to obtain more accomplices and to share with them his secret [plans], namely, those whom he knew felt irreconcilable hatred towards the Romans and enviously and gluttonously coveted their fortune. The opportune moment arose of its own accord when certain high-born nobles began to make plans for Palestine. He united them in the common enterprise and won them over as fellow conspirators for his insurgence against the Romans. These men were [539] marquis Boniface of Montferrat, count Baldwin of Flanders, count Hugh of St Pol and count Louis of Blois and many other daring warriors who took pride in their stature which was as long as their lances.⁴

Consequently, after three full years, 110 cavalry light transports and 60 warships were built in Venice, while huge merchant ships, more than 70, were also assembled. One of these was called *Universe* because it surpassed the others in size greatly. One thousand knights clad in full iron armour and 30,000 infantry, which included a very large number of heavy infantry and especially the so-called crossbowmen, were ordered to embark on them.

When the fleet was ready to be put to sea, trouble after trouble fell upon the Romans and, as the saying goes, wave after wave dashed upon them. For Alexios, the son of Isaac Angelos, was supplied with letters from the Pope of Old Rome and from Philip, king of Germany, which promised the greatest favours to this gang of pirates, should they take up with Alexios and restore him to his paternal imperial rule.⁵ After some time, Alexios was gladly put in charge of the fleet which considered him not only the man to disguise and reshape a naval operation of plunder against the Romans as something well-founded and justified, but also to appease their greed and avarice with heaps of money. Therefore, since they were all cunning

---

    commercial support, restored the privileges and offered compensation for the losses but Alexios III was apparently dragging his feet in paying up.

3 Enrico Dandolo was chief magistrate or doge of Venice (1192–1205).

4 Boniface, marquis of Montferrat, had been elected as leader of the Fourth Crusade in June 1201. Baldwin, count of Flanders, Hugh IV, count of St Pol, and Louis, count of Blois were prominent members of the expedition.

5 Alexios Angelos, the future Alexios IV, escaped from Constantinople to Italy in October 1201. He travelled to the court of the king of the Germans, Philip of Swabia, choosing this destination because Philip was married to his sister Irene. He also visited Pope Innocent III in Rome although Choniates errs when he claims that the pope encouraged the Byzantine prince. See Geoffrey of Villehardouin (2008), pp. 20–1; Brand (1968a), pp. 275–6.

men and fond of strife, they accepted Alexios, who was as immature in his thinking as in his age, and persuaded him to come under oath to an agreement with them which was by its nature impossible to fulfil. [540] For the lad agreed not only to their request for seas of money, but also to campaign with them against the Saracens with heavily armed Roman units and 50 triremes. The most significant and improper thing, however, was that in deviation from orthodoxy, which is embraced by the Latins, he agreed both to the abnormality of papal privileges and to the change and alternation of the established tradition of the Romans.[6]

The fleet untied the stern cables, sailed to Zara, disembarked there and laid siege to it, according to the wishes of Dandolo, the doge of Venice, because it had supposedly violated ancient treaties.[7] Alexios, the emperor of the Romans, even though he had been informed of the hostile plans of the Latins a long time ago, took no measure to strengthen the Romans. For his extraordinary laxity was equal to his slackness in matters of duty and public interest. Let me just tell you that when his advisors proposed that he take measures for an abundance of weapons, make plans for the preparation of war engines, and above all else see to the construction of warships, they took him for a dead man. He was to be seen engaging in after dinner laughter, as if he deliberately showed reluctance to act on the reports about the Latins. He occupied himself with lavish rebuilding of bathhouses, removal of hills for the creation of gardens, restoration of ravines, and rashly wasting time on these and other similar activities. The eunuchs who had charge of the thickly wooded mountains, which were kept untouched for the imperial hunt like sacred groves or like a paradise planted by God, kept a watch for those who wanted to cut any kind of timber suitable for shipbuilding and violently threatened them with death. [541] The emperor did not rebuke these foolish guardians; he was captivated by their chatter and gave his consent.

After the Latins had set a garrison at Zara, they disembarked at Dyrrachion and Alexios, the one who accompanied them, was proclaimed emperor by the people of the city.[8] [Emperor] Alexios [III now] perceived the reports about the Latins as genuine; he became the proverbial fisherman who recovers his right mind after he had had a shock.[9] Consequently, he began to repair the partly rotten and mostly worm-eaten small ships, barely twenty in number, and, surveying the walls of

---

6 As well as promising the Venetians and the crusaders a huge financial reward if they would restore his father, Isaac II, to the throne, Alexios undertook to end the schism between the Byzantine and Catholic Churches by recognising the authority of the pope. See Geoffrey of Villehardouin (2008), p. 26.
7 The fleet sailed from Venice in October 1202 and attacked and captured the Dalmatian port of Zara, modern Zadar, on 24 November. This action was on the insistence of the Venetians to whom the crusaders still owed a large amount of money for the hire of the ships. Zara had recently thrown off its allegiance to Venice and Dandolo agreed to postpone the payment of the debt if the crusaders forced the city to return to the fold.
8 The fleet reached Dyrrachion in May 1203. See Geoffrey of Villehardouin (2008), p. 31.
9 Possibly a reference to the fable where some fishermen were at first delighted when hauling in their very heavy net, only to be downcast to find that it contained nothing but stones. The oldest among them, however, soon recovered and advised that they must expect reversals of fortune in life. See Babrius and Phaedrus (1965), p. 424 (13).

the City, he commanded the destruction of the buildings which were outside the fortifications.

The [Latin] fleet sailed from Dyrrachion and blockaded the island of Corfu, delaying their voyage from that place for twenty days. Since they realised that the citadel was hard to attack, they spread their sails straight for Constantinople.[10] For the Westerners had long known that the emperor of the Romans was preoccupied with nothing else but intoxication and drunkenness and that Constantinople was another Sybaris, widely celebrated for its wantonness.[11] Since it happened that they had an unexpectedly fair voyage (for the sea breezes were constantly gentle and blew to fill the sails of their ships), they reached the City almost unnoticed. [542] After they had put in at Chalcedon, on the other side of the straits, east from Peraia and a small distance below the Double Columns, the large ships and the smaller ones soon arrived [at Constantinople] by oars and by sails respectively, and anchored a little more than a bowshot away from land.[12] Last but not least the dromons put in at Skoutarion.[13]

The Romans appeared on rising ground nearby, occupied the shores and fired missiles at the ships. Their shots, however, were utterly ineffective since most of them could not cover the distance and fell into the sea. Another detachment took position on the area north of Damatrys so as to hold in check the advance of the Latin cavalry. These men did not accomplish anything advantageous either though. For not only did they refrain from striking against the enemy, but rather dispersed and withdrew once the Latins attacked them.

After a few days, the Latins realised that there was nobody to resist them on land and they approached the shore.[14] Consequently, the corps of cavalry rushed forth a short distance from the sea, while the warships, the dromons and the merchant ships moved to the bay which ran inland. When both the cavalry and the ships attacked the fortress, to which the Romans usually bound the heavy iron chain whenever an enemy attempted a naval assault, they immediately overcame its defences. It came to be that part of the garrison was to be seen abandoning its post after offering a token resistance [543] Some were killed or captured, while several climbed along the chain, like some kind of well-rope, and embarked on the Roman triremes. Many, however, missed the chain and fell straight to the deep water. Then, after the chain was broken, the entire fleet streamed inside. Some of our triremes were overpowered on the spot and others, pushed towards the City's shore, were

---

10 The fleet departed from Corfu on 24–25 May 1203. See Geoffrey of Villehardouin (2008), pp. 32, 354.
11 In ancient times, Sybaris in Sicily was renowned for its inhabitants' luxurious way of life.
12 The fleet reached Chalcedon, modern Kadıköy, on the opposite side of the Bosporus to Constantinople, on 24 June 1203. See Geoffrey of Villehardouin (2008), pp. 35, 354. Peraia, now Hasköy, stands on the northern shore of the Golden Horn and the Double columns or Diplokionion was roughly where the Dolmabahçe Palace now stands.
13 The fleet moved to Skoutarion or Chrysopolis, modern Üskadar, on 26 June 1203. See Geoffrey of Villehardouin (2008), p. 36.
14 i.e. they crossed from the Asian to the European side of the Bosporus on 5 July 1203. See Geoffrey of Villehardouin (2008), pp. 41–2.

holed throughout after their crew evacuated them. The damage took many forms that a man's mind cannot fully comprehend. The date was July of the year 6711.[15]

[Choniates now describes how the crusaders moved up the Golden Horn to Blachernae and set up a position before the Land Walls of the city. On 17 July, they began an assault on the walls while the Venetian ships attacked the sea defences across the Golden Horn. Alexios III led a large army out of the Land Walls to confront the attackers but then inexplicably retreated before his numerically inferior enemies. The next day, he was found to have fled the city during the night. The courtiers promptly released Isaac II and restored him to the throne.]

[550] At once Isaac dispatched messengers to his son Alexios and to the leaders of the Latin army and revealed the flight of his brother, the emperor. The Latins, however, changed neither their plans against the City, nor dispatched Isaac's son to him when his father had requested them so, unless he agreed to fulfil all the arrangements which Alexios had agreed with them. The arrangements were, as I have stated above, that Isaac would omit none of the extraordinary agreements regarding doctrine and gifts which had been agreed with the Latins. [551] For Alexios, a thoughtless lad ignorant of reality, would do anything in order to succeed in ascending the paternal throne. He did not look critically at any of their claims, or take into account how hatred of the Romans is the Latin mentality. So by having subjugated the imperial crown, he purchased his entrance into the City; he was deemed worthy of sitting together with his father and of assuming the office of co-emperor.[16] Thus, all the citizens assembled at the palace to see the son with his father and to do obeisance to both.

A few days later, the leaders of the Latins visited the palace, not alone, but accompanied by men of distinguished Latin families. Benches had been set for them and all sat in council with the emperors. They were proclaimed benefactors and saviours and received every other noble title in recognition of the revenge they had taken on the power-loving Alexios for his inane deeds, and for coming to their aid when they were in trouble. That was not the end of it though; they enjoyed all sorts of kind treatment and gifts and experienced feasting and entertainments. For Isaac drained the imperial treasury and lavishly handed over both whatever little there was in it and whatever he had acquired after imprisoning Empress Euphrosyne and the distinguished men of her family.[17]

The beneficiaries regarded all this as merely a drop in the ocean, for they were constantly thirsting for all the waters of the Tyrrhenian Sea (since there is no other nation more greedy, voracious and consuming than this race). So, contrary to all legality, he laid his hands on sacred things. I think it was because of this that the affairs of the Romans were wholly overthrown and obliterated. For since there was a shortage of money, he had recourse to the holy churches. [552] One could see the holy icons of Christ cast down and chopped up with axes, while their decorations

---

15 The Kastellion tower on the northern side of the mouth of the Golden Horn was taken on 6 July 1203.
16 He was crowned as co-emperor Alexios IV on 1 August 1203. See Geoffrey of Villehardouin (2008), p. 51.
17 Alexios III's wife Euphrosyne was a member of the Kamateros family.

were carelessly and thoughtlessly removed by force and surrendered to fire. Moreover, the sacred and all holy vessels were snatched away from the churches without hesitation, set on fire and offered to the enemy troops as common silver and gold. This very frenzy against the saints was by no way perceived as such by the emperor himself, so that nobody spoke out about reverence. Yet, on account of our reticence or, to put it better, our lethargy we differed in no way from those frenzied men. Consequently, we suffered and witnessed so many of the most calamitous injuries because we were not blameless.

All the vulgar mob of the city, who did not support a praiseworthy course of action of their own accord, and who were not convinced by others who proposed a better response, unreasonably razed to the ground and reduced to ashes the dwellings of the western peoples located by the sea, without distinguishing friend from foe, for the enemy had already poured over the Roman districts. This misdeed and thoughtlessness annoyed not merely the Amalfitans, raised in the Roman manner, but also the Pisans who had chosen Constantinople as their home.[18] Moreover, before the Emperor Alexios [III] had been seen to flee, he had fed these peoples with high hopes and diminished much of their resentment. But when Alexios had fled and Isaac became emperor, the latter reconciled the Pisans and the Venetians and also contrived the following against us. [The Pisans] sailed across to Peraia where their opponents had been encamped and they became comrades and messmates with their former adversaries and agreed and united on all matters.[19]

[553] On the nineteenth of August in the sixth indication of the year 6711 some of the French (in the old days they were used to be called Flemings) were assisted by a company of Pisans and Venetians so as to carry away the money of the Saracens like a dish ready to be served or a gift about to be handed over. This wicked battalion put into the City on fishing boats for there was nobody who hindered them in any way from sailing against the City and in turn from sailing back from it. They treacherously attacked the synagogue of the Muslims, which is called Mitaton in the vernacular, and plundered what they could with their swords.[20] Since these unlawful acts took place so unexpectedly and beyond all anticipation, the Saracens defended themselves by arming themselves with whatever there was to hand. The Romans who had assembled there because of the reports of these misdeeds came to the assistance of the Saracens. They achieved far less than they hoped for but for a while the band of these men withdrew. Those who ceased holding their ground with weapons, now inclined towards inflicting a new conflagration on top of the one not long before, since they had learned from experience that fire is the best weapon and the most destructive of all when it comes to overpowering the City.

---

18 Like the Venetians, merchants from Amalfi, Genoa and Pisa had their own quarters inside Constantinople on the southern shore of the Golden Horn.
19 The Pisans were bitter commercial rivals of the Venetians and had fought alongside the Byzantines during the hostilities of July 1203. Now they were forced into the arms of their hereditary enemies.
20 The Mitaton mosque, which was used by visiting Saracen merchants, stood on the southern shore of the Golden Horn, outside the sea walls. The attack took place on 19 August 1203.

So they scattered over many locations and set dwellings on fire. Throughout the course of that night, the fire grew higher beyond imagination and spread everywhere for almost two days. The sight was unprecedented and totally surpassed any powers of description. As many other conflagrations had occurred in the City before, one cannot describe how many and how great they had been. This particular conflagration demonstrated that all the others had been nothing but small sparks. [554] For the flames, divided in many places and spreading out in different directions, then converged and formed into the trail of a fiery river. Porticoes were destroyed, the beauties of the forums collapsed, the massive columns were shattered as flammable brushwood. There was nothing mightier in this world than that fire. Even more remarkable though, was the fact that embers were detached from those roaring and stubborn flames. Carried by the wind, they burned up faraway buildings, since they were hurled over a great distance and stretched out in the sky like shooting stars. For a while, they left the intervening space untouched and unburned, but soon afterwards, returning to it, they overcame and obliterated it. Because the fire, advancing mostly in a straight course driven by a north wind, was soon diverted, as if a south wind dispersed it, and was perceived to take an oblique course, to destroy back and forwards and to consume everything which was thought to have been spared. The danger did not even spare the Great Church. Thus, all the buildings facing towards the Arch of the Milion and located next to the gallery of Makron and the so-called 'Synods' collapsed to the ground.[21] As baked bricks offered no protection, and deep foundations did not endure, everything was overwhelmed and met the fate of wicks on candles.

The first kindling of the fire began from the synagogue of the Saracens which is located towards the northern part of the City inclined towards the sea close to the church which is dedicated to the name of St Irene. Its lateral course towards the east subsided at the greatest of churches, while its spread towards the west extended from so-called district of Perama and then it expanded following the breadth of the City, halting its onrush at the southern walls of the City. The most extraordinary event was that while all this was happening and while the fire was spreading across the facades of the houses by leaping over them, embers were released and burned a ship which was sailing by. [555] The so-called colonnades of Domninos were also burned to ashes as well as the porticoed streets which began from Milion, with one of them leading up to Philadelphion.[22] The Forum of Constantine and everything south and north from it experienced the same fate. The Hippodrome itself did not remain unharmed, its whole section around the demes being destroyed by fire, including everything towards the [harbour of] Sophia up to Bykanon itself, and in turn everything neighbouring the areas of Eleutherios.[23]

Since the fire encompassed the City from sea to sea and divided it like a great chasm or river of flame flowing in its midst, it was dangerous to reunite with your

---

21 The Arch of the Milion and the Makron stood in the Augousteion square outside Hagia Sophia.
22 The Philadelphion took its name from a statue of emperors embracing fraternally which may be the one now in St Mark's Square, Venice.
23 i.e. the fire spread as far as Constantinople's southern shore on the Sea of Marmara.

loved ones, unless you were carried there by boat. At that time, the majority of the City's inhabitants were stripped bare of their properties. The fire consumed both the possessions of those who were caught off guard, and of those who transferred them to different hiding places. For the fire progressed in many twisting, rotating and returning motions, in the form of a spiral, and eliminated the goods which had been moved. Oh, these magnificent and fascinating buildings, laden with all kinds of charms and luxurious ways, envied by all!

Emperor Isaac and his son Alexios were not disturbed in the least by these terrible events. Yet the firebrands of our country, with blazing red faces, prayed for complete destruction, resembling in this manner the incendiary evil angel of the scriptures. [556] The fire had not yet completely ceased when the collection and melting down of sacred treasures was resumed, more so than before. The Latin army spent the gold and silver, bestowed on them in the aforementioned way for their bodily needs, as if it were profane metal and offered it to those who wanted to transact [with them]. Since they had received what was due, they proclaimed themselves blameless, although they were not ignorant of where their awarded money came from. Nevertheless, they brought down the wrath of heaven on the Romans because the latter cared for their own properties but defiled those of God.

Alexios also thought it necessary to secure the assistance of the Latin forces, because Alexios, his uncle and former emperor, departed from Develtos, captured Adrianople and he did not cease to covet and to struggle anew for the sovereignty which he renounced, he who had abandoned it to mad coveters. [Alexios IV] enticed marquis Boniface to lead a campaign with him, but only after Alexios agreed to pay him 1,600 pounds of gold.[24] Then he marched against Alexios and forced him to withdraw and to escape more rapidly and much farther than before. He made a circuit of the Thracian cities, so as to restore them to his rule, or to put it better, to plunder them since the army which accompanied him frequently desired to draw water from the golden streams, and could not satisfy itself, even though it was drinking, like those bitten by the venomous serpent whose bite causes intense thirst. He marched as far south as Kypsella, then returned to the palace, thoroughly dependent on this faction, those who had played their part, with Alexios his uncle, in rendering his father impotent and in overthrowing him from power.

49. Nikephoros Chrysoberges: Epiphany speech to Alexios IV (1204)

Nikephoros Chrysoberges (c.1160–c.1215) was prominent at the court of Alexios III and remained so after the emperor's flight and the restoration of Isaac II on 18 July 1203.[25] On 6 January the following year, Chrysoberges gave the traditional Epiphany oration before the emperor, addressing it to Isaac's son and co-emperor, Alexios IV. After his return from Thrace as described by Choniates [48], relations between Alexios and his former allies had deteriorated rapidly, when it became

---

24 Alexios IV and Boniface set out from Constantinople in late August 1204. Geoffrey of Villehardouin (2008), p. 54.
25 On Chrysoberges, see Brand (1968b), pp. 463–4.

apparent that the emperor would not be able to clear his outstanding debt. In late November, the emperor rejected the ultimatum sent by the crusade leaders and desultory hostilities began. Only a few days prior to Chrysoberges' speech, the Byzantines had tried to set fire to the Venetian fleet by sending fireships across the Golden Horn.[26] This encomium is a valuable source in that it was compiled before the sack of Constantinople in April 1204 and is therefore free of the hindsight that colours Choniates' account. Moreover, like many overtly laudatory speeches, there is an element of advice, possibly even criticism. In this case, the orator warns the emperor not to allow the crusade leaders to overawe him but rather to use them for his own purposes and those of the state.

Chrysoberges (1892), pp. 24–35:

Oration by the same author to emperor lord Alexios Angelos, son of the celebrated emperor Lord Isaac Angelos. It was read as is customary for orators in the palace of Blachernae at the feast of Holy Epiphany in the month of January, seventh indiction, year 6712.

[24] Emperor of great deeds, named after Alexander due to your boasting the same abilities and equalling him in prosperity.[27] I am your unskilled and wooden orator today, merely a soulless imitation of ancient rhetoric. Nevertheless, you had only to appear before me and profuse sweat poured over me. Anguish immediately broke through me from the moment that I opened my mouth. For indeed there is much sweat and labour for all historians and for the lips of all rhetoricians who wish to sing your praises. Where is the expressive Xenophon? He would have described your expeditions in a lively way and glorified your [25] restoration to the imperial throne.[28] He would have examined your youthful venerability, your virility and vehemence in your teenage years, and elaborated your successful journeys and transmigrations. Where is Thucydides the historian? He would have organised your naval and cavalry battles well with elegant techniques.

[. . .]

For you have taken your place on the throne as a newcomer, after living neither in the shade, nor in luxury as is usually the case with those who stay at home. Instead, you have travelled on many roads much like those who have great passion in their soul. You have honed your hands in the fire like iron for war and, hardened like a double edged [sword], you have arrived from there strong and tempered with the cargo of wisdom, [26] having gathered much of it from many cities just as those who are merchants are accustomed to do [. . .].

Of course, that was no ignoble contribution to your prosperity. For when the Italians offered to you their servitude and agreed to assist you, their voyage was

---

26 See Geoffrey of Villehardouin (2008), pp. 58–9.
27 i.e. Alexander the Great.
28 In his *Anabasis*, the Athenian soldier and historian Xenophon (c.428–c.354 BCE) described an expedition into Asia Minor in 401 BCE.

free from difficulty and the journey of their merchant vessels was easy. So many times, their cargo ships and their warships have attempted expeditions to these waters; but since they were not carrying your gentle [people] for your service, emperor, they were quickly stricken in the sterns and turned to cowardly flight. So many times, he who watches over Aquileia with great arrogance blackened his oared ferryboats and light war vessels with nautical coating, and after he had sailed beyond the Ionian Sea and crossed that of Malea, he nautically plied the dashing oar upon our waters.[29] Since, however, he was not serving Christ the Lord for your purposes, he was utterly repulsed and shattered on reefs and watersheds. But now that you, the mighty one, have marked all the Latin ships with your seal, as is fit for a lord, they sail quickly in waveless seas and cut through the calm flow of water. [27] Rendering service to you, they undertake the task of fulfilling your commands.

The legend about halcyons goes as follows. They are creatures which travel on wings but mate at sea. Until they are pregnant, the tumultuous sea remains calm, and they dwell and play around in gentle water.[30] Those who were present at the occasion of your voyage were able to observe the same phenomenon. Observing these sunny and bright days during which you set sail, one could appropriately call them halcyon days. Dipping the keel in the waters, the well-benched trireme was carrying you, and the other many-benched ships were following and attending like handmaid servants to a mistress. During this period the sea smiled and spread like a bed. It simply opened its watery arms and, one might even say, 'parted with delight'.[31] In the words of the poet, from every direction the dolphins and the seals leapt up from underwater, since they probably knew that you were the emperor. The winds at the stern resembled skilful soft-blowing trumpeters and gently guided the bow forward with western breezes.

Through these things you realised your majesty, oh Emperor, and you are able to tow along the foreign-tongued Italians. For you will surely teach wisely that the sea and the land are determined to accept them only in this case, when they are determined to fight side by side with you, and to defend you, the emperor chosen by God, under the laws of obedience. Above all, you will counsel them to be firm only when they serve so mighty a Roman emperor [. . .].

[28] Through such teachings, the mighty one, will exchange their boiling passion for submission. For surely, once and for all God thought it fit to glorify you again. Just as before, you were able to subject their brow and their fleet to your service, so God assembled for you all sorts of obedient servants from everywhere so that they do not swell their cheeks against us like Olympic champions, but lower their gaze as servants of Your Majesty. They should not be arrogant because they escorted you, oh Emperor. It was a matter of divine providence in your case. Instead, they should be subject to the laws of servitude, since they fulfilled their servile duties when they escorted the lord emperor.

[. . .]

---

29 Chrysoberges is referring to the Venetians and their doge here.
30 The halcyon was a mythical bird, sometimes identified with the kingfisher.
31 Homer (1924), ii. 4–5 (*Iliad* XIII. 29).

Let Solomon come from our court and assist me, and let him inform you about the sun. He reports that it travels to the south; it circles coming around to the north.[32] We witnessed you hastening from one place to another in such antithetical courses. Escaping from Constantinople to the southern part of Europe, you returned from there once more to this north, our very own, with gleaming radiance. Thus, after you had changed your direction from the western Adriatic to our Thracian Propontis you appeared as a rising star. Surely, it was necessary for you to bathe in the streams of the ocean, so as to shine brightly where you had bathed, just as they say of the sun when they see it [29] dropping into the sea towards the west. These might be the words of an orator narrating this explanation from the amusements of myths. I, on the other hand, refrain from describing the prodigious ocean as something greater than a natural thing, and devote myself to perceiving your crossing as a modern Jordan. Just as the incarnate Lord was revealed from the streams of Jordan, you arrived [and] you appeared divinely radiant from the sea. You, the morning star, set and turned your attention towards the west. You have risen proclaiming your coronation. And if you carry along with you a certain haze, by haze I mean the foreign regiments, we all regard this as the sun's natural property. Because the sun, as it is about to mount the horizon for the first time and to shine gracefully, draws along with it into the air misty and smoky vapours from the water, but then scatters them with its far-reaching light and dissolves what has been disbanded [. . .].

This is what we think, oh mighty one, and we expect the same thing from you, from our luminary. For by casting your far-striking rays at the right moment, you will diminish the vaporous crowds of foreigners and dissolve them. The more care you show towards the empire, the more shall they reduce to nonexistence. And yet we perceive you, oh emperor, in this way, both urging cheerfulness and driven by manliness, possessing two different virtues, much like your two hands with which you hold the imperial authority of the Romans. You stretch out cheerfulness as if it were your right hand without so far bringing forth your concealed manly impetus, and, with this right hand, you want to cajole the wicked men first. The lion, king of the beasts, does the same, whenever it stretches out its right paw, through mysterious natural counterbalance it withdraws its left one. If they are satisfied by your right hand, you regard them as excellent and enlist them as your servants; otherwise they experience the unfavourable left hand and you impose on them your imperial valour in a more pressing way. Proof of this constitutes the foreign-speaking Latin people. If they are happy to be received as friends, they shall join your servants in your favour, [30] but the senseless ones shall experience your courage. If you are challenged, I know very well that their dark blood will at once rush forth on your spear[33] and that against these senseless servants and murmurers you will employ other, absolutely loyal ones.

[. . .]

---

32 Ecclesiastes 1:6.
33 Homer (1924), i. 34–5 (*Iliad* I. 303–4).

184 *The Fourth Crusade*

Indeed I should also mention your hunting expeditions which take place alongside your drills, oh emperor, and now bring as much delight to the spectator's eyes as sweetness to the tongue and voice of us who compose orations. A spirited Arab horse breathing battle, made for war, receives you, running beside it with your hunting gear, very readily as it trots along. King Alexander's riding skill is unworthy of mention compared to yours. For he was also still a teenager and not having yet become a full man, mounted and rode Bucephalus, who had not accepted the command of any of the senior grooms, and caused the spectators to shed tears of joy. You, however, by riding alone, excite tears of dread, especially from those wicked foreigners. And so, one said to another the following: 'Oh, what a young branch of heroic spirit has risen in the garden of the Roman empire'.

[...]

[33] Judge now the same case yourself, God-crowed emperor, between these two mothers, namely your own New Rome and the first, the foreign-tongued one.[34] For today they have [34] come to quarrel for power as if for a child. Now, however, the new one is being represented by me and she reports to the judge as follows. She claims that both gave birth to and raised the supreme power and majesty. The first in the course of more ancient times, when the Augusti and the Caesars ruled her, while the second later, when the truly greatest Constantine, after he had prepared a fertile field for her, transformed it into a noble source of such splendour.[35] That is how she reports her the affair, but as for the old one she reports that after she had fallen into a depraving sleep, she lay on her own offspring and has been carrying a dead child ever since.[36] The new one, on the other hand, is awake and proud of her living Roman emperors, who are skipping, as a poet would say. It is a lively and spirited offspring, vigorous in its leaps. And so, she claims that recently the weakly one has been attempting to become young again, to steal that which is still moist and living and to substitute it with something dry and dead. She is trying to snatch our imperial authority with her treacherous concealed hand. Bring about judgment with your sword, oh mighty one! For the honest mother laments, and in her peroration she asks for your mercy one last time. Namely that when you give your decree, you will condemn the greedy hand and that you will take the chance to judge justly and to deliver her. Let us regard you as Solomon on all accounts, due to your venerable conduct alongside your youth, your skilful deliberation, your wise legislation. If you mediate and spiritually reconcile the two hostile mothers, after you have used the patriarch's wise mouth and spoken through him, you will be heard, you will counter propose and you will rejoin. And finally, after you have interposed your intercession as a bond of union between them, at once the mothers shall embrace one another wholeheartedly and the Gospel of Christ shall also include your praises.

---

34 i.e. Constantinople and Rome. Chrysoberges is comparing them to the two mothers who came before King Solomon, both claiming to be the mother of the same child. See I Kings 3:16–28.
35 i.e. Constantine the Great, who founded Constantinople in 324.
36 A reference to the western emperors who were crowned by the pope in Rome and whose legitimacy the Byzantines did not recognise.

Behold, here is one greater than Solomon, not only punishing the greedy seizure but even reconciling the hostile parties. And so, the children of oratory, having listened to the mothers about the two disputed infants, lament for them, and jump around towards the tribunal. They interrupt the new trial of Solomon and my own words and they are restless to proclaim to you with their own voice their deliverance which they have grounded on the practices of sophistry. The first argument is demonstrated with rhetorical syllogism, the second by consequence.

[35] May you pay heed to these as well, most judicious emperor, which take delight in your triumphs. May you be victorious, mighty one, by seizing your spear, by being munificent when it is fitting, by terminating our feuds. Reconcile, triumph, accept the annual rhetorical offerings on your victories and live long, guarded by God.

50. Niketas Choniates: The Capture and Sack of Constantinople (1204)

Just three weeks after Chrysoberges gave his speech, on 29 January 1204, Alexios IV was deposed. The leader of the rebels, Alexios Doukas Mourtzouphlos, was then crowned emperor as Alexios V. Alexios IV was murdered in prison just over a week later and Isaac II died around the same time, probably of natural causes. Choniates' narrative is resumed at the point where the new emperor, who had come to power on a wave of anti-Latin feeling, was preparing to defend Constantinople against the inevitable attack by the crusader force encamped at Blachernae and the Venetian fleet in the Golden Horn.[37]

Choniates (1975), pp. 566–91:

[566] Since the imperial treasury that he had acquired was neither full nor half-full, but decidedly meagre, emperor Doukas garnered wealth by reaping where he had not sown and by gathering where he had not scattered.[38] He brought to court with heavy charges those who had formerly been girded with the highest offices under the Angeloi as well as those elevated to the high dignity of Sebastokrator and Caesar. The money he levied from these people he spent on public matters.

He was second to none in resisting the Latins in a haphazard way. For he raised up the sea walls of the City with beams, surrounded the land gates with small fortifications and revived the army by his own example. On many occasions, with sword at hand and armed with a bronze mace, he checked the sallies of the enemy and spontaneously volunteered to attack those who periodically marched out to acquire provisions.

---

37 On Alexios V, see PBW (2016): Alexios 5; Phillips (2004), pp. 231–44. His nickname of Mourtzouphlos (Μούρτζουφλος) meant 'the frowning one'.
38 Matthew 25:26.

Without a doubt, he was hailed by the citizens for the above deeds, even though he was suspicious of the people and in disagreement with his relatives. For since they were nurtured in luxury and raised in softness, they avoided uplifting austerity and prudent habits and became difficult and recalcitrant like a patient who puts up with a nurse. Therefore, they avoided Doukas' criticism and indignation like the taste of raw octopus, a meal of hellebore, or a glass of bull's blood (because he had by birth a deep and heavy voice as well as a husky throat) and they perceived his ruin as a divine intervention.

[567] For instance, the emperor campaigned against Baldwin, count of Flanders, because he was ravaging the regions around Phileas and collecting tribute from them. Since the Romans were moving forwards and the opposing army was withdrawing, they came to blows with one another. The Romans were overwhelmed by awe and turned zealously to headlong flight, whereas the emperor, left behind all by himself, nearly perished and the icon of the Mother of God, which accompanies Roman emperors as a fellow general, fell to the hands of the enemy.[39] These were not the only calamities though; what was expected to follow was much worse and grievous. For once more frightful ladders and all kinds of siege engines were constructed and erected in the larger ships. Banners flew on top of them, and great rewards were offered to those who ascended the ladders so as to fight.

A portion of suffering had begun; more was almost underway and still more followed. Arguments in favour of amity were not given proper attention and were completely dismissed. Or rather, certain wicked backbiters often confounded them.[40] For Enrico Dandolo, the doge of Venice, undertook to discuss peace terms with the emperor and boarding a trireme, he brought his ship at the shore at Kosmidion. When the emperor too arrived at this place on horseback, they discussed on matters pertaining to peace, giving priority to nothing else. The doge of Venice and the other leaders demanded an immediate payment of five thousand pounds of gold and other additional terms. To those who have experienced freedom and usually impose, rather than accept orders, the terms would seem as violent Spartan lashes, unbearable and unacceptable. [568] To those, however, for whom the risk of captivity was imminent and public ruin loomed, the first partly a while before and the second opening its mouth presently, the terms were surely tolerable and not at all oppressive. Nonetheless, as the terms for peace were set for discussion, Latin cavalry forces suddenly appeared from higher ground and attacked the emperor with a headlong charge. Although the emperor barely escaped danger after wheeling about his horse, some of his associates were captured.[41] For their extreme hatred towards us and our excessive disagreement with them had absolutely no chance of resulting in a mutual turning of the scales towards benevolence.

Later, the largest ships of the enemy, on which the ladders had been fixed and as many of the siege engines as had been prepared, sailed away from the shores

---

39 This incident took place around 5 February 1204. Cf. Geoffrey of Villehardouin (2008), pp. 60–1.
40 Choniates calls these critics Telchines: legendary islanders who had a reputation for alchemy and sorcery.
41 The abortive meeting took place on 7 February 1204.

and stretching in line, like a yoke, they moved towards the walls. So as to draw up in sufficient intervals from one another, they occupied the space extending in a line from the monastery of Evergetes to the palace of Blachernae, the area around which had been burned, with its buildings destroyed, and deprived of every pleasant sight. When Doukas noticed these movements, he took measures to counter the enemy. He commanded that the imperial tent be pitched on the hill close to the monastery of Pantepoptes, whence the warships were visible and the actions of their crews clearly discernible.

At the dawn of April the ninth in the seventh indiction of the year 6712,[42] the transport ships and the dromons approached the walls. [569] Some daring adversaries ascended the ladders and released all kinds of missiles against the troops on the towers. Throughout that day, a battle raged, filled with loud cries. The Romans prevailed to some degree. For both the ladder-ships and the light horse-transport ships were repulsed from the walls, having achieved nothing at all, while the City's stone-throwing engines killed a great number of men.

The enemy, therefore, took a break throughout the next day and the day after, which was the Lord's day. On the following day, namely Monday of the sixth week of the Lent, twelfth of April, they sailed once more against the City and beached on the shores. By midday, our troops had the upper hand, even though the strength of the evil was fiercer and more intense than three days before. Because it was destined for the Queen of Cities to put on the yoke of slavery, God deemed it right to constrain our jaws with muzzle and rein since all of us, both clergy and laity, had gone astray like a stubborn and unyielding horse. From one of the ladders, which was nearest the Petria and operated under pressure in front of the emperor, two men, first among their comrades, surrendered themselves to fortune, leaped down onto the tower opposite them and put the Roman garrison which consisted of allied peoples to flight. Then they urged on their countrymen by vigorously waving their hands from above as a sign of joy and courage. Matching those who had leaped onto the tower, a certain knight called Peter entered through the nearby gate. It was proven that he was more than sufficient to drive all of our formations into confusion. [570] He appeared as a giant, with a bodily stature of nearly nine fathoms and he wore a helmet on his head which was fashioned in the manner of a well-towered city.[43] Consequently, the highborn men around the emperor and the rest of the army could not bear so much as to lay eyes on the front of a helmet belonging to a knight so striking to look at and spectacular in stature. They accepted their usual flight as an effective means of producing salvation. On the spot, as if they were united and melded into one cowardly entity and, due to their timidity, they were pursued by the thousands from the fortified positions that they had been assigned for them (for they had drawn up on tall mounts) by a single man. As soon as they reached the Golden Gate in the land walls, they pulled down the City's newly built wall at that section, ran forth and scattered, taking the road of ruin and utter destruction that

---

42 i.e. 9 April 1204.
43 Choniates may be referring here either to Peter of Bracieux or to Peter of Amiens, both of whom distinguished themselves in the fighting on 12 April 1204. See Phillips (1204), pp. 250–2.

188 *The Fourth Crusade*

they deserved! Since there was nobody to oppose them, the enemy ran to and fro in all directions and drew their swords against every age and sex. Most of them did not form a unit, standing next to each other as if in formation, but poured out in a scattered way, since everybody was already terrified of them.

In the evening, they set fire to the eastern districts of the City a short distance from the Monastery of Evergetes. The fire spread to the nearby sections of the City which slope down towards the sea and end in the area of the Droungarios. After they had despoiled the imperial tent and easily seized the palace of Blachernae by assault, they turned back again and established their camp at the Monastery of Pantepoptes.

The emperor, going about throughout the City's narrow streets, attempted to rally and call upon the people, who were wandering about for no good reason, to form a contingent. But they were neither persuaded when he urged them, nor obeyed when he encouraged them. Quite the opposite, the storm of desperation fell on everybody.

[Unable to rally any resistance, Alexios V fled the city. The following day, 13 April, the sack of Constantinople began.[44]]

[573] What took place in the Great Church is unacceptable even to be heard of. The table of the offering, a fusion through fire of every kind of precious materials into one mass and patterned one after the other to form the perfection of a multicoloured beautiful thing, truly remarkable and marvelled by all peoples, was chopped into little pieces and divided among the looters. They did the same with all holy treasures which were so numerous in quantity and splendour. They thought it necessary to carry out as booty items like the all-hallowed vessels and furniture, unmatched in elegance and craftmanship, [made from] rare materials, as well as to remove the pure silver which overlay the frieze of the altar, the pulpit and the gates [574] and a great many other gilded adornments, forming patterns along with gold everywhere. Mules and asses saddled with packs were brought inside the Church right up to the sanctuary. When several of the animals slipped, since they were unable to stand on their feet due to the polished marble floors, they were impaled by daggers. Thus, the sacred floor was defiled by the excrement from the bowels and the spilled blood. In addition, they sat on the throne of the bishop a foolish woman laden with sins, a priestess of the Erinyes,[45] a handmaid of demons, a practitioner of unspeakable witchcraft and infamous spells. Behaving wantonly towards Christ, she sung a broken rhythm and after she had whirled about many times, she swung her feet to and fro in dance.

It was not the case that [some of] these deeds were unlawful, while others were not, nor that some were more illicit than others. Every completely lawless act was wickedly committed at the same time. Would men raging against God in this way really spare pious women and girls of marriageable age, or those who had devoted themselves to God and chosen to live a life of chastity? In general, it was

---

44 See Phillips (2004), pp. 258–80.
45 Also known as the Furies, these were wild spirits of vengeance.

troublesome and difficult to appease the barbarians with supplications or to find a way to make them sympathetic, totally irascible as they were, morose and unwilling to listen to anything. They regarded everything as fuel to their anger or as deserving to be made fun of and laughed at. Consequently, he who did not hold his tongue was rebuked. In most cases, he who disputed with them a little or was reluctant towards their desires often had a dagger drawn against him.

As a result, the whole head was sick.[46] There were lamentations, woe and weeping in the narrow streets, mourning at the crossroads, lamentations in the churches, men wailing, women screaming, people being dragged away, enslavement, rape, abduction and separation of people which were formerly related. Those of illustrious families wandered about naked; the venerable in their old age were lamenting and the rich were left without possessions. This was the case in the squares, [575] on the corners, in the churches, in the hiding places. For there was no place whatsoever which was not searched, nor able to offer safety to those who streamed in.

Christ our Emperor, what distress and affliction did people experience back then! The roaring of the sea, the gloom and darkening of the sun, the turning of the moon into blood, the fall of the stars, did they not in this manner foretell the final evils themselves? And yet we have seen the abomination of desolation standing in the holy place, repeating lascivious petty words and other things which were, even if not entirely, still surely contrary to that which is deemed sacred by Christians and promotes the word of faith.[47]

To cut a long story short, such were the crimes that the Western armies committed against the inheritance of Christ. They showed no mercy whatsoever to anyone, denying everybody their money, estates, houses and clothes, and leaving no kind of share to the owners. These were the deeds of the brazen neck, the arrogant mind, the lifted eyebrow, the ever shaved and youthful cheek, the bloodthirsty armed hand, the wrathful nostril, the haughty eye, the insatiable jaw, the hateful disposition, the piercing and unfiltered speech that mostly dominated the lips. To a higher degree though [these were the acts] of their learned and wise men, who hold to their oaths, who are truthful, who hate evil and are very pious, righteous and stricter keepers of Christ's ordinances than us, the Greeks.[48] To an ever greater degree [these were the deeds] of those who had raised the cross to their shoulders, who had repeatedly sworn on it and on the Bible to pass through Christian lands without shedding blood, diverting neither to the right, nor to the left, to arm their hands against the Saracens, and to dye their swords crimson in blood of those who had pillaged Jerusalem, [who had sworn] neither to marry a woman, nor to have relations with her for as long as they bore the cross on their shoulders, so as to be purified by God and to follow in his footsteps.

[576] In reality, they proved to be taletellers. Although they sought to avenge the Holy Sepulchre, they plainly raged against Christ and with their cross they sinfully

---

46 Isaiah 1:5.
47 There are numerous biblical allusions here. See Matthew 24:15, 29; Mark 13:14–26; Luke 2:25–8; Revelation 6:12–17.
48 Interestingly, in this instance, Choniates does not refer to the Byzantines as Romans but as *Graikoi*.

brought about the downfall of the cross, exhibiting no fear to trample this that they bore on their shoulders for the sake of some gold and silver. To snatch pearls, they rejected Christ, the most valuable pearl and squandered him, the most all-hallowed, to the most sinful living beings. The Muslims did not commit such atrocities. Even though they did not behave in an entirely kind and humane way towards the Latins when they conquered Jerusalem, still the Muslims did not neigh after Latin women, neither did they transform the Christ's cenotaph into a mass grave for the fallen, nor the entrance of the life-bringing tomb into a descent towards Hades, nor life into death, nor resurrection into fall. Instead, they fixed the ransom money into a few gold coins per man and allowed every single soul to depart. They laid no claim to the rest of their possessions, even though they equalled the grains of sand. That is how generously the enemies of Christ had treated the Latin infidels, bringing against them, neither sword, nor fire, famine, persecution, nakedness, ruin and oppression.[49] The Christ-loving people, however, our fellow believers, treated us in the manner which we briefly described above, even though we were guiltless of any injury against them.

[Choniates now moves into a series of laments, written in the style of the Old Testament prophet Jeremiah. When he resumes the narrative, he recounts his own experiences during the sack of Constantinople.]

[586] On that day, the day on which the City fell, the looters took up quarters in the houses here and there. They plundered what they found inside and interrogated the owners about hidden treasures, attacking some with blows, speaking kindly toward others and threatening everybody. They took possession of what they found inside, as some [goods] were exposed to their eyes and brought out by their owners, while other were revealed after the looters looked for them, [587] nothing whatsoever was spared and no portion of the belongings was left to their owners. In addition, there was no sharing of roof or food, but only contempt, cold-shouldering, shameful captivity and dismissal. On account of that, the leaders decided to permit all those who so wished to depart from the City. Consequently, they assembled into companies and went out clothed in rags, gaunt with hunger, pale, corpse-like in appearance and with bloodshot eyes, since they shed more blood than tears. Some lamented for their wealth, while others spoke nothing of it as if they had experienced no distress whatsoever. Some bewailed a beautiful marriageable girl, snatched away and deflowered by an unknown man, or lamented over the loss of a spouse, while others walked on and wailed about some other calamity.

To combine my own affairs with the historical narrative, while the sun shone that truly hateful and gloomy day, many of my friends gathered at my house, the entrance to which was arcaded, dark and difficult to approach. For our house which had been erected at the district of Sphorakion, second to none in beauty and great in size, had been completely destroyed by the second fire. In addition, it was also convenient to reach the Great Church from my place since it was situated next to

---

49 A reference to Saladin's restrained behaviour when Jerusalem had surrendered to him on 2 October 1187.

the temple area. There was nothing left unsearched by the troops though. No place which offered security due to its holiness or position preserved unharmed the people who flocked there. Wherever one ran to, the enemy entered that place, dragged him out and carried him off wherever they wanted to. Perceiving these lawless deeds, we pursued what was best for us, as best as the circumstances allowed us.

[588] There was a friend and associate of mine, a Venetian by birth, who had been considered worthy of protection and along with him his wife and possessions enjoyed complete immunity. He proved to be of service to us in those difficult times. For having put his armour on, he transformed himself from merchant into soldier and very aggressively he drove away every single looter who entered our house, pretending to be their fellow soldier and claiming that he had seized the place first. He spoke with them in their own foreign language and discussed appropriate matters with them. Since they were swarming around in great numbers, he gave up resisting them and especially the French who were approaching. Their mindset and body frame were different than the others and they boasted that they feared nothing but heaven. As he was unable to confront them, he proposed that we withdraw from that place so as to avoid being captured by the barbarians, we men on account of our money, and the women to avoid being mistreated and raped.

Consequently, this honest former dependent and client, now our worthy helpmate and champion in those troubled times, led us to another house which was inhabited by some Venetians, acquaintances of ours. Shortly afterwards, we departed from that place, dragged away by our arms, sorrowful and ill-dressed, we were led along as if we were his spoils of war.

As this area of the city had been awarded to the French, we became wanderers once more. Since our servants had scattered all over the place and everybody had inhumanly abandoned us, we were compelled to carry the children who could not yet walk on our shoulders and to hold a suckling boy in our arms, and to traverse the streets in this manner.

[589] Thus, having remained in the City for five days after its capture, we too departed. It was Saturday and the weather stormy.[50] I think that this circumstance was neither random, nor simply a coincidence which occurs without meaning, but in accordance with God's will. Since my wife had not yet experienced the pains of childbirth, it was as if the prophecy of Christ, pray that your flight does not take place on a stormy day or on Saturday! and woe to those who are pregnant on these days![51] had been foretold for us and truly fulfilled. As we were walking, a considerable number of friends, relatives and a multitude of other people joined us as soon as they saw us. We were traversing the crossroads like a host of ants. Some soldiers walked towards us. They were not armed in the strict sense but long swords hung down from their sides, alongside their horses, and they bore daggers attached to their belts. Some were laden with spoils, while others searched the passing exiles in case they had on them a magnificent garment wrapped inside a torn

---

50 17 April 1204.
51 Matthew 24:19–20.

tunic or even had hidden a silver or gold coin in their breasts. Still others examined the women who excelled in beauty with fixed stares, difficult to avert, so as to seize and rape them on the spot. Consequently, since we were worried about the women, we enclosed them, like a sheepfold, with the rest of us all round them. We instructed the younger ones to rub mud into their faces just as they once had cosmetics and thus quench the fiery red of their cheeks so as not to signal, like a beacon fire at night, to the vagabonds, first as observers, then as admirers and finally as ravishers, who believed that that their selfish desire was blameless. At once we lifted our hands as one in supplication to God, beating our chests with distressed hearts, soaking our eyes with tears so that all of our men and women might escape those savage beasts unharmed. It was vital for us to pass through the Golden Gate.

[590] When we arrived near the Church of the excellent martyr Mokios, an insolent and unholy barbarian snatched away from our midst, as a wolf does a lamb, a fair-haired maiden, the young daughter of a judge. In response to this lamentable sight, the whole company was frightened and cried aloud. The father of the girl, worn out by old age and sickness, stumbled on a pothole and laid there on his side, wailing and covered with mud. He looked at me in desperation for help and repeatedly begged me by name to assist him in any possible way to rescue his child. Indeed, having turned around immediately, as quickly as I could, I began to follow the tracks of the abductor. Calling for aid against this violent act with tears in my eyes and gestures of supplication, I compelled those of the soldiers who were not totally ignorant of our language to help me. I managed to attach myself to them with my hand and thus I succeeded in prompting their pity and in enlisting their assistance in seeking for that lewd and shameless man.

So I myself led the way and the others followed. When we arrived where that womanizer lodged, he had already sent the maiden inside and he stood at the entrance so as to repel his opponents. I pointed at him with my finger and said: 'This is the man who inflicts injury in front of the martyr in broad daylight and neglects the commands of your lords. For you have decreed and taken the most holy oaths that you will not have intercourse with and, as far as possible, not even look in an adulterous manner on any women who are married, completely untouched by men and devoted to God. This man, having disregarded your mandates in the presence of many witnesses, was not afraid to bray like a donkey at maiden girls. Protect, therefore, your own laws and us who are in your hands and be appeased by these tears of which God approves and which nature has brought to our eyes as a great resource to arouse compassion for each other. If you are fathers of children, [591] give a hand to those who supplicate you; do it for the sake of your wives and your beloved children, do it for the sake of the God-receiving tomb and the preaching of Christ which admonishes everybody who follows him to do to others whatsoever you would that they should do to you'.[52]

Using these words as my line of reasoning, I moved the hearts of those men, so that they insisted on demanding the girl. Initially the captor disregarded them since

---

52 Matthew 7:12.

he was seized by those two most tyrannical passions, lust and anger. However, when he saw the men infuriated, proposing to hang him from a stake as an unlawful and shameless man, and talking to him from the heart and not merely from the lips, he capitulated reluctantly and returned the maiden. When the father gained a glimpse of his daughter, he was filled with joy. Making a libation of tears to God for the fact that this passion remained without a wedding crown and bed, he stood up again and marched with us.

51. Ephraim of Ainos: The Fourth Crusade and the fall of Constantinople (1203–4)

Looking back on these events a century later, Ephraim based his account on that of Choniates but added a few independent elements. These include extra details about Theodore Laskaris, the future Emperor Theodore I of Nicaea, and a surprisingly complimentary portrait of Baldwin of Flanders.

Ephraim of Ainos (1990), pp. 238–56:

That is what had taken place up to that point.
Already from earlier years, some man called Enrico Dandolo,
the doge of Venice, was a destructive Erinys for the city,
a thievish man, famous for his wickedness,
[6715] a sinful Hadad,[53] an injury for the Romans.
He secretly kept the embers of envy burning,
and bore inside his heart the spark of vengeance,
like a heap of ashes,
due to an alleged past penalty for insulting
[6720] behaviour by the Romans towards his fellow-countrymen.
He was waiting for the moment when the wind would blow
so as to kindle his malice like a torch,
greater and seven times as bright,
against the Roman empire and imperial authority.
[6725] And so, seizing this opportunity,
he stoked the fire of envy into great height,
since the circumstances supplied jealousy with fuel.
In support of his evil plans, he had as fellow conspirators
Latin noblemen who were rulers of districts
[6730] and about to sail away towards the region of Palestine
to avenge the life-giving tomb;
he plotted with them against the Romans.
These were noble men experienced in matters of war:
Montferrat named Boniface
[6735] who held the dignity of marquis and was in the full bloom of his might,

---

53 Hadad, king of Edom, was an adversary of David and Solomon, kings of Israel. See I Kings 11:21–5.

Baldwin, count of the region of Flanders,
also Hugh, count of St Pol,
and Louis, count of the land of Blois,
along with a great number of other daring men.
[6740] To put it succinctly, the total ships of the fleet
that were constructed in Venice in three full years
were one hundred and ten light vessels which could carry horses,
fashioned according to the rules of the craft,
and sixty large warships.
[6745] In addition, great merchant ships were assembled
from all around the land of Italy,
numbering more than seven hundred.
Among these was a huge monstrous ship,
the biggest one had ever seen,
[6750] and for this reason, it was called *Universe*.
And so, one thousand knights clad in full armour embarked on them,
as well as approximately one hundred thousand infantry,
divided into all kinds of men at arms,
[6755] most of them being crossbowmen.
When the fleet was ready to set sail,
an abyss of evil burst forth
and a sea of troubles full of waves,
with the city being afflicted by injury after injury.
[6760] For Alexios, the fireraiser of Constantinople,
son of the emperor Isaac,
who had earlier escaped from Byzantion secretly,
backed by letters from the Pope of the Old Rome
and the king of the Germans,
[6765] requested that those who were about to sail to Palestine
with their fleet should set sail with him for his homeland.
The pope and the king supported his request
and they promised to owe them favours,
if they restored the lad
[6770] to his paternal imperial rule.
'In addition to the aforementioned things, he will probably pay court
to you and reward you with heaps of money
if he regains authority thanks to you'.
Thus, the cunning men,
[6775] trained in matters of guile,
admitted a naive boy, prone to be cheated,
an alien wanderer, as ship and mess mate
and persuaded him to agree to a sworn covenant with them
which by its nature could under no circumstances be fulfilled.
[6780] For not only did he consent to grant them
a sea of money but also fifty allied war ships filled with

heavily armed men to sail against the Hagarenes.
In addition to the above, alas his ignorance, he promised,
[6785] the pope the annulment of ancient customs,
to make innovations in the customs of the Church,
and to bring about the distortion of the faith,
the one which is deemed acceptable by the disciples of the Latins.
The fleet untied the stern cables,
[6790] came down to the fort of Zara,
and attacked its inhabitants, according to the wishes of Dandolo.
When the fleet subdued the fort,
it came to anchor at the city of Dyrrachion,
and there the young Alexios, the one who sailed with the Italians,
[6795] was proclaimed emperor of the Romans.
Since the ruler of the Romans was well informed of these events,
he begun to restore with skill
the old and rotten warships,
barely twenty in number.
[6800] The fleet left the anchorage of Dyrrachion,
and since it encountered a very favourable wind
and a keen sea breeze at its stern,
it very rapidly arrived at the city of Constantine.
Almost nobody from the City anticipated
[6805] the sailing of the hostile Italians.
Why should I prolong my account?
The Latins, knowing the cowardice of the Romans,
noticed that the latter had an utter dread of them.
They most readily moved against the shores, free from fear
[6810] and disembarked a cavalry army on land.
In turn, the warships, the light vessels and the transports
immediately sailed into the nearby bay.
They made an assault against the fort of the chain
from all sides, both from land and sea.
[6815] They made one part of its garrison flee
while the other they sent to the bottom of the sea,
killing in battle those who resisted.
After the chain had been broken in two,
the entire fleet poured in easily
[6820] and became an irresistible and unbearable bane.
All the army, cavalry and infantry,
and the whole fleet arrived at Kosmidion.
The land army fixed a camp there,
a hill overtopped the area,
[6825] and they surrounded it with an encircling ditch
and with lines of wooden palisade.
From there, one could see the palace.

The fleet once again lay in wait on the shores.
And so, from both sides, many times in a day,
[6830] one witnessed severe fighting.
Heavy armed men, noble generals,
friends and relatives of the emperor,
bravely engaged the Latins in battle,
with cavalry and infantry forces,
[6835] demonstrating, on one level, that the city
possessed a garrison of vigorous and warlike soldiers
and on the other, their courage in battle.
From the above, it is possible to note that the Romans were not cowards
nor strangers to martial deeds.
[6840] And especially in this case, there was the emperor's son-in law
who led and commanded in battle in a marvellous way,
Theodore Laskaris, a lion in battle.[54]
For since he conducted battle in an excellent way,
he struck the enemy both with blows and amazement.
[6845] After the army of the Latins, both naval and land,
had assembled in close order, oh their frenzy,
they knew they had to strike against Byzantion in some way or another,
so as either to conquer it, or to make a treaty
and then go on their way.
[6850] And so, those of the enemy Latins
who had ships halted in front of Petrion,
[attacked] by unusual ladders made of ropes tightened together,
skilfully fastened at the top of their masts.
The others built a ram, a siege-engine
[6855] which could destroy walled cities.
All around they deployed heavily armed men
and crossbowmen to oppose [us] in battle.
And in this manner, they joined the fight
which was truly fierce, and utterly dreadful.
[6860] The city-storming ram easily
demolished the wall overlooking the sea
even though it was repulsed by the allies of the Romans.
Those who were on board in ships released
stones, lances and daggers from the ladders above
[6865] against the guards of the towers and the champions of the walls
and easily turned them to flight.
Finally, they captured the towers of the walls
and set on fire the buildings situated
from the Blachernae as far as the monastery of Evergetes.

---

54 Theodore Laskaris was married to Anna, daughter of Alexios III.

[6870] When the emperor perceived this misfortune and
distress and became anxious
about the tears of his subjects and their reproaches even more,
he turned himself into a warrior but barely and this against his will.
He departed from the palace armed
[6875] and gathered around him many keen cavalrymen
and an infantry phalanx of brave young men.
Had he achieved something glorious with his men,
it would have brought salvation to the city and his rule,
if he had engaged the enemy in battle,
[6880] or if he had at that time agreed on fighting
with Laskaris, his son-in-law, a man of noble birth and very eager [in battle].
But on this occasion, the excessive cowardice of the army
forced the city into utmost danger.
For he had armed himself just for show,
[6885] the emperor came forth as a soldier only for a while
and immediately he disappeared, having done nothing.
As soon as he went forth for battle with joy,
he returned from it greatly dishonoured,
and rendered the enemy Latins bolder.[55]
[6890] However, when Alexios Komnenos,[56] the emperor of the Romans,
secretly entered the imperial palace,
he knew that it was prudent and advantageous
never to oppose the most critical danger.
Therefore, he departed secretly at night
[6895] and went to Develtos, a fortress in Thrace
where he set up his residence.
He had ruled as emperor for eight years,
three months and ten days.
Then Isaac assumed the crown[57]
[6900] with Alexios, his beloved son.
[. . .]
Shortly after, the leaders of the Latins
[6915] came to the imperial palace,
received honours and plentiful grants,
and then they were dismissed in good order.
Every day the emperor bountifully granted
them a sea of money,
[6920] even though they regarded it as a mere drop.

---

55 Ephraim is describing the events of 17 July 1203, when Alexios III sallied out of the Land Walls to confront the crusaders at Blachernae, only to retreat without a blow being struck.
56 i.e. Alexios III, who used the surname Komnenos.
57 On 18 July, following the flight of Alexios III.

198   *The Fourth Crusade*

Then, as he was in need of more to spend,
he laid his hands on the holy relics,
sacred vessels and the revered icons, alas!
He took their adornment unlawfully
[6925] and offered them generously to the enemy Italians
as if they were common silver or gold.
At that time, alas, to the detriment of all the Roman empire,
the emperor made special efforts to reconcile
the Venetians and the Italians of Pisa who lived in the city and to make them friends,
[6930] since they were previously hostile to one another!
Those who had previously turned towards one another in hostile manner,
thereafter always conducted their affairs as allies and messmates.[58]
And so, the French, supported by some contingent
of Pisans and Venetians who went over to them,
[6935] sailed against the City with light ships.
Along with heavily armed swordsmen,
they secretly rushed against the mosque of the sons of Hagar,
and robbed absolutely everything there was inside.[59]
Shortly after, they were repulsed by the Muslims
[6940] and the citizens who assisted them.
Those Latins went mad and set fire to buildings.
Through the all-consuming fire they burned
the greatest and the finest parts of Constantinople.
On that day, the touch of fire began
[6945] from the mosque of the sons of Hagar, as I have said,
which everybody also called Mitaton
and had been established by sea,
very close to the honoured church of St Irene.
After the fire burned everything and consumed what was around,
[6950] it died away, destroying everything all around the area
as far as the great and renowned church
of Hagia Sophia, the all-holy wisdom of God.
It also reached the other part of the sea,
burning at length and in breadth.
[6955] Under those circumstances, it was dangerous to meet your loved ones,
unless perhaps one used a boat.
Isaac was vexed to hear what had taken place,
but his son, the burner of the homeland,
rejoiced at its complete annihilation and destruction.
[6960] As events occurred the way they did,

---

58 Ephraim is being sarcastic here: the Pisans and Venetians were only reconciled because a Byzantine mob attacked the Pisan quarter in Constantinople.
59 19 August 1203.

the ex-emperor of the Romans departed from Develtos
and captured Adrianople.
When Alexios [IV], the fireraiser of the homeland, was informed about this,
he left Byzantion with an army,
[6965] taking with him as a co-general
Boniface of the Latins, the marquis of Montferrat.
Alexios persuaded him to join him in campaign
with a total amount of nearly 1000 pounds of gold.
And so, he ran around the Thracian cities
[6970] and put everything well in order, according to his interests.
He marched south as far as the fort of Kypsella
and then returned to Byzantion.
Then he depended on the wicked faction,
the one which had assisted his uncle
[6975] in the blinding of his father and his overthrow from authority.
The blind autocrat felt suffocated by the above.
For during that time he waited for the opportunity to
avenge fully those who had inflicted harm on him in broad daylight.[60]
And so, he did not cease to revile his son,
[6980] above all because he heard that he took delight
and rejoiced greatly in the company of corrupted men
and that he played dice with the Latins every day,
that he became intoxicated with them and that he defiled the crown,
altogether performing things unworthy of imperial majesty.
[6985] Thus, everybody hated him, the office holders included.
[...]
The Latin cavalry and naval army
[7015] which lay in ambush for the Queen of Cities
was exceedingly fond of gain,
a genuine insatiable cask, like in the proverb.[61]
They often fell upon Propontis
and all the areas around Byzantion,
[7020] plundering and burning
holy churches and renowned buildings to the ground.
On account of this a mass of citizens assembled
demanding an army from the palace
and a man to lead them against the opposing enemy.
[7025] But everyone turned a deaf ear to these requests
and the crown bearers were especially unyielding,
judging in their ignorance that battle with

---

[60] i.e. Isaac II was annoyed that his son was collaborating with individuals who had been involved in his overthrow in 1195.

[61] A reference to the mythological story of the Danaids, who were punished for the murder of their husbands by having to fill a vessel full of holes with water for eternity.

the Latins should not be heard of, even by the tip of the ears.
Only Doukas Mourtzouphlos came out
[7030] engaging the Italians in battle to some degree,
and without anyone supporting him,
due to the emperor's order out of envy.
Perhaps he would have been in danger, unless the archers
aided him with missiles from afar.
[7035] Because of this, all the citizens of Byzantion
closed ranks and hurled insults
against both rulers of the Romans,
and diligently searched for somebody to proclaim emperor.
They seized one called Nicholas Kanavos,
[7040] a young man who was unwilling to take up the position,
and anointed him emperor of Rome.
When the above took place, Alexios [IV] knew that
Latin forces along with the marquis
ought to be admitted to the palace.
[7045] For Isaac lay there breathing his last,
unable to comprehend earthly matters.
And so, when the mass of the citizens was informed of the above
and was in tumult with upheaval and disorder,
Doukas seized the opportune occasion
[7050] for what he had planned in his mind.
He deceitfully approached Alexios at night,
and he misled and scared him with his tale,
that a mob was supposedly hastening to get rid of him,
because he had participated in the machinations of the Latins,
[7055] and was standing by the gates, consisting entirely of swordsmen.
On account of this, the lad beseeched Doukas
to find a way to assist him in these matters.
Doukas took him alone,
and went secretly through a hidden postern gate,
[7060] to one of the deep-hidden lodgings.
He imprisoned and bound him in that place
and shortly after he put him to death by strangulation.
Doukas adorned himself with the imperial insignia
and was proclaimed Roman emperor.
[7065] When Doukas assumed the rule,
he found the treasury hardly in surplus.
After he had arrested the tax-collecting officials, he took from them
a huge bulk of money from previous exactions,
and employed it for the public administration.
[7070] He marched against the Italians like a soldier,
and easily checked their raids.
Thus, he was loved by his subjects,

especially so by the bands of soldiers.
The emperor also marched swiftly against
[7075] Baldwin the count of Flanders
who had laid waste to the quarter of Phileas.
A battle broke out between the two
and the Roman army turned tail.
The emperor barely made it back alive on this occasion
[7080] and the revered icon of the lady who became a mother without a husband,
through which the emperors thrive by having as their co-general,
was captured by the enemy in this battle.[62]
Truce agreements were neglected and dismissed,
and so, a Latin phalanx was prepared
[7085] for the capture and sack of the City.
The ships which sailed away from the shores,
on top of which were ladders and siege engines,
navigated towards the shore of the monastery of Evergetes,
and arrived one after the other as far as Blachernae.
[7090] In turn, Doukas brought his tent and fixed it
on the hill close to the Pantepoptes,
whence the enemy ships were visible.
The ships approached the walls with men at arms.
The engagers joined in fight and battle with both
[7095] the bands on the walls
and the soldiers who guarded the towers.
On this day the defenders were the more successful.[63]
The next day they attacked the City with all their forces.
From one of the ladders which had been set up
[7100] very near the place of Petrion,
two men jumped off to the adjoined area
and terrified a guard post with their swords.
To the delight of their fellow countrymen, they raised their banner
and all the masses of the Italians joined them.
[7105] The emperor's guard and the
squadrons of the Roman army
all vanished, leaving the place out of fear,
a thousand men were routed by one.
They reached the Golden Gate,
[7110] readily destroyed the new wall
and left the City, running in the most inglorious manner.
The enemy, oh the novel tragedy,
dispersed in many parts of Byzantion,

---

62 Around 5 February 1204.
63 9 April 1204.

202   *The Fourth Crusade*

sacking and robbing the sumptuous houses
[7115] and inflicting all the worst calamities on the City.
They also occupied the imperial buildings
and plundered all the wealth found in them.
The emperor went about throughout the main highways
and attempted to assemble the people into squadrons
[7120] so as to resist the enemy in battle.
The people did not obey their leader
who suggested what was best and advantageous both for them and the City.
Instead, each rather quickly acted on his own accord
in order to move and bury their wealth.
[7125] Doukas realized that nothing profitable had come from his efforts
and was very much afraid
that he would suffer a miserable punishment if he were captured.
He quickly entered the imposing imperial buildings
and, taking with him empress Euphrosyne
[7130] and her daughters, he embarked on a boat,
since he was excessively in love with one of them.[64]
He departed from his homeland, the City of Byzantion to escape.
He was a man similar to Ares in battle,
a steadfast warrior, noble and virile,
[7135] a trickster and dissembling in his way of thinking.
He bragged about all his natural characteristics,
even though he lacked an adequate and normal body size.
He took pride in the fact that his eyebrows were very close to one another.
His throat was defective and the sound of his speech unpleasant.
[7140] He was middle-aged and tortuous in nature,
unjust in matters of the marriage-bed, a lover of women and lustful.
He held the dignity of protovestiarios
when he assumed the rule of the imperial state.
He held imperial authority
[7145] for two months and sixteen days.
When the emperor [Alexios III] escaped, as I have said,
Doukas and Laskaris had occupied the great house of God
and quarrelled for power,
both good young men and warriors.
[7150] Laskaris obtained the imperial office by lot
and at that point denied the imperial symbols.
Nevertheless, he left the temple with the patriarch
towards Million and the neighbourhoods of Byzantion,
and went to entreat the crowd graciously
[7155] and to exhort them to fight the enemy.

---

64   Alexios V Mourtzouphlos had married Eudokia, the daughter of Alexios III and Euphrosyne.

From among the elite, he especially urged
the Celtic imperial guard, who shake their
Ares-like swords in their shoulders, not to desert.
Since, however, his flattery and exhortations
[7160] found absolutely nobody in agreement,
and one of the phalanxes of the Latins was already visible,
he swiftly moved away from there, as he had to,
and sought safety in flight.
The enemy, possibly lacking any adversary,
[7165] proceeded with their unchecked ravaging,
slaying mercilessly with the sword
whoever they happened to meet and looting by force,
plundering and setting the city on fire
and committing all kinds of acts. What an unbearable sight!
[7170] They pillaged the holy ornaments of the houses of God,
sacred relics and holy veils.
They cast down to earth
the icons of Christ, of his all-pure mother, and of other saints.
The transgressors also plundered the
[7175] decorations of the icons, since they were made of gold and silver.
They forced chaste, devoted and virgin women
into shame and defilement
and inflicted various wicked acts, these were
almost consonant with them, absolutely like them.
[7180] And so, in lanes, crossroads, avenues, quarters,
in temples, monasteries and hidden corners, and
in streets, narrow and wide,
one could hear a variety of lamentation, moaning,
wailing, weeping and other ominous dirges
[7185] from men and women.
When the spoils were deemed adequate,
the most hateful nation of the bloodthirsty Italians
ceased plundering and despoiling.
Their most prominent generals decided
[7190] to allow everybody
who was willing and eager to depart from Byzantion.
Thus, they left in their thousands,
lamentable, depressed, and ragged,
shedding blood rather than tears, as the saying goes,
[7195] for their present condition.
The Italians, on the other hand, oh their immense arrogance,
as if they had seized the whole world,
or were established as rulers over
all the kings in the earth,
[7200] divided up the empire among themselves!

204   *The Fourth Crusade*

Each received, theoretically, the ownership of
and authority over lands and cities.
It was the decision of Dandolo, the doge of the Venetians,
a man blind in terms of eyesight
[7205] but very formidable in the perception of mind
that the leader of the Latins would be proclaimed by vote.
The chosen noble voters
of the French, the Venetians and the Lombards
appointed Baldwin, the count of Flanders,
[7210] as king of Constantinople,
a very fine young man, with beautiful characteristics,
very pious and a lover of Christ,
mild, gracious and very prudent,
who played heed to the afterlife,
[7215] a reservoir of many God-given virtues
a fervent lover of good judgment and justice.
He ordered a herald with a piercing voice to
proclaim twice a week that
none of the king's men,
[7220] who did not have a legal bond with a wife,
and who chose instead to live with a harlot lawlessly, was to stay in the palace in the evening.
He was also a guardian of laws and legal justice,
he never wished to pay heed to women,
not even to glance at them passionately,
[7225] for as long as he was separated from his wife.[65]

52. Joel: On the fall of Constantinople (1204)

Nothing is known about the author of this extract apart from his name. He was probably actively in the mid-thirteenth century and wrote a chronicle of events from Creation to 1204. The passage that follows comes at the end of the work and although it is brief and adds no additional information to that given by Choniates, it gives a good impression of how Byzantines looked back on the sack of Constantinople in the mid-thirteenth century.[66]

Joel (1836), p. 66:

Alexios Komnenos reigned for 37 years and four months. John, his son, for 24 years. Manuel, the son of John, reigned for 38 years, and, Alexios, the teenage son of Manuel for one year. Andronikos, the uncle of Alexios from his father's side, murdered him and became a tyrant for three years. His nephew, Isaac Angelos,

---

65 Baldwin's wife, Marie of Champagne, set out to join him but died at Acre in August 1204.
66 On Joel see Neville (2018), pp. 216–8.

killed him and ruled for nine years. Alexios, his own brother, blinded him and then he ruled for nine years too. Alexios, his nephew, the son of Isaac, although he was still a teenager, drove him away from the throne and from Constantinople and ruled for six months. His cousin, Alexios Doukas, also [known as] Mourtzouphlos, murdered him and ruled for two months. Alas! That [is] what Christians [did] to Christians. Indeed, how likely would it be that justice would stand aside and not deliver us up to captivity and destruction? This was what happened and, due to such impiety, magnificent Constantinople was given over to the Latins.

VII After the Fourth Crusade

After the fall of Constantinople, a number of Byzantine successor states emerged, which contested the attempts being made by the crusaders to subdue all the Byzantine territories. Alexios Komnenos, a grandson of Emperor Andronikos I, seized power in Trebizond and took over much of the Black Sea coast. Michael Angelos, a cousin of Alexios III, seized Arta and came to rule much of Epirus and Thessaly. Theodore Laskaris, the son-in-law of Alexios III, established himself at Nicaea and gradually extended his rule over much of western Asia Minor. It was this 'empire of Nicaea' that was ultimately to recapture Constantinople from the Latins in 1261.[1]

53. Niketas Choniates: Speech to Theodore Laskaris (1206)

Niketas Choniates was one of many dispossessed Byzantine grandees who made their way to Nicaea and the court of Theodore Laskaris. This laudatory speech was probably composed in an attempt to gain Theodore's favour and a place at his court. He does not appear to have been successful, perhaps because his past in the service of Alexios III, now Theodore's rival for power, was held against him.[2]

Choniates (1972), pp. 129–47:

Oration published to be read to lord Theodore Laskaris, emperor of the eastern Roman cities, when the Latins had occupied Constantinople and John from Moesia ravaged the western Roman lands along with the Cumans.[3]

[129] They say of Alexander, he who was Philip's son, who marched a mighty army against Darius and was the only one who prevailed over all the east, that he eagerly pursued learning and associated himself with the very best of wise men.[4] On many occasions, he was accustomed to declare that it was especially because of this that

---

1 On these events, see Harris (2022), pp. 190–6.
2 Simpson (2013), pp. 63–5; Chrissis (2019), p. 249.
3 John of Moesia is better known as Ioannitsa or Kalojan, tsar of Bulgaria. On 14 April 1205, he and his Cuman allies had defeated the army of Baldwin of Flanders at Adrianople.
4 Alexander the Great, son of King Philip of Macedon, invaded the Persian empire of King Darius III in 334 BCE.

DOI: 10.4324/9781003015345-9

he willingly chose to do his greatest deeds and he became brave against dangers and courageous, so that the Greeks might prevail over the barbarians and that he might be proclaimed immortal by the Greeks and be so for ever, even though he was a mortal. I think that Alexander spoke and acted in an appropriate manner, and not only Alexander, but every other ruler eager for distinction, like Alexander. For just as every object of praise flourishes and travels all over the earth when elevated by the wings of discourse, so when it is not preserved by speech and writing it wastes away and is dragged into the depth of oblivion. To put it another way, deeds need hands and hands need Muses so as in the first case to perform deeds of war by their natural strength, while in the second to traverse the massive open sea of time conveyed on a page as if on a fishing boat. In accordance with this, I think that what the affairs that distinguish Hermes from Ares have not been examined properly, nor how things themselves relate to their reflection. For if discourse is the shadow of deeds which ever accompanies them just like bodies, it goes without saying, I presume, that Hermes the messenger goes hand in hand with the noblest of deeds and the kings who are virtuous in war, and he appears to be their partner and companion. I think that Orpheus, the son of Calliope, constitutes an undisputed proof. In his bronze-fitted portraits, drenched all over with sweat, he shares the same concern as Alexander who is crowned by his brilliant armed victories.[5]

[130] Consequently, since this is the case, most powerful emperor, and you have returned to us victorious and the most prominent of trophy-winners, come, lay aside your weapons for a while, rest your horse, recover from hardship, wipe your brow, brush clean the dust which covers your holy head as dew the halo of the moon. In fact, do not allow the loud trumpet to sound the note of battle, but that of parade and procession, and listen to the words of Hermes. You fought well, you distinguished yourself splendidly, you struggled bravely. You should, therefore, receive praise for your deeds, just as in the past athletes received a crown and an inscription. Words will not make you effeminate in any way; do not be afraid of this. Rather they will strengthen you even more and urge you on greater and higher deeds, just as in the past the melodies of Timotheus inspired Alexander to take up arms.[6] Now praise is slackening and effeminising to those who are indolent and effeminate. One may note a similar case with the above in domesticated pigs which have their bellies rubbed down, since praise tickles their ears and they somehow wholly commit to unmanliness. To those who are manly and excellent, however, whose hands are ever on duty and whose life is steadfast and eager, eulogy is a goad towards virtue and an incitement to the realisation of more deeds of prowess. For through discourse, they recognize again their achievements as if in realistic

---

5 According to Plutarch (1914–26), vii. 260–1 (*Life of Alexander* XIV), a statue of the mythological lyre-player, Orpheus, sweated when Alexander set out on his Persian expedition, which was considered a good omen.
6 A Theban aulos player during the reigns of Philip II and Alexander.

images and plain mirrors, in the same way that Electra recognised her brother's lock by comparing it to her own braids.[7]

Consequently, it is right that your prowess be handed over to discourse and praise be received as a kind of due payment and reward. For if you ever rank victories as the worthiest thing and you win trophies by drilling and planning, discourse will certainly not neglect to grow on the brilliance of your deeds and to make them famous everywhere. Because you did not receive rulership from family succession, but from God, as prize for your virtue and repayment for your toils and wounds. For to start with, He summoned you to become emperor, to rule over everything, to marry into the imperial family, to flourish and to distinguish that family and to be made second only to the Angeloi who held the sceptre of the Romans. Things, however, turned out differently and a mixture of peoples from the west conquered the most important and most beautiful of cities. Our aristocrats scattered here and there and all ran for their lives. Some emigrated and others remained in our country, without, however, coming to its aid, [131] but rather invading it and further disgracing themselves since they willingly submitted to the ruling peoples and ignobly exchanged freedom for a piece of bread and something to drink. Only the right time let its voice loose like a prominent herald: 'Emperorship is not to be granted as a game of fortune, nor as family heritage, but as a gift for bravery and a reward earned by sweat, you have been the only one who opposed the intentions of all the others'. For you did not run away from the enemy, even though you were stripped bare of everything but your virtue and body, like another clever Odysseus against the roar of the sea [. . .]. You [did not] seek mountains and lodgings in the most remote areas taking care to benefit yourself above everyone else like the others, the cowards.

How can it be otherwise? You did not allow your eyes to sleep, nor did you grant rest to your temples.[8] You lamented like the tearful prophet for all the misfortunes which befell the new Zion, and perceiving from the present state of affairs what will take place in the future, as well as recognising the dangers which are clearly approaching, for attack followed attack from every side.[9] You now administer some things in a beneficial way, while you take actions to secure others for the future and give all your attention to them. You made a circuit of the eastern cities, you conversed with the inhabitants, you made them realize all the terrible things they would suffer if they did not follow you sooner. Some you rebuked, others you warned. On some occasions you held an assembly with the communities of the common folk, while on others, speaking privately to prominent men and summoning them to dinner, you proved to be experienced in conduct and flexible in your way of thinking, so that you might revive in this manner the already dying Roman spirit. For everyone looked fearfully at the lances of the Latins, as heavenly apparitions, casting

---

7 According to Greek mythology, Electra was the daughter of Agamemnon, king of Mycenae. In Sophocles' play *Electra*, she is shown a lock of hair found on her father's tomb, which she recognises as belonging to her brother Orestes, whom she had believed to be dead.
8 Psalms 132:4.
9 An echo of the *Iliad*. See Homer (1924), ii. 170–1 (*Iliad* XVI. 111).

beams of light.[10] You endured even though you were slandered. In some cases, after you had threatened with the stick, you granted the staff of office, and after you had established enmity, you strengthened friendship, not seeking anything for yourself but pursuing the salvation of all cities through warfare. [132] You sought not to wear the purple garments and to put on the crimson shoes, but to drive away the ominous barbarians and to help the fatherland which suffers badly and endures the most grievous of all calamities. You prayed like the herald of God from Tarsus, risking yourself for the freedom of all and being slandered for the defence of your race and stock.[11]

Oh Emperor, your perspiration into which you were frequently plunged, contesting the lance bearers in the city of Pegai![12] Our salvation gushed forth from this toil, and you, like a sun which had bathed in the ocean stream, rose before us even more graceful! Oh, your spear-throws there, by which you drove away the impending horrors! Oh, your firm countermarching and the straight-thrusting of your long lance which cast shadow against the enemy, by which you revived our cause, which had collapsed to the ground, but fixed a penumbral death to the heads of the enemy. Indeed, your riding there was deliverance for us, in that place you proved to be unmatched in the melee, second to none in thrusting with the lance, brave and rapid as a proud lion and undetectable like a swift-flying eagle. For as if you were walking in the air, or rather carried by wings of the winds, or even supplied with the sun's ability to be always on the move, you surveyed and rode around from one place to another faster than a quick thought.[13]

[Choniates now turns Theodore's dealings with David Komnenos, the brother of the emperor of Trebizond, Alexios Komnenos. The pair were attempting to extend their power further along the Black Sea coast into Paphlagonia.]

[145] That is how things took place. The lad, washed away at Pontus by the waves of the sea like refuse, thought that if he employed the Italians as helpers, he would overthrow you with new and irresistible hardships and that he would save himself in the end, through a reversal of fortune. Wickedness, however, lies to itself.[14] Thus, as soon as they learned about your operations in the area of the Pontus, they took advantage of your absence and attacked Nikomedeia by land and sea. You, however, who are unshaken by sudden changes, and neither elevated beyond measure when things are favourable, nor ignobly frustrated by misfortunes, left the lad aside as he was easy to overcome and you could many times best him anew. Instead, you turned your bridle and looked for his allies, desiring to destroy both the wall and those who built it. What however, did the brave warriors and unshaken knights, unyielding, high-minded and haughty, do? You just charged against them in open battle with part of your army and since their minds were seized with fear,

10 i.e. They were like comets.
11 i.e. St Paul, who was from Tarsus. See Romans 9:3.
12 Pegai, modern Karabiga, had been captured by Peter of Bracieux in late 1204.
13 Choniates is putting a very positive gloss here on Theodore's defeat by Peter of Bracieux at Poimamenon on 6 December 1204.
14 Cf. Psalms 27:12.

they fled with all haste, covering themselves with shame and the [darkness of] night.[15] What is even more strange is that they did not withdraw in the same manner as they had come, but they entered Constantinople in one breath, after having lost many men and horses and abandoned all their campaign baggage like a load dragging them down to Hades. Therefore, he who puts his trust in God and binds his deeds to Him should not be frustrated when sudden terrible things occur.

For truly, emperor most devoted to Christ, while in the evening you spent the night in the camp with the quiet annoyance of a brief vexation due to the reports of the invasion of the Italians [146], much fervent joy sparkled in the morning due to their repulse and withdrawal. The words of Isaiah find their realisation with you, the Lord will put his hand on them, and the helpers will grow weary and those who are helped will fall, and all will be destroyed simultaneously.[16] Therefore, not only you did receive once more benefits from God, but you also added well to what had been previously acquired. For your enemies were mistaken about the extent of your power, even though they were skilful in cunning and hastened to oppose your march. And the man against whom you declared the campaign, you managed to drag him anew, as before, out of the districts of Pontus like a fish pierced by your spear, and to mock him like a pitiable sparrow desiring to fly away, but unable to escape. By plundering their weapons, as if they were their wings, and by the young men, who bore these weapons, going over to you and submitting to Your Majesty. Therefore, having taken the summit and occupied the middle part, and so possessing the majority [of the empire's former territory], you will see the rest of it following and joining in.

Triumphant emperor, may you strike and prevail as above! Let it be that you succeed in being glorified with the greatest triumphs not only on land, but let it be that you also pride yourself in battles on the salty sea! May we, your subjects, perceive your achievements on land and sea evenly matched for the first prize! May all the foreign peoples fall and submit one after the other, whether they attack us from warships or contrive against us from land!

Let it also be that you come to the aid of your native city as well,[17] which remains without a helper and suffers those things that are most unbearable to be said and heard at the hands of its mad rapists and cruel lovers of wickedness! Oh, how she was stripped of its purple and fine linen! How her famous ornaments were destroyed! How was her head, which had been adorned with a golden hairnet and glorified with a bright-shinning face, sprinkled with ashes! How despised, declined and full of open wrinkles is the city which surpassed and reigned over all other cities and was red-cheeked, glittering in appearance and fair to look at.

Consequently, lifting her hands and turning her eyes towards you, oh Emperor, she pleads with distress and speaks the words of David: [147] 'My bliss, deliver me

---

15 David Komnenos and his Latin allies were defeated at Tracheiai, near Nikomedeia, in the autumn of 1206.
16 Isaiah 31:3.
17 i.e. Constantinople.

After the Fourth Crusade 211

from those who have surrounded me![18] Be a Moses, my deliverer! Appear to those who caused me to be burned and consumed by flames, like a fire, which burns down a thicket! Do not spare those who did not spare me! May the Italians pay the price of my tears through your missiles! I have exceeded or matched in misfortune the ancient Zion which was destroyed by the Babylonian army. Just as, however, Zerubbabel restored Zion,[19] you take care of me and restore me from this grievous calamity. Take up your weapon and shield and come to my aid![20] Your hardship will not be without recompense, but your reward will be paid in full. I will crown you with the brightest imperial crown, I will gird you with the most splendid wreath of victory. I will portray you in wall sculptures as Rome did Brutus, I will honour you as Sicily did Timoleon, I will applaud you in eternity and mount you on a pillar as Athens did Harmodius.[21] I wish I could see you, whom I have longed to see for a long time and ever more! Let us be cheerful like a mother holding her child and like a son his mother and let it be so, that because of you I put on the cloak of salvation and the tunic of joy'.[22]

The city which raised you and the homeland of all the Romans, oh Emperor, utters these words lamenting and beating its breasts. May the Lord of Consolation[23] hear its loud cry and render your sovereignty cheerful and long-lived.

54. Niketas Choniates: Lament for the death of his brother-in-law (1206)

Choniates' wife (whose name is not recorded) was a member of the Belissariotes family and her two brothers, Michael and John, were his close friends and colleagues in the palace administration. They accompanied Niketas and his family to Nicaea but John seems to have died there in 1206. The text that follows may be an expanded version of a eulogy delivered at his funeral, in which Choniates reflects on the catastrophe of April 1204.[24]

Choniates (1972), pp. 148–66:

Lament for the death of his brother-in-law, John Belissariotes, who passed away in the city of Nicaea. He held the offices of epi ton oikeiakon, logothetes ton sekreton, megas logariastes and, finally, protasekretis and orphanotrophos

---

18 Psalms 32:7.
19 Zerubbabel led the first group of Jews back to Israel from captivity in Babylon at some point between 538 and 520 BCE.
20 Psalms 35:2.
21 Brutus led the uprising which overthrew the last king of Rome in around 509 BCE. Timoleon established a democratic constitution in Syracuse in the fourth century BCE. Harmodius was one of the assassins of the Athenian tyrant Hipparchus in 514 BCE.
22 Isaiah 61:10.
23 2 Corinthians 1:3.
24 On John Belissariotes and this speech, see PBW (2016): Ioannes 341; Simpson (2013), pp. 16, 24–5; Chrissis (2019), pp. 250, 252.

[148] Oh, this miserable era! The magnitude of tortuous misfortunes! The compilation and mixture of manifold difficulties! Oh, fortune, diverse in distress and generous with afflictions, which often trampled over me with various misfortunes that were extremely difficult to deal with! It has now inflicted the highest calamity and allowed the grave to engulf a man who by nature was more fit to live than to die and who should have been added to the heavenly granary as a ripe grain, after many years of old age, when most of his hair had turned the colour of silver.

Why this departure from us, excellent man, and dear friend? Why this change which cannot be undone? Very often, being close together, we moved around from place to place and lived in foreign districts. We were driven away from our homeland and I myself from the city which cultivated my learning, after it had fallen to the hands of the barbarians. We became wide roamers like migratory birds and wandering stars, [149] but not even once during all these [occasions] did we choose to be separated completely. One would have called us Pylades and Orestes, if he saw us accompanying one another and travelling together, or rather united like the Moliones, or like a shin connected to the knee, or even like hands washing one another.[25]

Now that Hades has looted us and caused a plunder more harmful than that of the Western peoples, however, we face this lamentable parting. Hereafter, we shall no longer meet each other, we shall never again both dwell in the same city or under the same roof. These of all things were our respite and a balm for our afflicted souls in the times when the greatest adversities came one after another.

[...]

Apart from that I would also like to offer you the following words of Hector which agree with my painful mourning for you, now utter ruin is certain, now holy Troy has been completely ruined.[26]

For it is fitting to mourn the fair city of Constantine in the same way. Because even if a hostile western crowd insulted it and it was utterly destroyed and razed to the ground by lance and fire, and emerged as imposing ruins, [150] it is now laid even lower and inflicted with greater sufferings than before. For in the past, as much as it measured its misfortune by the beauty of its courts, its gold-coated houses and its heaps of all kinds of wealth, these things could be easily plundered, stolen, and carried away at any time by anyone. Now, however, it suffers the most grievous misfortune of all, since it has been deprived of its men and to a great extent sadly despoiled of those who rendered it the most prosperous of all cities. Hector understood this and took to complain and to mourn lamentably for the leading men who had been defeated in battle by the Achaeans and whom he had recognised as the finest in generalship, defending Troy better than walls and ditches. For men who are governed by reason and know how to administer cities in a suitable way, believe that there is nothing more beneficial than those who can fashion

---

25 Pylades and Orestes, nephew and son of Agamemnon, were close friends. The Moliones were the twin sons of Poseidon, the god of the sea.
26 An echo of Homer (1924), ii. 60–1 (*Iliad* XIII: 772–3).

perfectly all those things which pertain to public preservation and bring about the observance of the laws, which differentiates human conduct from the constant fury of wild beasts. Because men who carry weapons with only a barbarian mentality, think of nothing else but Ares' dust, and strive to engage in close combat with swords, can be bought quickly by anyone (the Massagetae, the lance-bearing Italians, the tent-dweller Persians will fill the gaps of the battle arrays).[27] Those who sacrifice to Hermes and the three Graces, however, and conduct warfare prudently are obtained with great difficulty (Solomon argues that the prudent man conquers the fortified cities and overpowers the fortress in which the irreverent man puts his trust).[28] Such men are scarcer than the Phoenix bird which is reborn every five hundred years.

Consequently, the Queen of Cities which gave birth to you, raised you up and distinguished you, deemed you worthy of the greatest of honours, gave you a share of its greatest gifts and honoured you with remarkable promotions, you most excellent man, the disciple of wisdom, the companion of graces, the servant of Themis and the fervent supporter of the Muses![29]

[...]

[159] So long as imperial rule was in order and was given an emperor who was not like the senseless ruler of Tanis but realised his duties to the full, [men like] you held the most prominent offices and were perceived as men who adorned them.[30] To put it otherwise, so long as you devoted yourselves to public administration, the state flourished, triumphed over the waves and sailed safely over rough water. When, however, the envy of the stupid and those unsuitable for praise or the frivolous and malicious plan of certain men frustrated good government, the fine state of things was expelled with you and behaviour which destroys life predominated. Henceforth, the shameless and insolent part of the class of labouring men and those who only yesterday were bankers and mostly engaged in weighing with the scales, as well as those who dealt with well-woven cloths, and with them the tanners and those who work with needles, became more important than those who were rulers. They sat down like a new Clotho and Lachesis,[31] chiselled who would put on the crimson shoes and inquired closely with the eye of their needles, like a prediction, as to who would be summoned to the imperial sceptre. Some of these groups desired fervently an appointment to imperial office and tried to obtain it very openly. Oh righteousness, what a lawless scheme! Oh prudence, what a reckless resolution! Oh brightness, what silliness! Others, acting more like youths than like their age with regard to prudence, established connections with foreign peoples and learned of their practices, failing to notice that they appointed pirates for us as prosecutors, robbers as judges and vagabonds as chastisers, [160] and that

---

27 The Massagetae were an ancient tribe who lived to the east of the Caspian sea. Choniates is using the term rhetorically to denote any group of uncivilised foreigners.
28 Proverbs 21:22.
29 Goddess of law and custom.
30 Tanis or Zoan was a city of Ancient Egypt. Isaiah 19:11 observes that 'the princes of Zoan are fools'.
31 Two of the three Fates who spun the thread of life.

they put the sea-going peoples into our harbour as looters of the fatherland. Ah the ambitious mind and the harsh soul which betrays everything! Oh this pitiable exchange, the sluggish mind and the eye blinded by ceremonial robes, the silver trumpets which sound the rider's signal and the colour of the shoe which is different from all the others!

Woe, woe the kinds and multitudes of evils you have experienced, imperial city, eye of the earth, talk of the whole world, bliss of the whole earth from noble roots,[32] wet nurse of wisdom, guide of faith, home of all that is fair! How did you become a widow, you the most populous of all cities, and full of open wrinkles like an old woman who cooks at a furnace,[33] you who had a glittering face, clothed in purple and fine textiles, and bearing luxurious jewels? How are you scorched and razed by fire and subjected to the same misfortunes as Troy, you who were renowned everywhere for your gleaming buildings and your golden palaces? How did you become a camp for foreign people, obscure, scattered and lowly in station, you who received the submission of all peoples and were called the Queen of Cities? How were you ploughed like a field and then became overgrown like a thicket grove?[34] Who shall save you, who shall comfort you and who shall return to greet you in a friendly manner?[35] Which of the four winds shall assemble your children?[36] Who shall come for you as a saviour like Moses or shall be seen to restore you like Zerubbabel? For you have now become a song, a parable and a shaking of the head for those beyond the strait.[37]

At that time, therefore, when everyone was lamenting about something different that had befallen them and was weeping because of them, those of aristocratic status owning only themselves (namely, what the ancients customarily called souls and bodies), considered everything else as a clearance of garbage and, bringing the blessed words of Job in their mouths, they sang along with him joyfully the Lord giveth and the Lord taketh away.[38] They proved their solidarity and their sensitive and mournful hearts and they were moved to pity more by the misfortunes of their fellow-men than by their own sufferings, even though their hands were tied with ropes by their captors so as to extort money and they were caught by that bastard barbarian army, which was fonder of gold than of Christ, as if by a net spread upon [161] Tabor and by a trap on a mountain watch.[39] Without a doubt, deciding that they would not put up with that particular situation, they moved away from the murderous tyrants, bivouacked a short distance away from the city and wrestled against the forces of nature. Consequently, I did not postpone departure either. Like Clement

---

32 Psalms 48:2.
33 An echo of Homer (1919), ii. 202–3 (*Odyssey* XVIII. 27).
34 Jeremiah 26:18.
35 1 Kings 2:13.
36 Zechariah 2:6.
37 Psalms 44:14.
38 Job 1:21.
39 Hosea 5:1. Mount Tabor was the scene of a battle between the Israelites and the Canaanites in Judges 4:13–25 and 5:1–25.

with Peter, Timothy with Paul, or even Strophius with Agamemnon,[40] I accompanied them; I offered my share of effective comfort and received theirs. This wandering was not for long though. For after a while, they proved that virtue does not accept a tyrant, as somebody argued in another book,[41] imitating the inviolate doves, they flew with light heart over that unclean piece of wreckage. They preferred to offer their gaze to the mountains and to set up their nests in holy precincts, rather than to be admitted to the tents of sinners.[42] For that is how they called our lance-bearing captors, the greedy jaws, the hands insatiate for blood, the upright necks, the uneducated minds, the ever fierce and furious faces, the men who pierced Christ with the lance a second time, who spilled his precious blood on the ground, who played dice for his garment and cross, which they bore on their shoulders and sewed on their clothes, trampled them with their feet and threw them in worthless places.

Consequently, when they hid themselves in a monastery near the straits of Hellespont, they sang with David our souls have been saved from the hunter's trap.[43] They made themselves equal to the best of the monks, differently dressed and like-minded, and meditated on bitter joy, which is pleasing to God, preferable to them and much better than the satirical smiles mingled with tears looked for by some.

[. . .]

[166] Even though I was almost speechless and shocked because of what had happened and closed my mouth with my hand, just like the countrymen of Job,[44] this should not be considered as something new. Even if I gabble like them once I have begun to speak, the envious should not criticize me in this way either. For the many eulogies which flow to me from all directions almost compel me to speak in a distracted way. Because I now feel a conflagration and burning stronger than when the fire, that abyss, burned to the ground our houses, which were ventilated by the wind on three stories and filled with golden surfaces, and consumed them like flammable fuel, spearing not even the deep-rooted foundations. Now I have truly experienced plunder, spoliation, lamentable captivity. I am carried away as booty, I am despoiled, I am taken captive. There is no sword, only death, no arrows only oblivion.

55. Theodore Laskaris: Speech written for him by Niketas Choniates (1208)

Although Choniates did not succeed in securing a senior post for himself at the court of Theodore Laskaris, he was entrusted with certain minor tasks, such as travelling to Cilician Armenia to bring back Theodore's bride Philippa in 1213/14.

---

40 Clement I was the second or third bishop of Rome. According to tradition he was instructed and consecrated as a priest by St Peter. Timothy was a close companion of the Apostle Paul. Strophius was Agamemnon's brother-in-law.
41 A reference to the Athenian philosopher Plato, who explored the link between virtue and good government. See Plato (2013), ii. 294–7 (404e–405d).
42 Psalms 12:1 and 84:10.
43 Psalms 124:7.
44 Job 29:9.

He also wrote this speech for Theodore to deliver, in which the emperor compares himself to David, the biblical king of Israel. Just as David had first been king of Judah and then extended his rule over Israel too, so Theodore would someday come to rule over all Byzantines and recover the lost city of Constantinople.[45]

Choniates (1972), pp. 124–8:

Imperial oration compiled to be read by lord Theodore Laskaris, ruler of the eastern Roman regions, when Constantinople had been conquered by the Latins and was occupied by them as conquered territory along with the western Roman regions.

[Theodore Laskaris begins by urging the Byzantines to abstain from pleasures and corruption. He admonishes them to fight the good fight, both spiritually and physically. Once the people fast and demonstrate genuine repentance, Christ will side with them and assist them in their struggles].

[125] The people of the other classes and the common folk should partly be incited to the same zeal [as the monks] and partly cultivate repentance. They ought to pick up the light cross of Christ, as He himself affirms,[46] and to cultivate extraordinary virtue, irrigated by streams of tears. Those who practice weighing at the scales and exchanging based on transactions, remembering the money which the Lord distributed among his followers, ought to fear the judgement of the timid and worthless servant and to imitate quickly in most things the progress of the one who is faithful and virtuous.[47] In addition, everyone, unless they can cover all kinds of virtues, ought to choose the fulfilment of at least some of them in order to accomplish deeds pleasing to God which are arranged for an ascent towards Him as a ladder with many rungs.

Thus, in the past generals and tribes surrendered to peoples with strange languages. Three children proved to be more refined than gold and more powerful than a fire which burned sevenfold.[48] Daniel made lions resist famine. Elijah saw God in Horeb and Moses saw God, or rather was named god over Pharaoh, flogging Egypt with natural calamities, and turning myriads to flight with a stretch of his hands. The people of Nineveh complied with God's judgement. The people of Israel, supplying themselves only with flour from Egypt, undoubtedly a token of fasting, crossed the Red Sea on foot without getting wet, while the Egyptian officers, their pork meats and their cauldrons, sank into the violent water like lead and were destroyed.[49]

Yesterday we were crawling in pleasures like some kind of fickle . . . papyrus with ever growing foliage and a water-loving reed. [126] Today, however, let us

---

45 On the 1208 speech, see Simpson (2013), pp. 22–3, 63; Chrissis (2019), pp. 249, 253–5.
46 Matthew 11:29–30.
47 A possible reference to Jesus' Parable of the Talents (Matthew 25:14–30; Luke 19:11–27).
48 Shadrach, Meshach and Abednego were cast into a furnace but miraculously survived. See Daniel 3:19–25.
49 For these incidents, see Daniel 6:16–26; 1 Kings 19:11–18; Jonah 3:1–10; Exodus 3:1–12, 7:1, 7:14–25, 7:8–15, 12:34, 14:15–24.

burst from the ground like well-rooted palm trees, planted in the house of God, fed by the saltiness of tears, and just as the cedar trees in Lebanon, let us grow in virtue.[50] We, who follow God's calling, are instructed to live piously and prudently. Season and occasion do not define our God-pleasing conduct, but our whole life is assigned as one day dedicated to a proper way of living and to strict conformity to the Commandments. Since not everybody is strong enough to accept such teaching, let us at least not pass the period of fasting as carelessly as in previous days, since it is set aside as a time of reconciliation and payment of what is due. Rather, just as Christ was obedient to his Father to the death, death by crucifixion,[51] let us, in the same manner, comply with Christ and purify our passions along with our food.

If righteousness truly exalts the state, but sins diminish it, as demonstrated by Solomon and by truth, our race would, without a doubt, not have been humiliated, diminished and subjected. If righteous deeds had not been forgotten, our Queen of Cities would not have been destroyed by fire and would not have experienced the very worst of things which mankind [had suffered] so far, trodden down by the feet of bloodthirsty foreign peoples. Each of us, however, had conducted his life in the pursuit of wicked deeds.[52]

Which Jeremiah would have lamented for our [misfortunes] or what sort of time would sweep away with its stream of oblivion those things which were in store for us to experience and suffer? The fall of cities, devastation of churches, desecration of the most sacred vessels, the lamentation of men, the weeping of women, looting, migration, and so many other things which make death preferable to being alive. You saw it Lord, do not keep silent! Seize your weapon and shield and rise up to help us! Do not cast us off forever! Lift your arm against their arrogance and make them suffer in the same way that they made us suffer![53]

Presumably, the regions east of Constantinople would have experienced and suffered worse calamities than those the west had suffered, and more grievous than those which befell the capital, had not God left Our Majesty behind as a seed and saved these regions from the hands of another Herod, just as in the past he unexpectedly delivered the disciple who walked on waves from prison.[54] As Paul says, inspired by the Holy Spirit, 'But if I wish to boast, I will not be a fool'.[55] [127] For you should recognize, recognize every toil, night vigil, the change from those lands to others, the concealed and wicked plans of some, the frequent migration to neighbouring peoples, their assistance, the sources of sweat in the Pegai of

---

50 Psalms 92:12–13.
51 Philippians 2:8.
52 Proverbs 14:34; Jeremiah 16:12.
53 Psalms 35:2 and 22, 74:3.
54 For Peter's deliverance from prison, see Acts 12:5–18 and for his walking on water, see Matthew 14:28–33.
55 2 Corinthians 12:6.

Hellespont.⁵⁶ All these things occurred and were accomplished by Our Majesty, not to achieve personal gain (otherwise I [would have been] more of an opportunist than a patriot), but to scare off from the eastern cities the accursed western corps, which entered the Roman realm imperceptibly with great ease, like a swarm of locusts, to destroy and plunder. I shall check in a pitched battle the advance of the Latin army which constantly feeds on the locality like the disease of gangrene.

With this plan and resolve, Our Majesty hastened from one place to another, as if in a double course, sometimes turning back the whippersnappers who rendered the Black Sea inhospitable⁵⁷ just by flying my banner, sometimes mingling with the mixture of peoples,⁵⁸ learning their practices, taking vengeance on them and putting them in chains up to their necks, and on other occasions attacking them in other way and destroying their companies like the drawings children make in the sand. God, however, the perfect rewarder, who weighs what is in the heart of each man, having welcomed my reign's burning desire and zeal for the defence of what is right, raised me up to this imperial summit, granting me the anointment of David and his calling.⁵⁹ Just as David first had ruled over the tribe of Judah and then over all Israel, my reign has now succeeded in being established over the eastern Roman cities. Just as God placed David the firstborn at the summit of earthly kings and later granted him the territory of other tribes as well and the possession of Zion, so shall He guide my royal plans and actions. He shall grant me the power to trample over serpents and scorpions and he shall allow me to take courage against the peoples who have occupied the land of the Romans, more fervently than bees do with honeycombs.⁶⁰

[128] Without a doubt, these matters will be realised if we worship God through prayer, fasting and virtuous deeds, and, I might add, through obedience to my rule. For God desires his subjects to submit and to comply easily and readily to those who rule in his name, expressing no disagreement whatsoever with those who handle public matters. For there is a good order which holds everything together, in time, in the sun and the stars, and, more importantly of course, in the spirits, for the spirit of the prophets is subject to the prophets,⁶¹ and nothing beneficial escapes it. Consequently, if we deal with public affairs in this way, we shall say to this mountain, to the stony-hearted race of the Italians, raised in arrogance as high as the hills and mountains, who took the course of the sea, overran our land and spread widely over it, 'Be lifted up and thrown into the sea'.⁶² And let us take back our native cities from which we were expelled because we had sinned. These are our

---

56 A word play since pegai (πηγαί) means 'sources' but it is also the name of the town of Pegai on the Dardanelles.
57 A word play; the Black Sea was called Εὔξεινος (hospitable) by the ancient Greeks but Theodore's enemies had made it κακόξεινον (inhospitable). The whippersnappers are Theodore's younger rivals for power, Emperor Alexios I Komnenos of Trebizond and his brother David.
58 Psalms 106:35.
59 Theodore had been crowned emperor in Nicaea in April 1208.
60 Psalms 37:23 and 89:27; Luke 10:19.
61 1 Corinthians 14:32.
62 Matthew 21:21.

ancestral and original dwelling places: the paradise and city of the Lord of hosts at the Hellespont, the city of our God, the well-established joy of all the earth, the highly prized, renowned to all nations.[63]

Make it so, oh Christ the King, who crushes conflict with your spiritual arm, who disperses war-desiring peoples, who ends and brings life, who punishes and heals, who steers human affairs to the left and to the right and administers them excellently, that from the moment when we have completed 40 days in accordance with your commandments, we may chant for you the resurrection from the dead, and from then on applaud you for the defeat of our enemies! If we also celebrate our entrance into the city from which we had been driven out, and my rule proves to be like [that of] Moses the liberator and Zerubbabel who restored Zion from captivity, this shall be most remarkable of Your deeds and the most extraordinary thing which ever took place. When the rest of the flock, which is not gathered into our fold today, listens to the voice of Our Majesty, it will assemble once more under one rule, as in a single fold. There will be one flock and one shepherd to glorify You and to boast about Your inheritance. Greatness and veneration are fitting to You, and to the Father and the Holy Ghost, now and for ever, and unto the ages of ages, Amen!

56. Constantine Stilbes: Memorandum against the Latins (c.1215)

Constantine Stilbes was a teacher at the patriarchal school in Constantinople who became archbishop of Cyzicus in around 1204. Following the fall of Constantinople, he attached himself to the court of Theodore Laskaris at Nicaea, where he was apparently acquainted with Niketas Choniates.[64] It was there that he compiled his *Memorandum against the Latins*, a list of Catholic theological errors and of atrocities committed during the sack of Constantinople and its aftermath. Only a small selection of his 104 points has been translated in the following extract.

Stilbes (1963), pp. 70–1, 77, 81–6:

Issues with their high-ranking priests, the rest of their clergy and similar matters

38. The high-ranking priests array themselves for war too and fight in the very first rank, ahead of the other [soldiers]. They stain their hands with blood, they kill and they are killed, and the disciples of gentle Christ become murderers: they who with the very same hands consecrate the sacramental body and blood.

Issues with the saints, sacred things and similar matters

60. Their high-ranking priests and especially the pope approve of the slaughter of Christians and they declare deliverance for those who participate in it.

---

63 These are echoes of Psalms 24:10 and 48:2.
64 On Stilbes, see Choniates (1972), p. 215; Stilbes (2015), pp. 9–10.

61. They consider any Latins who have been killed in battle to have achieved salvation, and they argue that they go directly to heaven, even if they have fallen while fighting out of greed, bloodlust, or some other excessive type of malice.

[Regarding] the things they had the audacity to perform against the holy [places] during the capture of Constantinople and similar matters

76. They set on fire countless holy churches whose beauty and grace of the Spirit that dwelt there were inexpressible.
77. They turned the churches which were spared and the remnants of the others into stables.
78. They introduced mules into the holy altar of the great church of the Wisdom of God itself, so as to overload them with the riches from there, and these animals, devoid of reason, excreted dung and urine in the holy sanctuary forbidden to laymen.
79. They cut the throat of one of the mules they had introduced into that very same holy altar, committing an act of unmentionable vice.[65]
80. They introduced an immoral woman impure in every sense into that very same holy altar, and, after she had taken a seat on the so-called *synthronos*, she blessed the Latins who were present, mocking the gestures of the patriarch. In the end she left the place, after she had danced and disrespected the saints with her actions. This was another unspeakable act of theirs.
81. They broke the holy table of the very same altar into fragments, which was an extraordinary piece with regard to its craftmanship and material as well as most sacred on account of the consecration, and they misused the fragments as worldly [objects].
82. Some of their distinguished heavily armed men entered into the same divine church on horseback, and their horses neighed and trampled the all-holy floor.
83. They made common use of sacred plates and chalices as [if they were] objects from a brothel or a tavern, and they brought them to their private tables where, alas, they even had their beloved dogs as dinner guests!
84. They poured the consecrated blood and bread out of the sacred vessels and they threw them away as garbage.
85. From the material of the gold and silver sacred vessels they fashioned for themselves spurs, belts, and what common people call trouser straps. For their courtesans [they made] rings, bracelets, earrings, and, sometimes, jewellery for the feet.
86. They converted fine linen cloths of the sacred tables, sacred cloths, priestly and high-priestly robes into clothing, ornaments for men and women, bed coverings and saddle cloths for horses.

---

65 Niketas Choniates [50] says that one or more mules slipped on Hagia Sophia's marble pavement and impaled themselves on the objects that had been strapped to their backs.

After the Fourth Crusade 221

87. They valued the sacred marble slabs, those of the altar table, and the columns the same as cobblestones, and they treated them as if they were the latter.
88. They cast the saints' relics out of their precious chests into unclean places, like some kind of trash.
89. They took the altar screen in the hospice of St Sampson which was covered in sacred scenes, and having pierced it throughout, they set it into the so-called Covent in order for their patients to have a bowel movement through these holes. Alas, this is an audacious thing even to be said![66]
90. Some of the icons of the saints they burned, others they trampled on or cut into pieces with axes and delivered to their servants as fuel for the domestic fireplace. Some they attached to their houses as panels, some they put on seats, and others they nailed in the floor of their buildings, or even, alas, in the feeding troughs of their horses!
91. While they were performing holy service, their priests and bishops were frequently seen treading upon holy icons which had been laid on the floor.
92. They defiled the tombs of saints and, if they could not find any, those of emperors and empresses. They uncovered the mysteries of nature and they looted whatever was in there, even a chip of gold or silver or some piece of cloth. They even carried on their shoulders the very tomb of the saint and great emperor Constantine.[67]
93. They slaughtered many of our priests and laymen in the churches and the holy altars since they had fled for refuge to the holy sanctuaries.
94. An armed bishop bearing a cross in both his hands as some kind of standard rode in front of the Latins during the battle and the taking of the City, as well as during the aforementioned impieties which took place the same day.
95. A cardinal went into the church of the Archangel at Anaplous and plastered over many icons of saints in there with lime.[68] After the icons, he cast the relics of the same saints at the nearby sea so as to acquire something for himself later. Then, when he was about to perform holy service, he brought along inadequately clad boys, in the manner we have described above.[69]
96. Let us not write about the defilement of young girls and consecrated nuns, the adulteries with women and boys, the enslavement of freemen and aristocrats and their sale to foreign lands, and especially to those of the Saracens, alas for a felonious reason, so as for the slave traders to make a greater profit from this act!

---

66 The hospital of St Sampson was situated on the Acropolis of Constantinople.
67 Emperor Constantine the Great was buried in a marble sarcophagus in the church of the Holy Apostles.
68 Anaplous and the church of the Archangel Michael lay to the north of Constantinople and the western shore of the Bosporus. The cardinal responsible for this alleged vandalism may have been either Benedict of Santa Susanna, who was in Constantinople in 1206, or Pelagius of Santa Cecilia, who was there in 1213–14.
69 In his point 27, not translated here, Stilbes had claimed that Catholic clergy used to perform a ceremony at which they would sprinkle scantily clad young men with water, claiming that this would endow them with invulnerability in battle.

97. Let us not mention this huge injustice against people who are Christians and have done no wrong. How they marched from a vast distance and from a faraway land against a foreign country, and, even though they too declare that they follow Christianity, they burned, slaughtered, and stripped naked those who still breathed so as for them to suffer a life more bitter than the death of those who had been killed instantly, and to suffer a prolonged death. Why should I enumerate indescribable things, when those I have already mentioned are sufficient to demonstrate the magnitude of the tragedy?

98. On account of all these crimes committed by the soldiery against God and mankind, no kind of castigation whatsoever [was announced] by their so-called holy Church against the criminals. If all these matters are true, then it is a foregone conclusion that their Church approves of unlawful acts of such magnitude, and, thus, it is answerable for the accusations.

Bibliography

Primary Sources Translated in the Volume

Alexios I (1901), 'Letters to the Abbot of Monte Cassino (1097 & 1098)', in *Die Kreuzzugsbriefe aus den Jahre 1088–1100: Eine Quellensammung zur Geschichte des ersten Kreuzzuges*, ed. H. Hagenmeyer (Innsbruck: Wagner), pp. 140–1, 152–3.
Alexios I (1913), in P. Maas, 'Die Musen des Kaisers Alexios I', *Byzantinische Zeitschrift* 22: 348–69.
Basilakes, Nikephoros (1984), *Nicephori Basilacae Orationes et Epistolae*, ed. A. Garzya, Bibliotheca Scriptorum Graecorum et Romanorum Teubneriana (Leipzig: Teubner).
Choniates, Niketas (1972), *Orationes et Epistulae*, ed. J.A. Van Dieten, Corpus Fontium Historiae Byzantinae 3 (Berlin and New York: de Gruyter).
Choniates, Niketas (1975), *Historia*, ed. J.A. Van Dieten, Corpus Fontium Historiae Byzantinae 11, 2 vols (Berlin and New York: de Gruyter).
Chrysoberges, Nikephoros (1892), *Nicephori Chrysobergae ad Angelos Orationes Tres*, ed. Maximilian Treu (Breslau: Gutsmann).
Ephraim of Ainos (1990), *Ephraem Aenii Historia Chronica*, ed. O. Lampsides, Corpus Fontium Historiae Byzantinae 27 (Athens: Institutum Graecoromanae Antiquitatis).
Glykas, Michael (1836), *Annales*, ed. I. Bekker, Corpus Scriptorum Historiae Byzantinae (Bonn: Weber).
Italikos, Michael (1972), *Lettres et discours*, ed. Paul Gautier (Paris: Institut français d'études byzantines).
Joel (1836), *Ioelis Chronographia Compendiaria*, ed. I. Bekker, Corpus Scriptorum Historiae Byzantinae (Bonn: Weber).
Kinnamos, John (1836), *Epitome rerum ab Ioanne et Alexio Comnenis gestarum*, ed. A. Meineke, Corpus Scriptorum Historiae Byzantinae (Bonn: Weber).
Manasses, Constantine (2017), Ὁδοιπορικόν, ed. K. Chrysogelos (Athens: Sokoli).
Neophytos (2005), 'On the Misfortunes of the Land of Cyprus', in Ἁγίου Νεοφύτου τοῦ Ἐγκλείστου Συγγράμματα, ed. A. Karpozilos, vol. 5 (Paphos: Monastery of St Neophytos), pp. 405–70.
Nicholas of Methone (2018), 'Βίος τοῦ ὁσίου πατρὸς ἡμῶν Μελετίου τοῦ ἐν τῷ ὄρει τῆς Μυουπόλεως ἀσκήσαντος', in Οἱ Βίοι του ἁγιου Μελετίου του Νέου, ed. I. Polemis (Athens: Kanaki), pp. 30–149.
Phokas, John (2008), ῎Εκφρασις ἐν συνόψει τῶν ἀπ', in Ἀντιοχείας μέχρις Ἱεροσολύμων κάστρών καὶ χωρῶν Συρίας Φοινίκης καὶ τῶν κατὰ Παλαιστίνῃω Ἁγίων Τόπον, ed. A.E. Fadi (Thessaloniki: Aristotle University).
Prodromos, Manganeios (1881), *Recueil des historiens des croisades: Historiens grecs*, ed. E. Miller, vol. 2 (Paris: Imprimerie nationale), pp. 188–759.

224   Bibliography

Skoutariotes, Theodore (1894), 'Synopsis Chronike', in Μεσαιωνικὴ Βιβλιοθήκη, ed. C.N. Sathas, vol. 7 (Paris: Maisonneuve), pp. 1–556.
Stilbes, Constantine (1963), in J. Darrouzès (ed.), 'Le mémoire de Constantin Stilbès contre les Latins', Revue des études byzantines 21: 50–100.
Theodosios of Byzantion (1884), 'Laudatory Speech to Our Pious Father Christodoulos', in Ἀκολουθία ἱερὰ τοῦ ὁσίου καὶ θεοφόρου πατρὸς ἡμῶν Χριστοδούλου τοῦ Θαυματουργοῦ, ed. C. Boines (Athens: Perri Brothers), pp. 163–208.
Theophylact of Ohrid (1986), Lettres, ed. Paul Gautier, Corpus Fontium Historiae Byzantinae 16/2 (Thessaloniki: Association des recherches byzantines).
Tzetzes, John (1972), Epistulae, ed. P.A. Leone (Leipzig: Teubner).
Urban II (1853), 'Letter to Alexios I Komnenos (1096)', in Patrologia Latina, ed. J.-P. Migne, vol. 151 (Paris: Garnier), col. 485.
Zonaras, John (1897), Epitome Historiarum, ed. T. Büttner-Wobst, Corpus Scriptorum Historiae Byzantinae, vol. 3 (Bonn: Weber).

Other Primary Source Texts and Translations

Albert of Aachen (2013), History of the Journey to Jerusalem, trans. S.B. Edgington, 2 vols (Farnham and Burlington VT: Ashgate).
Babrius and Phaedrus (1965), Fables, trans. B.E. Perry, Loeb Classical Library (Cambridge MA and London: Harvard University Press).
Choniates, Niketas (1958a), Die Krone der Komnenen: Die Regierungszeit der Kaiser Joannes und Manuel Komnenos (1118–1180); Abenteurer auf dem Kaiserthron: Die Regierungszeit der Kaiser Alexios II, Andronikos und Isaak Angelos (1180–1195) aus den Geschichtswerk des Niketas Choniates (Graz: Styria).
Choniates, Niketas (1958b), Die Kreuzfahrer erobern Konstantinopel: Die Regierungszeit der Kaiser Alexios Angelos, Isaak Angelos und Alexios Dukas, die Schicksale der Stadt nach der Einnahme sowie das 'Buch von den Bildaulen' (1195–1206) aus den Geschichtswerk des Niketas Choniates, trans. F. Grabler (Graz: Styria).
Choniates, Niketas (1966), Kaisertaten und Menschenschicksale im Spiegel der schönen Rede: Reden und Briefe des Niketas Choniates, trans. F. Grabler (Graz: Styria).
Choniates, Niketas (1984), O City of Byzantium: Annals of Niketas Choniates, trans. H.J. Magoulias (Detroit MI: Wayne State University Press).
Choniates, Niketas (1994–1999), Grandezza e catastrofe di Bisanzio: Narrazione cronologica, trans. A. Pontani, F. Pontani, and J.-L Van Dieten, 3 vols (Milan: Mondadori).
Choniates, Niketas (2021), Νικήτα Χωνιάτη, Χρονικὴ Διήγησις, trans. G.T. Tserevelakis (Thessaloniki: Stamouli).
Diogenes Laertius (1925), Lives of Eminent Philosophers, trans. R.D. Hicks, Loeb Classical Library, 2 vols (Cambridge MA and London: Harvard University Press).
Ephraim of Ainos (1984–1985), Εφραίμ του Αίνου, Χρονογραφία, trans. O. Lampsidis, Βιβλιοθήκη Ελλήνων Συγγραφέων, 2 vols (Athens: Academy of Athens).
Eustathios of Thessalonica (2013), Secular Orations 1167/8 to 1179, trans. A.F. Stone (Brisbane: Australian Association for Byzantine Studies).
Geoffrey of Villehardouin (2008), 'The Conquest of Constantinople', in Chronicles of the Crusades, trans. C. Smith (London: Penguin), pp. 1–135.
Herodotus (1920–5), The Histories, trans. A.D. Godley, Loeb Classical Library, 4 vols (Cambridge MA and London: Harvard University Press).
Hill, R. (1962), Gesta Francorum: The Deeds of the Franks and the Other Pilgrims to Jerusalem (Oxford: Oxford University Press).
Homer (1919), Odyssey, trans. A.T. Murray, and G.E. Dimock, Loeb Classical Library, 2 vols (Cambridge MA and London: Harvard University Press).

Homer (1924), *Iliad*, trans. A.T. Murray, and W.F. Wyatt, Loeb Classical Library, 2 vols (Cambridge MA and London: Harvard University Press).
Joel (1979), *Joel: Cronografia compendiaria*, trans. F. Iadevaia (Messina: EDAS).
Josephus (1928–9), *The Jewish War*, trans. H.S.J. Thackeray, 3 vols (Cambridge MA and London: Harvard University Press).
Kinnamos, John (1976), *Deeds of John and Manuel Comnenus*, trans. C.M. Brand (New York: Columbia University Press).
Kinnamos, John (2021), *Ιωάννης Κίνναμος, αὐτοκρατορικός γραμματέας τοῦ Μανουήλ Α´ Κομνηνοῦ, Ιστορία 1118–1175 μ.Χ. Ἐπιτομή τῶν κατορθωμάτων τῶν αὐτοκρατόρων Ἰωάννη Β´ καὶ Μανουήλ Α´ Κομνηνοῦ*, trans. N. Nikoloudis (Athens: Labyrinthos).
Komnene, Anna (1928), *The Alexiad of the Princess Anna Comnena: Being the History of the Reign of Her Father, Alexius I, Emperor of the Romans, 1081–1118 A.D*, trans. E.A. Dawes (London: Routledge and Kegan Paul). Available at: https://sourcebooks.fordham.edu/basis/AnnaComnena-Alexiad.asp.
Komnene, Anna (2009), *The Alexiad*, trans. E.R.A. Sewter, revised Peter Frankopan (London: Penguin).
Mesarites, Nicholas (2017), *Nicholas Mesarites: His Life and Works (in Translation)*, trans. M. Angold (Liverpool: Liverpool University Press).
Neophytos (1864), 'Neophytus De Calamitatibus Cypri', in *Chronicles and Memorials of the Reign of Richard I*, trans. W. Stubbs (London: Longman), pp. 174–9.
Odo of Deuil (1948), *De Profectione Ludovici VII in Orientem*, trans. V.G. Berry (New York: Columbia University Press).
Phokas, John (1889), *The Pilgrimage of Joannes Phocas in the Holy Land*, trans. A. Stewart (London: Palestine Pilgrims' Text Society).
Phokas, John (1988), 'John Phocas A General Description of the Settlements and Places Belonging to Syria and Phoenicia on the Way from Antioch to Jerusalem, and of the Holy Places of Palestine', in *Jerusalem Pilgrimage 1099–1185*, trans. J. Wilkinson (London: The Hakluyt Society), pp. 315–36.
Phokas, John (1994), 'Des Johannes Phokas kurzgefaßte Beschreibung der zwischen Antiocheia und Jerusalem begenden Städte und Ortschaften in Syrien und Phoinikien und der Heiligen Stätten in Palästina', in *Peregrinatio graeca in Terram Sanctam: Studien zu Pilgerführern und Reisebeschreibungen über Syrien, Palästina und den Sinai aus byzantinischer und metabyzantinischer Zeit*, trans. A. Külzer, Studien und Texte zur Byzantinistik 2 (Frankfurt: Peter Lang), pp. 287–305.
Plato (2013), *The Republic*, trans. C. Emlynn-Jones, and W. Preddy, 2 vols (Cambridge MA and London: Harvard University Press).
Plutarch (1914–26), *Lives*, trans. B. Perrin, Loeb Classical Library, 11 vols (Cambridge MA and London: Harvard University Press).
Ralph of Caen (2005), *Gesta Tancredi: A History of the Normans on the First Crusade*, trans. B.S. Bachrach, and D.S. Bachrach (Farnham and Burlington VT: Ashgate).
Robert the Monk (2005), *History of the First Crusade*, trans. C. Sweetenham (Aldershot and Burlington VT: Ashgate).
Stilbes, Constantine (2015), *The Incineration of New Babylon: The Fire Poem of Konstantinos Stilbes*, trans. T. Layton (Geneva: La Pomme d'Or).
Tzetzes, John (2001), *Ιωάννης Τζέτζης Επιστολαί*, trans. I. Grigoriadis, Κείμενα Βυζαντινής Λογοτεχνίας 3 (Athens: Kanaki).
Von Leutsch, Ernst, and Schneidewin, Friedrich Wilhelm (1889), *Corpus Paroemiographorum Graecorum*, vol. 1 (Göttingen: Vandenhoeck and Ruprecht).
William of Tyre (1943), *A History of Deeds Done Beyond the Sea*, trans. E.A. Babcock, and A. C. Krey, 2 vols (New York: Columbia University Press).
Zonaras, John (1999), *Ιωάννης Ζωναράς Επιτομή Ιστοριών*, trans. I. Grigoriadis, Κείμενα Βυζαντινής Ιστοριογραφίας 5, vol. 3 (Athens: Kanaki).

Secondary Literature

Aerts, W.J. (2003), 'A Byzantine Traveller to One of the Crusader States', in *East and West in the Crusader States'. Context – Contacts – Confrontations III. Acta of the Congress held at Hernen Castle in September 2000*, ed. K. Ciggaar, and H. Teule (Leuven: Peeters), pp. 165–221.

Angelou, Athanasios (1981), 'Nicholas of Methone: The Life and Works of a Twelfth-Century Bishop', in *Byzantium and the Classical Tradition*, ed. M. Mullett, and R. Scott (Birmingham: Centre for Byzantine Studies, University of Birmingham), pp. 143–8.

Angelov, Dimiter G. (2006), 'Domestic Opposition to Byzantium's Alliance with Saladin: Niketas Choniates and His Epiphany Oration of 1190', *Byzantine and Modern Greek Studies* 30: 49–68.

Bloch, Herbert (1946), 'Monte Cassino, Byzantium and the West in the Earlier Middle Ages', *Dumbarton Oaks Papers* 3: 163–224.

Brand, Charles M. (1968a), *Byzantium Confronts the West, 1180–1204* (Cambridge MA: Harvard University Press).

Brand, Charles M. (1968b), 'A Byzantine Plan for the Fourth Crusade', *Speculum* 43: 462–75.

Chrissis, Nikolaos G. (2019), 'Ideological and Political Contestations in Post-1204 Byzantium: The Orations of Niketas Choniates and the Imperial Court of Nicaea', in *The Emperor in the Byzantine World*, ed. Shaun Tougher (Abingdon and New York: Routledge), pp. 248–63.

Chryssogelos, Konstantinos (2021), 'Several Notes on John Phokas' Brief Ekphrasis', in *Byzantine Authors and their Times*, ed. V.N. Vlyssidou (Athens: National Hellenic Research Foundation), pp. 285–304.

France, John (1971), 'The Departure of Tatikios from the Crusader Army', *Bulletin of the Institute of Historical Research* 44: 137–47.

Frankopan, Peter (2012), *The First Crusade: The Call from the East* (London: Bodley Head).

Galatariotou, Catia (1991), *Making of a Saint: The Life, Times and Sanctification of St Neophytos the Recluse* (Cambridge: Cambridge University Press).

Harris, Jonathan (2022), *Byzantium and the Crusades*, 3rd ed. (London and New York: Bloomsbury).

Hobbs, Christopher (2020), 'John Kinnamos', in *Franks and Crusades in medieval Eastern Christian Historiography*, ed. Alex Mallett (Turnhout: Brepols), pp. 65–92.

Horrocks, Geoffrey (2010), *Greek: A History of the Language and Its Speakers*, 2nd ed. (Chichester and Malden MA: Wiley-Blackwell).

Jeffreys, Elizabeth (2019), 'A Twelfth-Century Perspective on Byzantium's Western Neighbours: The Witness of Manganeios Prodromos', in *Byzantium and the West: Perception and Reality (c.11th–15th)*, ed. N.G. Chrissis, A. Kolia-Dermitzaki, and A. Papageorgiou (Abingdon and New York: Routledge), pp. 128–40.

Jeffreys, Elizabeth, and Jeffreys, Michael (2001), '"Wild Beast from the West": Immediate Literary Reactions in Byzantium to the Second Crusade', in *The Crusades from the Perspective of Byzantium and the Muslim World*, ed. A.E. Laiou, and R.P. Mottahedeh (Washington DC: Dumbarton Oaks), pp. 101–16.

Jeffreys, Elizabeth, and Jeffreys, Michael (2015), 'A Constantinopolitan Views Frankish Antioch', *Crusades* 14: 49–151.

Jeffreys, Michael et al. (2017), *Prosopography of the Byzantine World, 2016* (London: King's College London). Available at: http://pbw2016.kdl.kcl.ac.uk.

Kraft, Andreas (2012), 'The Last Roman Emperor "Topos" in the Byzantine Apocalyptic Tradition', *Byzantion* 82: 213–57.

Lilie, Ralph-Johannes (1993), *Byzantium and the Crusader States, 1095–1204*, trans. J.C. Morris, and J.E. Ridings (Oxford: Oxford University Press).

Magdalino, Paul (1993), *The Empire of Manuel I Komnenos, 1143–1180* (Cambridge: Cambridge University Press).

Magdalino, Paul (2005), 'Prophesies on the Fall of Constantinople', in *Urbs Capta: The Fourth Crusade and Its Consequences*, ed. A. Laiou, Réalités byzantines 10 (Paris: Lethielleux), pp. 41–53.
Mullett, Margaret E. (1981), 'The Classical Tradition in the Byzantine Letter', in *Byzantium and the Classical Tradition*, ed. M.E. Mullett, and R. Scott (Birmingham: University of Birmingham), pp. 75–93.
Mullett, Margaret E. (2012), 'Whose Muses? Two Advice Poems Attributed to Alexios I Komnenos', in *La face cachée de la littérature byzantine: le text en tant que message immédiat*, ed. Paolo Odorico, Dossiers byzantins 11 (Paris: Centre d'études byzantines, néo-helleniques et sud-est européennes), pp. 195–220.
Mullett, Margaret E. (2013), 'How to Criticize the Laudandus', in *Power and Subversion in Byzantium*, ed. Dimiter Angelov, and Michael Saxby (Abingdon and New York: Routledge), pp. 247–62.
Neville, Leonora (2018), *Guide to Byzantine Historical Writing* (Cambridge: Cambridge University Press).
Phillips, Jonathan (2004), *The Fourth Crusade and the Sack of Constantinople* (London: Jonathan Cape).
Phillips, Jonathan (2007), *The Second Crusade: Extending the Frontiers of Christendom* (New Haven CT and London: Yale University Press).
Simpson, Alicia (2013), *Niketas Choniates: A Historiographical Study* (Oxford: Oxford University Press).
Treadgold, Warren T. (2013), *The Middle Byzantine Historians* (Basingstoke and New York: Palgrave).
Vranousi, Era L. (1966), *Τα αγιολογικά κείμενα του οσίου Χριστοδούλου ιδριτού της εν Πατμω μονής: Φιλολογική παράδοσις και ιστορικαί μαρτυρία* (Athens: Historic and Folklore Society of the Dodecanese).
Zafeiris, Konstantinos (2011), 'The Issue of the Authorship of the Synopsis Chronike and Theodore Skoutariotes', *Revue des études byzantines* 69: 253–64.

Index

Abu'l Kasim, governor of Nicaea 9
Abydos (Çanakkale) 62, 124
Acre (Ptolemais, Akko) 103, 116, 134, 160
Adana 46, 56, 121
Adhémar, bishop of Le Puy 10
Adrianople (Edirne) 62, 73–4, 83, 156, 180, 199, 206
Aeschylus 106
Aimery of Limoges, Latin patriarch of Antioch 92–3
Aleppo (Berroia) 41, 42–3, 48, 57, 59, 90, 93
Alexander of Gravina 60
Alexander the Great, king of Macedon (336–323 BCE) 49, 54, 88, 162, 181, 184, 206–7
Alexios I Komnenos, Byzantine emperor (1081–1118) 3, 7–27, 30–1, 34–9, 88, 204
Alexios I Komnenos, emperor of Trebizond (1204–22) 206, 209, 218
Alexios II Komnenos, Byzantine emperor (1180–3) 151, 167, 204
Alexios III Angelos, Byzantine emperor (1195–1203) 42, 173–5, 177–8, 180, 196–7, 199, 205
Alexios IV Angelos, Byzantine emperor (1203–4) 3, 174–5, 177, 180–5, 194–5, 197–200, 205
Alexios V Doukas Mourtzouphlos, Byzantine emperor (1204) 185–8, 200–2, 205
Alp Arslan, Great Seljukid sultan (1064–72) 7, 44
Amalric I, king of Jerusalem (1163–74) 121–7, 129
Amaseia (Amasya) 27
Anazarbos (Ain Zarba) 40, 46, 57, 92
Andronikos I Komnenos, Byzantine emperor (1183–5) 151, 161, 167, 174, 204

Ankyra (Ankara) 27
Anselm IV, archbishop of Milan 26
Antioch (Theoupolis, Antakya) 18–19, 22–6, 34, 88–9, 99–100, 103, 121, 169; principality of 30–1, 39–58, 90–8, 131–2, 159
Apros (Kermeyan) 15
Arimathea 149
Ascalon 30, 122–3
Assassins 132
Athanasios I Manasses, patriarch of Antioch 100
Athens 28
Athyra 13, 63
Attaleia (Antalya) 55, 57, 61, 91, 145

Baldwin I, king of Jerusalem (1100–18) 10, 30
Baldwin I, Latin emperor of Constantinople (1204–5) 174, 186, 193–4, 201, 204
Baldwin III, king of Jerusalem (1143–63) 93–6, 99
Baldwin of Marash 40
Basilakes, Nikephoros 50–5
Bathys 76
Beirut (Berytus) 103, 132–3, 160
Belissariotes, John, logothete 211–15
Belissariotes, Michael 211
Benedict, cardinal of Santa Susanna 221
Bernard, bishop of Lydda and Ramla 149
Bernold of St Blasien 7
Beroë (Stara Zagora) 9
Bertha of Sulzbach (Irene), Byzantine empress 69, 98, 104, 121
Bertram of Toulouse 95
Bertrand of Blancfort, Grand Master of the Templars 95
Bethlehem 108, 146–8
Blachernae 1, 13, 177, 188, 196–7

Bohemond I, prince of Antioch
    (1098–1111) 10–11, 14–17, 20, 22–3,
    24, 26, 27, 30–5, 39
Bohemond II, prince of Antioch
    (1126–30) 39
Bohemond III, prince of Antioch
    (1163–1201) 90
Boleslav IV, high duke of Poland 68
Boniface, marquis of Montferrat 174, 180,
    193, 199–200
Boutoumites, Manuel 12, 20–1
Branas, Alexios 154
Branas, Michael 61, 67, 91
Branas, Theodore 154
Bryennios, Nikephoros 8, 13, 100
Byzantion *see* Constantinople

Caesarea Maritima (Keysariya) 149
Caesarea Philippi (Baniyas) 149
Cana 134
Capernaum 109, 114, 135
Carmel, Mount 134, 149–50
Chaka, emir of Smyrna 37
Chalintzes, Niketas 31
Choirobacchoi 63, 74–5, 83–5
Choniates, Niketas 2–3, 19, 42–5, 55–6,
    71–9, 97–8, 123–9, 151–65, 173–80,
    185–93, 206–16
Chouroup 70
Choziba 143
Christodoulos of Patmos 170–2
Chrysoberges, Nikephoros 3, 180–5
Cilicia, Armenian principality 39–58,
    90–2, 215
Clermont, council of (1095) 7, 9
Conrad III, king of Germany (1138–52)
    59–76, 79–86
Conrad, imperial constable 26
Conrad of Montferrat, king of Jerusalem
    (1190–2) 154
Constance, princess of Antioch 39,
    90–1, 99
Constantine I, Roman emperor (306–37)
    41, 81, 184, 221
Constantinople (Byzantion,
    Istanbul) 1–2, 11–17, 62–8, 75, 80–1;
    Fourth Crusade at (1203–4) 176–80;
    sack of (1204) 185–93, 195–205,
    212–16, 219–22
Corfu (Kerkyra) 79, 170, 176
Crete 37, 170
Cyprus 22, 37, 55, 91–2, 111–21, 124,
    164–9
Cyrus the Great, king of Persia (559–530
    BCE) 54

Damietta 122–9
Dandolo, Enrico, doge of Venice
    (1192–1205) 174–5, 186, 193, 195
Danishmend, emir of Sebasteia 25, 27,
    31–2, 34
Darius III, king of Persia (336–330
    BCE) 206
Dasiotes, Nikephoros 69
Demosthenes 1, 46
Develtos 180, 197, 199
Devol, treaty of (1108) 35, 39
Dorylaion (Eskişehir), battle of (1097)
    21, 67
Dositheos, patriarch of Constantinople
    (1189–91) 153–4
Doukas, Alexios, governor of Cyprus
    111–12, 120
Doukas, John, caesar 25
Doukas, John, grand hetairiarch 129
Dyrrachion (Epidamnos, Durazzo, Durrës)
    12, 15, 35, 124, 175–6, 195

Edessa (Urfa) 44, 59; county of 30
Emmaus (Abu Ghosh) 149
Ephraim of Ainos 3, 19, 34–5, 56–8,
    79–80, 121, 168–9, 193–204
Euboea 124
Eudokia, Byzantine princess 202
Eugenius III, pope (1145–53) 59
Euphrosyne, Byzantine empress 177, 202
Eustace III, count of Boulogne 10
Euthymios the Great 142

Fatimid caliphate 121
Ferep 43, 57
Firuz 22, 24
Frederick, duke of Swabia 159–60, 168–9
Frederick I Barbarossa, German emperor
    (1152–90) 62, 69–70, 73–4, 151–61,
    168–9
Frederick I, duke of Swabia 70
Fulk, king of Jerusalem (1131–43) 40

Gallipoli 156
Gerasimos monastery 144–5
Gesta Francorum 14
Gibelet 132
Gidos, Alexios 153
Glykas, Michael 18
Godfrey of Bouillon, duke of Lower
    Lotharingia 10–11, 13–14, 30
Greek language 1–3
Gregory VIII, pope (1187) 151
Guy of Lusignan, king of Jerusalem
    (1186–92) 165, 169

Hama 41
Hattin, battle of (1187) 130, 151
Hebron 148
Henry V, German emperor (1106–25) 70
Herakleios, Byzantine emperor (610–41) 80
Herod Antipas, tetrarch of Galilee 136–7
Herodias 136–7
Herodotus 46
Herod the Great, king of Judaea (37–4 BCE) 126
Homer 1, 33, 48, 162
Hugh, count of St Pol 174, 194
Hugh, count of Vermandois 10, 12–14

Ikonion (Konya) 39, 103, 129, 157–8, 167, 169
Innocent III, pope (1198–1216) 173–4, 194
Irene Angelina, queen of Germany 174
Irene Doukaina, Byzantine empress 8
Irene the Sebastokratorissa 100
Isaac II Angelos, Byzantine emperor (1185–95, 1203–4) 42, 151–6, 160–4, 166, 168, 170, 173, 177–8, 180, 197, 199, 204
Ishmael, son of Danishmend 25
Isocrates 46
Italikos, Michael, bishop of Philippopolis 3, 45–50, 73

Jaffa, treaty of (1192) 165
Jericho (Tell Es-Sultan) 108, 143
Jerusalem 9, 18, 26, 58, 106–8, 138–41, 190; kingdom of 30, 151
Joel 3, 204–5
John II Komnenos, Byzantine emperor (1118–43) 3, 36, 39–58, 61, 204
John Chrysostom monastery 144–5
John Roger 90–1
John the Baptist monastery 144
Joscelin II of Courtenay, count of Edessa (1131–49) 43
Julius Caesar 105

Kafarthab 41, 43, 57
Kalamon monastery 143–5
Kalojan, tsar of Bulgaria (1197–1207) 206
Kamateros, Andronikos Doukas 100
Kamateros, Basil 99–100
Kamateros, John Doukas, logothete 152, 168
Kamytzes, Manuel, protostrator 153–4
Kanavos, Nicholas 200
Kantakouzenos, Andronikos 152
Kapniskerti 41
Kasianos, Alexios 91

Kerbogha *see* Qiwam al-Dawla abu Said
Kibotos (Mudanya) 27
Kilij Arslan II, sultan of Ikonion (1156–92) 157–8
Kinnamos, John 2–3, 39–42, 55, 59–71, 90–7, 98–100, 121–3
Kistramos 92
Kition 116
Kitros, bishop of 10
Komnene, Anna 3, 8–17, 19–20, 22, 24–8, 30–1, 100
Komnene, Maria, daughter of Manuel I 104
Komnenos, Alexios, son of John II 61
Komnenos, Alexios Bryennios 100
Komnenos, David 209–10, 218
Komnenos, Isaac, brother of John II 52
Komnenos, Isaac, brother of Manuel I 55
Komnenos, Isaac, usurper on Cyprus 165–9
Komnenos, John, nephew of Manuel I 91
Kontostephanos, Andronikos 122–9
Kontostephanos, John 99–104, 110, 117–18
Kosmidion monastery 13, 15, 186, 195
Kutb al Din Malikshah, son of Kilij Arslan II 157–8

Lamos 92
Laodikeia-on-the-Lykos 157, 168
Laodikeia-on-the-Orontes (Latakiah) 31, 34, 132, 160
Larissa, battle of (1083) 39
Lefkosia (Nicosia) 91
Leo I, prince of Cilician Armenia (c.1129–37) 39–41, 51, 56
Longinias 92
Lothair III, German emperor (1125–37) 70
Louis, count of Blois 174, 194
Louis VII, king of France (1137–80) 59, 67–71, 76–9
Lucullus 49–50
Luke Chryoberges, patriarch of Constantinople (1157–70) 100
Lysias 46

Makrembolites, Demetrios 60
Malik Yaghibasan, emir of Sebasteia (1142–64) 93
Mamas, martyr 87–8
Mamistra (Misis) 46
Mamplanes, Turkish commander 67, 76
Manasses, Constantine 3, 99, 100–21
Manuel I Komnenos, Byzantine emperor (1143–80) 3, 18, 39–40, 55, 59–69, 104, 139, 144, 146, 151, 167, 173–4,

204; and Antioch 90–100; and Egypt 121–7; and Second Crusade 71–89
Manzikert (Malazgirt), battle of (1071) 7, 44
Maria of Antioch, Byzantine empress 99–100, 104–6, 117, 121, 151
Marie of Champagne 204
Marius 79
Marqab 167
Mary of Egypt 145–6
Masud I Rukn al-Din, sultan of Ikonion (1116–56) 47
Mavrozomes, Theodore 124
Meander, battle of (1147) 76–9
Melangeia 67
Melania the Younger 141
Meletios the Younger 28–9
Melisend, daughter of Raymond III of Tripoli 98–9, 117
Melitene (Malatya) 32
Mersivan, battle of (1101) 27, 30
Michael I Angelos, despot of Epirus (1204–15) 206
Michael VII Doukas, Byzantine emperor (1071–8) 10, 21
Monte Cassino Abbey 21
Montferrand 40
Muhammad II, Great Seljukid sultan (1153–9) 93

Nablus (Neapolis, Sychar) 106, 137
Nain 136
Naissos (Niš) 61
Nazareth 108–9, 116, 134–5
Neocaesarea (Niksar) 33, 42
Neophytos 165–8
Nicaea (Iznik) 18–19, 20, 68, 206, 211, 218–19
Nicholas, bishop of Methone 28–9
Nicholas IV Mouzalon, patriarch of Constantinople (1147–51) 68
Nikomedeia (Izmit) 9, 12, 209–10
Nistrion 43, 57
Novatus (Novatian) 12
Nur al-Din, sultan of Aleppo and Damascus (1154–74) 90, 92–3, 95–7, 121

Oderisius, abbot of Monte Cassino 21, 23
Odo of Deuil, abbot of Saint-Denis 21, 71
Ohrid 10, 143, 155
Opos, Andronikos 62

Palaiologos, George 20
Palaiologos, Michael 61, 67

Paphos 116, 165
Paschal II, pope (1099–1118) 35
Pasgouse (Lake Beyşehir) 57
Patmos 130, 170–2
Pegai (Karabiga) 209, 217–18
Pelagia of Antioch 140–1
Pelagius, cardinal of Santa Cecilia 221
Pelekanon (Eskihisar) 14, 19–20
Peraia (Pikridion, Hasköy) 64, 75, 86, 176, 178
Peter of Amiens 187
Peter of Aulps 25
Peter of Bracieux 187, 209
Peter the Hermit 10–12
Philadelphia (Alaşehir) 68, 156, 168
Phileas 13, 186, 201
Philip I, king of France (1060–1108) 10, 12, 35
Philip II Augustus, king of France (1180–1223) 164–5, 169–72
Philip of Swabia, king of Germany (1198–1208) 174, 194
Philippa, daughter of Raymond of Poitiers 99
Philippa, empress of Nicaea 215
Philippopolis (Plovdiv) 12, 73, 82, 150–6, 168
Philomelion (Akşehir) 24–6, 66, 68, 157, 168
Philopation 64, 67, 154
Phokas, John 3, 129–50
Piacenza, council of (1095) 7
Pikridion see Peraia
Pindar 46
Piraeus 28
Piza (Buza) 41–3, 57
Plato 1, 45, 215
Plutarch 2
Poimamenon, battle of (1204) 209
Pompey 49
Pons, Count of Tripoli (1112–37) 40
Prakana 59
Prodromos, Manganeios 81–9
Prosouch 62–3, 65, 74
Prousenos 154

Qiwam al-Dawla abu Said (Kerbogha), atabeg of Mosul 22, 24–5

Ramla 149
Raymond I, count of Tripoli (1102–5) 10, 14, 17, 26–7, 30–1
Raymond II, count of Tripoli (1137–52) 40, 57

Raymond III, count of Tripoli (1152–87) 98–9, 117
Raymond of Poitiers, prince of Antioch (1136–49) 39–43, 57, 90, 99, 121
Reynald of Châtillon, prince of Antioch (1153–61) 89–95, 97–8
Richard I, king of England (1189–99) 164–8, 169, 171
Robert I the Frisian, count of Flanders 9
Robert II, count of Flanders 10
Robert Curthose, duke of Normandy 10
Robert Guiscard, duke of Apulia and Calabria 15, 35
Roger II, king of Sicily (1130–54) 72, 79
Roger Borsa, duke of Apulia and Calabria 10
Romanos IV Diogenes, Byzantine emperor (1068–71) 44, 57

Sabas 139, 141
Saladin, sultan of Egypt and Syria (1169–93) 151, 155, 165–7, 190
Samaria (Sebasteia) 103–6, 136–7
Sarepta 133
Sebasteia (Sivas) 25, 27
Seleukeia (Silifke) 91
Sepphoris 134
Serdica (Sofia) 61–2
Shaizar (Larissa) 41, 43–4, 48
Sidon 103, 133
Skoutariotes, Theodore, archbishop of Cyzicus 7–8
Smyrna (Izmir) 25
Socrates 45
Sophronios III, patriarch of Alexandria 100
Soudi (St Simeon) 22
Stephen, count of Blois 10, 25
Stephen the Akolouthos 66
Stilbes, Constantine, archbishop of Cyzicus 219–22
Strymon, battle of (1185) 162
Suleyman, Turkish commander 59
Sychar *see* Nablus
Symeon Stylites 131

Tabor, Mount 135–6
Tancred, nephew of Bohemond 20, 24, 31

Taronites, Gregory, duke of Trebizond 31–4
Tarsus 25, 46, 56, 92, 121
Tatikios 19–20, 22–4, 31
Theodore I Laskaris, emperor of Nicaea (1208–22) 193, 196–7, 202–3, 206–11, 215–19
Theodore of Petra 142
Theodosios of Byzantion 170–2
Theodosios the Cenobiarch 142
Theophylact Hephaistos, archbishop of Ohrid 10–11, 31–4
Theophylact the Exoubitos 99
Thessalonica 69
Thomas, deputy clerk 41
Thoros II, prince of Cilician Armenia 90–2, 94, 121
Thremithos 116
Thucydides 2, 46, 106, 181
Tili (Toprakkale) 92
Tortosa (Tartus, Antarada) 132
Tripoli 98–100, 132; county of 30–1
Tyre 103, 109–10, 133–4, 160, 165
Tzetzes, John 80–1
Tzikandeles, Basil 63, 65
Tzintziloukes, Basil 61
Tzitas 27

Urban II, pope (1088–99) 7–10, 21

Vahka (Feke) 40–1, 56
Vatatzes, Theodore 92
Vempetz 43
Vladislav, duke of Bohemia 68

William, archbishop of Tyre 55, 122
William II Jordan, regent of Tripoli (1105–9) 30–1
William of Grandmesnil 25

Xenophon 181
Xerxes, king of Persia (486–465 BCE) 61

Zara (Zadar) 175, 195
Zengi, ʿImad al-Din, atabeg of Mosul and Aleppo 44, 59
Zonaras, John 17–18